Being Up-To-Date

Studies in European Thought

E. Allen McCormick
General Editor

Vol. 20

PETER LANG
New York • Washington, D.C./Baltimore • Boston • Bern
Frankfurt am Main • Berlin • Brussels • Vienna • Oxford

Neil Levy

Being Up-To-Date

Foucault, Sartre, and Postmodernity

PETER LANG
New York • Washington, D.C./Baltimore • Boston • Bern
Frankfurt am Main • Berlin • Brussels • Vienna • Oxford

Library of Congress Cataloging-in-Publication Data

Levy, Neil.
Being up-to-date: Foucault, Sartre, and postmodernity / Neil Levy.
p. cm. — (Studies in European thought; vol. 20)
Includes bibliographical references and index.
1. Postmodernism. I. Title. II. Series.
B831.2 .L48   149'.97—dc21   00-057698
ISBN 0-8204-5118-5
ISSN 1043-5786

Die Deutsche Bibliothek-CIP-Einheitsaufnahme

Levy, Neil:
Being up-to-date: Foucault, Sartre, and postmodernity / Neil Levy.
–New York; Washington, D.C./Baltimore; Boston; Bern;
Frankfurt am Main; Berlin; Brussels; Vienna; Oxford: Lang.
(Studies in European thought; Vol. 20)
ISBN 0-8204-5118-5

The paper in this book meets the guidelines for permanence and durability
of the Committee on Production Guidelines for Book Longevity
of the Council of Library Resources.

© 2001 Peter Lang Publishing, Inc., New York

Printed in the United States of America

Table of Contents

Preface

It is often claimed, and even more often implicitly assumed, that the kind of philosophy which came to prominence in the France of the 1960s, and which has subsequently established itself across the world as perhaps the single most important current in contemporary continental philosophy, represents a fundamentally new style of thought. The implicit claim seems to be this: that this kind of thinking is the first truly *radical* development in philosophy since at least Descartes; indeed, perhaps the most radical turning of thought since Plato. This kind of thinking— call it poststucturalism for want of a better word— is so radical, and so important, because it attempts to rethink the basis of the metaphysics which has held Western thought in its grip since the Greeks; and because it dethrones the epistemological subject, placed at the center of philosophy by Descartes, replacing it with codes and contingencies.

It is important to note that the claim made for post-structuralism is not simply that it opens up new roads for us to travel, but that it institutes a fundamental break in the history of philosophy. From this perspective, most earlier thinkers are more or less *passé*. The only philosophers worth retaining from the canon are those which it has always had the most trouble containing: thinkers like Nietzsche and Heidegger, who had prefigured this revolution in philosophy by thinking the roots of the metaphysics we now wish to displace.

Poststructural thinkers are thus incommensurable with the thinkers who preceded them. Indeed, post-structuralism is often seen to be the self-consciousness of a new historical epoch, an epoch we might call postmodernity. Post-structural thought is thus no mere academic exercise, but opens the way for new ways of being, new political arrangements, a more fluid subjectivity.

Yet it has been noted almost as frequently that the themes which postmodernism claims are distinctively its own are largely shared with modernism. The concern to decenter the subject, the attack upon Cartesian dualism, even the rhetoric of fundamental breaks— all seem to belong as much to the great modernists as to Lyotard or Derrida. It is this puzzle with which this book is concerned.

I aim, therefore, to establish the relationship— if any— between modern and postmodern styles of thought. I have approached this problem through the comparison of two philosophers, each of whom has a good claim to being paradigmatic of one of the two opposed epochs. Our modern philosopher is Jean-Paul Sartre: his self-confessed Cartesianism, his embrace of Marxism and of humanism, his relentless totalizing all combine to make him irresistible for my purposes. Our representative of postmodern thought is Michel Foucault, selected for his explicit attack upon the epistemological subject, upon the notion of continuous history and his attention to difference.

Of course, many of these features are equally characteristic of other post-structural thinkers. But what tips the balance decidedly in Foucault's favor is the direct and central concern of his work with the political. Given the centrality of ultimately political controversies to the postmodern debate, the chance of contrasting the implications for political theory and practice of the alleged transformation in thought via the confrontation of two of France's leading political philosophers could not be passed up.

Thus I will be concerned with the continuities and discontinuities between modern and postmodern philosophy, as represented by Sartre and Foucault. More particularly, I want to examine how well Sartre stands up to the attacks launched against modern thought by Foucault, especially Foucault's penetrating diagnosis of the aporias of modernity in *The Order of Things*. I shall also be concerned with the adequacy of each man's philosophy from a political and ethical point of view. Such concerns will remain largely in the background until the second half of the book, but the extent to which they remain a constant reference point should be clear.

Chapter One attempts a definition of postmodernism, the better to situate our thinkers. As we shall see, the very idea of postmodernity is paradoxical, even contradictory, which renders the attempt to measure the extent to which a thinker can fairly be described as postmodern that much more difficult. I suggest, though, that an adequate understanding of postmodernism will need to grasp the epoch's relation to time and the present precisely *as* paradoxical. The grammatical tense we call the future perfect captures this postmodern sense of time.

Chapter Two focuses on the explicit confrontation between Sartre and Foucault, as the older man's star fell and a new generation of thinkers took center stage in France. Right from the very beginning, we shall see, Foucault himself saw his generation as inaugurating a radical break with Sartre and his concerns. Already by the mid 1960s all the accusations which continue to be repeated today had been formulated by Foucault: that phenomenology, and Sartre's version of it in particular, is subject-centered and therefore cannot adequately think the being of language, that Sartre's thought is totalizing and therefore inattentive to difference, that his Marxism is unable to provide the tools for effective political critique. These accusations, and Sartre's replies to them, set the stage for the substantive comparison to come.

Chapters Three and Four are concerned largely with Heidegger. Heidegger's thought is unavoidable for any consideration of the roots of philosophical postmodernism; it was Heidegger who first announced the necessity of retrieving the history of Western philosophy in order to understand the fateful turn toward metaphysics undertaken by the Greeks; it was Heidegger who first decentered the speaking subject in favor of language itself, "the house of Being." Moreover, Heidegger is acknowledged by both our thinkers to be their most important philosophical predecessor.

Chapter Three demonstrates the extent of Foucault's debt to Heidegger. But it also shows that so long as this influence lasted, Foucault was unable to formulate a style of thought which could coherently criticize his own time. Archaeology was either an ineffectual antiquarianism, or an incoherent critique of the present. Chapters Four and Five analyze the root of this dilemma, by examining Foucault's diagnosis of the aporias of modern thought, in *The Order of Things*. In Chapter Four I demonstrate that Heidegger's work is vitiated by his nostalgia for a lost origin. In Chapter Five I turn the spotlight back onto Foucault, and examine the extent to which his archaeological work escapes from the aporias of modernity. I show that, on this score, archaeology is above reproach. But the necessity this places Foucault under, of keeping the transcendental and the empirical poles (or the thinker and her object) rigorously apart condemns Foucault's thought to contemporary irrelevancy. I then read Sartre's existentialism through the prism of Foucault's doublets. I conclude that Sartre shows us the way forward here. If thought is to be *critical*, we must give up the hope of avoiding the doublets. Instead, we must center our thought upon them, entering into their grasp lucidly, rather than scrupulously avoiding them (like Foucault) or backing blindly into them (like Heidegger).

Chapter Six begins the thematic and substantive comparison of Foucault and Sartre. It focuses upon the gaze as simultaneously subjectifying and objectifying. For Sartre, the power of the gaze is founded upon the ontology of the subject. I show how Foucault historicizes the gaze, and demonstrates that its functioning is embedded in concrete relations of power. But Foucault shares with Sartre a fundamental hatred of such structures, insofar as they impose upon subjects a fixed identity. I suggest that to this extent, at least, we ought to see Foucault as continuing to mine a vein of thought opened up by existentialism.

Chapter Seven focuses on the power of criticism and the place of freedom in the work of Foucault and of Sartre. I show that, on this score, Sartre's existential thought is incoherent. Despite the fact that the motivating force behind *Being and Nothingness* is the conviction that the subject is free, Sartre is unable coherently to think that freedom. Paradoxically, his subject is unable to choose because he grants it too much latitude for choice I then turn to the re-examination of Foucault's archaeology from this perspective. I show that Foucault's work is here the mirror image of Sartre's. Of course, freedom is not a concern of the 1960s Foucault. But the repetition of the structures of the for-itself at the level of the *episteme* make the fact of change between *epistemes* fundamentally mysterious.

Chapter Eight begins the examination of the ethico-political thought of our two philosophers. Sartre's early ethics is untenable, for much the same reasons as is his philosophy of freedom. If the for-itself is the source of all its values, then the very concept of value is incoherent. The condition of ethics, then, is that the subject inhabit an independently meaningful world. As we shall see, Sartre himself came gradually to accept this. But at the same time, the subject needs to be able to be able to distance herself, to some extent at least, from her world. It is was on this score that archaeology had failed. Genealogical critique, however, can be understood as the resolute affirmation of both these conditions.

I then turn to the status of the subject in Foucault. I show that he, as much as Sartre, is opposed to essentializing the subject. I suggest a way in which Foucault's last works can be read as giving us the tools to think subjectivity without the necessity of essentialization.

Chapter Nine examines the potential for intersubjectivity in Sartre and Foucault. It was on this head that Merleau-Ponty had based his scathing attack upon Sartrean existentialism. I show that the later Sartre has the means to reply to many of Merleau-Ponty's criticisms. Moreover, he can reverse the burden of proof, by showing that without a substantive conception of power, relations between subjects cannot be coherently conceived. This conception is missing from Merleau-Ponty's last works, but is provided for us by the genealogical Foucault.

Chapter Ten returns to the explicit confrontation between Foucault and Sartre, within the context of the debate over postmodernism. The postmodern, I suggest, is an *untimely* notion, as is suggested by its etymology. Since it is untimely, we can expect all the attempts made by each thinker to locate the other within time to be subject to unexpected slippages. I demonstrate these slippages at work in the pronouncements of each thinker on the other.

Chapter Eleven returns to the problems of ethics. I argue that Foucault and Sartre each separately develop an ethics in the future perfect— that is, an ethics which can neither be reduced to a set of rules, nor can dispense with such rules, but in which, instead, rules *will have been* followed. It is only when ethical thought has this equivocal relation to rules that it can be flexible enough to adapt to our rapidly and unpredictably changing (post)modern condition, yet still count as ethics. As I show, this parallels the postmodern ethics of Lyotard and of Derrida.

Finally, Chapter twelve turns to the examination of one of the crucial themes concerning which modern and postmodern thought are commonly believed to part ways: humanism. I show Sartre's humanism is not the crude Cartesianism often attributed to him, and I examine the possibilities for a properly postmodern humanism; that is, a humanism in the future perfect.

The cumulative effect of this study, I hope, will be to suggest that the notion of a fundamental rupture running between the thought of Sartre and Foucault is, at best, highly simplistic. Though at least some of the accusations levelled against him by Foucault's generation were justified, Sartre's thought had the resources to develop beyond these faults; indeed, to supply essential ingredients missing from the work of these very critics. I hope, too, that this conclusion is suggestive of a broader finding. I hope that the effect is not simply to rehabilitate Sartre, but to problematize the entire thematics of a radical break in recent thought. Though I do not necessarily hold that the very idea of postmodernism is incoherent, or that there is no evidence of a qualitative alteration in thought and society in recent years, I hope that my conclusions will suggest that the relation between postmodernity— if there is such a thing— and modernity are much more complex, subtle, and contradictory then the rhetoric of both its proponents and its detractors would have us believe.

This study has been a long time in the writing, and on the way I have accumulated a number of debts, both intellectual and otherwise. Elizabeth Grosz offered early encouragement. Andrew Milner inspired by his enthusiasm. Marie Maclean gave me an indispensable feel for intellectual life in France, and offered invaluable advice though she was gravely ill. Andrea Lobb read the entire manuscript and suggested many stylistic changes, but her influence on its contents is even greater.

Earlier versions of some of the chapters of this book have been published in a number of journals. Chapter three reprints material which was published in *The Journal of the British Society for Phenomenology* in May 1996, under the title 'The Prehistory of Archaeology: Foucault and Heidegger.' A version of chapter ten appeared in the journal *Symposium* in Summer 1998, under the title 'Untimely Meditations: Periodising Recent French Thought', while those portions of chapter eleven which concern Foucault formed the basis for 'Ethics and Rules: A Political Reading of Foucault's Aesthetics of Existence', *Philosophy Today*, June 1998. I thank the editors of all three journals for permission to reprint this material.

Publication of this book would have been impossible without the financial assistance of the Monash University Publications Grants Committee.

Abbreviations

Foucault:

AK	*The Archaeology of Knowledge* (Foucault, 1972b)
BC	*The Birth of the Clinic* (Foucault, 1973)
CS	*The Care of the Self* (Foucault, 1986d)
DP	*Discipline and Punish* (Foucault, 1986b)
ECS	"The ethic of care for the self as a practice of freedom" (Foucault, 1987c)
HF	*Histoire de la folie* (Foucault, 1972a)
HSI	*The History of Sexuality, Vol. I* (Foucault, 1990)
MC	*Madness and Civilization* (Foucault, 1971)
MIP	*Mental Illness and Psychology* (Foucault, 1987a)
OT	*The Order of Things* (Foucault, 1989a)
UP	*The Use of Pleasure* (Foucault, 1986c)

Sartre:

BN	*Being and Nothingness* (Sartre, 1956)
CDR	*The Critique of Dialectical Reason* (Sartre, 1976)
CP	*The Communists and Peace* (Sartre, 1969)
DF	"Determinism and Freedom" (Sartre 1974b)
EH	"Existentialism is a Humanism" (Sartre, 1975)
NE	*Notebooks for an Ethics* (Sartre, 1992)
SFM	*Search for a Method* (Sartre, 1968)
SG	*Saint Genet* (Sartre, 1988)
WD	*War Diaries* (Sartre, 1985)

Heidegger:

AWP	"The Age of the World Picture" (Heidegger, 1977b)
BT	*Being and Time* (Heidegger, 1962)
QCT	"The Question Concerning Technology" (Heidegger, 1977d)
MMM	"Modern Science, Metaphysics, and Mathematics" (Heidegger, 1977g)

ONE

Post Script

Literature today: a certain complex, multilateral and simultaneous relation to self where the fact of coming after (of being new) is not reducible to the linear law of succession.

— Foucault, "Distance, aspect, origin."

Philosophy owes its unity—insofar as it has one—not so much to shared problems, approaches or methods as to its history. It takes its coherence from a canonical set of figures, problems and texts. It is not surprising, therefore, that philosophy, as it is taught in universities, is virtually synonymous with the history of philosophy (Foucault, 1991: 44).[1] Given this fact, the reception and evaluation of new styles of thought takes places to an important extent through contextualization—the placing of a thinker in a historical tradition. Such contextualization, so it is argued, not only enable us to assess the originality of apparently new ideas, but, more importantly, it helps to reveal why a particular thinker at a particular time felt the need to break with previous modes of thought. We can thus get a clearer picture of what she hoped to achieve: of the problems to which she was responding, and the extent to which her solutions were adequate to these problems.

Today, however, the very possibility of contextualization seems thrown into doubt, especially within the tradition of Continental philosophy. For, on all sides, a fundamental rupture is proclaimed: we have left behind the old ways of thinking, we have broken with tradition. The modern era in philosophy, which began with Descartes, and more fundamentally the history of Western metaphysics, which began perhaps with Plato, are said to be over:

> if a project is finished today, or no longer sustainable (and the very idea of the postmodern appears to support such a view), it is (...) the philosophical project *itself* in general, is it was inaugurated for the West with the Greeks. (Lacoue-Labarthe, 1989: 11)

The story of Western thought suddenly appears in all its clarity, and for the simple reason that we are no longer caught in its aporias. Its problems are no longer our problems. Suddenly, comparison between ourselves and our predecessors is no longer of any use, for a radical break separates us from them. As Jean-François Lyotard, expresses it:

> since we are inaugurating something completely new, the hands of the clock should be put back to zero (...) it is both possible and necessary to break with tradition and institute absolutely new ways of living and thinking. (Lyotard, 1992a: 90)

From this new, disillusioned point of view, an examination of the history of philosophy reveals how, for a number of centuries or even millennia, philosophers have grappled with the wrong questions and have allowed themselves to be caught up in false problems which arise from not thinking their presuppositions through to the very end. But now we have laid bare the roots of philosophical enquiry and at one stroke escaped from the impasse. We have entered into a new age of thought.

The Problem of Postmodernism

This new age is 'postmodernity.' But no sooner is the break posited or asserted than new problems arise, the first arising from the definition of the term itself. In the first place, the dating of modernity is itself still a hotly contested topic— and the debate surrounding postmodernism only serves to intensify the controversy. Nevertheless, there is a degree of consensus as to the starting dates of both modernity and modernism. Modernity— the more encompassing term, referring to the era as a whole, at least as experienced in the West— is usually dated from approximately 1800; modernism— the artistic expression of modernity— is commonly regarded as beginning only around 1890 (McGowan, 1991: 3). But there is very little consensus as to what date to take as marking the *end* of modernity and modernism; this question is, of course, logically (but perhaps only logically) identical with that of defining the beginning of postmodernism.

The problem of dating the end of modernity is compounded by the meaning of the word *modern*, both etymologically and in its everyday usage outside the academy. It refers, of course, to the present time, to right now:

> Modernity, in normal usage, is something that progresses in company with and at the speed of the years, like the bow-wave of a ship; last year's modern is not this year's. (Bradbury and McFarlane, 1983: 22)

*Post*modernity, then, is that which claims to be after the present (McKenna, 1988: 229).[2] By definition, it is a phenomenon concerned centrally and self-reflexively with time and with presence, its relation to the time in which it appears being such that it is both in and after this present. It is fitting, then, that postmodernism should have been tentatively described as beginning "at some point in the nineteenth century, perhaps at the precise moment on January 3, 1889, when Nietzsche collapses into insanity" (Hoy, 1988: 12)[3]— fitting since such a dating would make the beginning of postmodernism simultaneous with that of modernism, making the latter a movement which has outlived its own period. The paradox contained in the name of postmodernity would thus reflect its paradoxical, anachronistic, origins.

Most writers, however, place the beginnings of postmodernity more logically, at the end of modernism; this date would perhaps mark the latest point at which such a logic of non-contradiction would necessarily hold. For one of the defining features of postmodernity, one of the few which serve to distinguish the later era from the modernism in relation to which it defines itself, is postmodernism's refusal of totalizing categories, whether logical or social. Thus the era itself would be marked precisely by the non-hegemonic nature of its dominance over the time in which it appears. In Jameson's terms, postmodernism would be the "dominant cultural logic"against which "genuine difference could be measured and assessed":

> I am very far from feeling that all cultural production today is 'postmodern' in the broad sense I will be conferring on this term. The postmodern is, however, the force field in which very different kinds of cultural impulses— what Raymond Williams has usefully termed 'residual' and 'emergent' forms of cultural production— must make their way. (Jameson, 1991: 6)

The period defined by— amongst other things— the intellectual dominance of thinkers who may be described as postmodern will thus allow also for the existence of other strains of thought. Postmodern thought itself, in turn, is marked by a similar refusal of totalization. The concepts and instruments it uses, as well as the ends to which they are applied, deliberately refuse the attempt to master the entire field in which they are at work. As Martin Jay puts it:

> if one had to find one common denominator among the major figures normally included in the post-structuralist category (...) it would have to be their unremitting hostility towards totality. (Jay, 1984: 514-5)[4]

For the postmodernist, existence and thought are composed of radically heterogeneous elements elements which cannot be simultaneously thought, nor subsumed in larger synthetic categories, nor even governed by all-encompassing rules. This is not a contingent failure of thought today, which might one day be overcome, but a necessary result of the structures both of thought and of reality. Moreover, postmodern theorists do not regard this inability of theory to master its field as a defect to be lamented. Rather, the recognition of irreducible difference is celebrated both as providing a way forward for thought—an escape from the aporias of modernism—and, more importantly, as a form of thought which could help to prevent a repetition of the two great tragedies which disfigure the face of the twentieth-century: Hitler's Germany and Stalin's Soviet Union. For the prime impetus behind the movement to find new forms of thought is a recognition that Enlightenment discourses of reason and freedom were themselves amongst the conditions of possibility for the Gulag and Auschwitz. As Linda Hutcheon puts it:

> 'to totalize' does not mean just to unify, but rather means to unify with an eye to power and control, and as such, this term points to the hidden power relations behind our humanist and positivist systems of unifying disparate materials, be they aesthetic or scientific. (Hutcheon, 1988: xi)

Thus an alternative date for the beginning of postmodernity suggests itself: 1945. This date has a certain consonance with the much earlier dates proposed above: as McKenna notes, following Blanchot, to live on after Auschwitz is to survive the end of the world, to be living on after life has ended - to be after now (McKenna, 1988: 234-5).

Postmodern Thought: Jacques Derrida

McKenna's definition of postmodernism leads him to define Derrida as the essential philosopher of the new era: Derrida has done the most to render the metaphysics of presence problematical (McKenna, 1988: 229). For Derrida, the structure of language itself prevents any element from ever being simply present:

> The play of differences supposes, in effect, syntheses and referrals which forbid at any moment, or in any sense, that a simple element be *present* in and of itself, referring only to itself. Whether in the order of spoken or written discourse, no element can function as a sign without referring to another element which itself is not simply present (...) Nothing, neither among the elements nor within the system is ever simply present or absent. There are only, everywhere, differences and traces of traces. (Derrida, 1981: 26)

Once again, this is not a matter for anxiety, but for celebration. Difference—or *différance*, Derrida's neologism whose inaudible *a* points to the lack of priority of speech over writing (an intention his translators subvert by maintaining the foreignness of this one French word, as indicated by the italics)—must be affirmed, must be highlighted, since the affirmation of difference helps to keep open the field of thought or action and so prevent a final, potentially tragic, totalization. *Différance*

> governs nothing, reigns over nothing, and nowhere exercises any authority. It is not announced by any capital letter. Not only is there no kingdom of *différance*, but *différance* instigates the subversion of every kingdom. (Derrida, 1982a: 22)

Derrida may also be regarded as paradigmatically postmodern in that his work betrays a strong sense of ending. Despite a proclaimed mistrust of "historical breaks" (Derrida, 1985: 84), he too, like Jameson, obviously believes that our era has something like a cultural dominant which marks it as decisively different from any preceding period in history. For Derrida, our period is defined in its difference by its rejection of humanism. According to his reading, "humanism or anthropologism" dominated philosophical and political thought from the time of the end of the Second World War:

> Of course, here I am picking out the dominant traits of a period. The period itself is not exhausted by these dominant traits. Nor can one say in absolutely rigorous fashion that this period started after the war, and even less that it is over today. Nevertheless, I believe that the empiricism of this cross-section is justifiable here only insofar as it permits the reading of a *dominant* motif. (1982b: 117)

Our period, by contrast, is defined by its attempt to think "the ends of Man", that is, the so-called death of the subject. Derrida thus proposes a much later date for the start of postmodernity than do the partisans of 1945; indeed, for him, that date marks the start of the period which preceded this. Nevertheless defining postmodern thought as the thinking of the ends of 'Man',[5] the thought which comes after 'Man', does have a certain consonance with the definition of postmodernity as the thought and the era which lives on after the present. Moreover, Derrida deliberately limits the totalizing effects of his periodization by interpreting the humanistic age in French thought as arising in part from a misreading of a number of German thinkers— Hegel, Marx, Husserl and especially Heidegger— who, although themselves perhaps not entirely beyond humanism, had already begun to break with its presuppositions. At the same time, Derrida appears to distinguish a much longer *durée*, within which the epistemic mutation dating from the end of the war takes its place as the last stage: for him, as for Rorty and Hoy, Nietzsche, who, with Heidegger, may have been "the last of the great metaphysicians" (1982b: 136), marks the end of an epoch in Western thought, an epoch dominated by the thinking of Being as presence and by the privileging of speech over writing; an epoch which dates back at least to Plato.

Jean François Lyotard

For Lyotard, perhaps the single most influential theorist of the postmodern, the period which has just passed is of much more recent origin than the epoch of Western metaphysics, though for him too its passing may well mark the end of a much longer era. Lyotard detects two relatively recent epistemic breaks in the history and thought of the West. The first, inaugurating modernity, is contemporary with the rise of the bourgeoisie and arises from the need of the newly dominant class to legitimate itself. In response to this exigency, bourgeois thought constructed two narratives of legitimation: the first, primarily political, narrative appealed to "humanity as the hero of liberty" (Lyotard, 1984: 31); in the other, primarily philosophical, narrative, "the subject of knowledge is not the people but the speculative spirit" (1984: 33). For Lyotard, these narratives are not so much *definitive* of modernity, which is not to be identified with specific narratives, but rather *paradigmatic* of it. Modernity designates any body of knowledge which utilizes a metadiscourse to legitimate itself:

> I will use the term *modern* to designate any science that legitimates itself with reference to a metadiscourse of this (philosophical) kind making an explicit appeal to some grand narrative, such as the dialectics of Spirit, the hermeneutics of meaning, the emancipation of the rational or working subject, or the creation of wealth. (xxiii)

Postmodernity, then, involves not so much a change in the narratives of legitimation as the end of grand narratives altogether: "Simplifying to the extreme, I define *postmodern* as incredulity toward metanarratives" (xxiv). This least paradoxical of definitions of the new age (which, however, poses the question as to whether it is not itself a grand narrative) remains consistent with Derrida's definition of "what is most irreducible about our 'era' (...) the place and time in which 'we' are" (1982a: 7). For incredulity toward metanarratives is the form the rejection of totalizing discourses takes in Lyotard. In the places of these metanarratives, there arises the thinking of difference:

> Postmodern knowledge is not simply a tool of the authorities; it refines our sensitivity to differences and reinforces our ability to tolerate the incommensurable. (xxv)

For Lyotard, as for Derrida, the subject is dissolved, precisely in those heterogeneous language games which replace the metadiscourses of legitimation:

> The social subject itself seems to dissolve in this dissemination of language games. The social bond is linguistic, but it is not woven with a single thread. It is a fabric formed by the intersection of at least two (and in reality an indeterminate number) of (sic) language games, obeying different rules. (40)

As noted above, for McKenna Derrida is the paradigmatic philosopher of postmodernism. But McKenna's own definition of this new period draws heavily upon Lyotard's essay, "Answer to the question: what is the Postmodern?" This slightly later refinement of the position presented in *The Postmodern Condition*, retreats from the notion of an absolute break between modernity and postmodernity. Here, Lyotard argues that postmodernism should be understood "according to the paradox of the future (*post*) anterior (*modo*)"[6] (Lyotard, 1992b: 24). Postmodernism will always be in the future perfect, as McKenna puts it (McKenna, 1988: 231), because the modern itself does not refer to a given historical period, but to that which the postmodern criticizes. Modernism in art, for instance, refers neither to a style nor to a collection of disparate styles, but to the sum of past attempts artists have made stylistically and formally to contest their predecessors. Postmodernism refers solely to all present and future attempts to contest these received modernisms— which attempts themselves are destined to become more modernisms. Thus postmodernism is

> undoubtedly part of the modern. Everything that is received must be suspected, even if it is only a day old (...) A work can become modern only if it is first postmodern. Thus understood, postmodernism is not modernism at its end, but in a nascent state, and this state is recurrent. (Lyotard, 1992b: 21-22)

It is thus postmodernity, not modernity, that "progresses in company with and at the speed of the years, like the bow-wave of a ship"; modernity is merely the wake that is left behind and becomes canonical. Or rather, modernity is that which is left *further* behind, since postmodernism itself, although progressing in company with the years, does so at a fraction of a pace behind the present; as Lyotard says, its practioners always "arrive too late." Postmodern artists, in their contestation of all pre-established formal conventions, work "without rules, and in order to establish the rules for what *will have been made*" (Lyotard, 1992b: 24). Postmodern art follows the logic of the future perfect, and is thus no more unproblematically present for Lyotard than for Derrida.[7]

Fredric Jameson

For Lyotard, this means that, to some extent at least, postmodernism (and thus modernism) is freed from any determinate historical period to become simply any attempt at a "shattering of belief", "whenever it appears" (Lyotard, 1992b: 19). For Fredric Jameson, on the other hand, postmodernism arises (as it had for Lyotard in *The Postmodern Condition* itself) from a mutation in Western—and thus, according to Jameson, global—society as a whole. Accordingly, postmodernism is "the cultural logic of late capitalism", the form thought and culture take in the new 'post-industrial' age of multinational capitalism. It is possible nevertheless to read Jameson against himself; to read his work as offering an account which, while more properly sociological and historical than Lyotard's, describes the same event: modernism becoming postmodernism *without changing its nature*. This despite the fact that Jameson explicitly rejects this position. For him, the view that "postmodernism is itself little more than one stage of modernism proper", fails to take into account "the social position of the older modernism (...) its passionate repudiation by an older Victorian and post-Victorian bourgeoisie for whom its forms and ethos are received as being variously ugly, dissonant, obscure, scandalous, immoral, subversive, and generally 'antisocial'." Today, however

> Not only are Picasso and Joyce no longer ugly; they now strike us on the whole, as rather 'realistic,' and this is the result of a canonisation and academic institutionalisation of the modern movement generally that can be traced to the late 1950s. This is surely one of the most plausible explanations for the emergence of postmodernism itself, since the younger generation of the 1960s will now confront the formerly oppositional modern movement as a set of dead classics, which 'weigh like a nightmare on the brains of the living', as Marx once said in a different context. (Jameson, 1991: 4)

To be sure, for Jameson this does not amount to quite the same situation of permanent revolution as for Lyotard. While Jameson's postmodernists may be in revolt against high modernism, their rebellion does not take them in the direction of the avant-garde Lyotard valorizes; that is, they do not attempt to "invoke the unpresentable in presentation itself" (Lyotard, 1992b: 24). For Jameson, postmodernism no longer has any such "protopolitical vocation." But if this is so, his remark that Joyce and Picasso strike us "on the whole, as rather 'realistic'" not only seems factually questionable, but seems to lead in the direction of a theory to which Jameson does not subscribe; that is, in the direction of Lyotard's characterisation of postmodernism as modernism "in a nascent state." As Jameson himself puts it, in his foreword to *The Postmodern Condition*: "This very commitment to the experimental and the new (...) determine(s) an aesthetic that is far more closely related to the traditional ideologies of high modernism proper than to current postmodernisms" (1984: xvi). Jameson's perfectly logical theory as to why postmodernism is essentially different from modernism thereby has the effect of reducing this difference to the point of disappearance: if postmodernism is different from modernism because modernism is now canonized, no longer shocking, then postmodernism is the same as modernism because: "Its own offensive features (...) no longer scandalize anyone and are not only received with the greatest complacency but have themselves become institutionalized and are at one with the official or public culture of Western society" (1991: 4). On this account, there may indeed be a difference between postmodernism as it is, and modernism as it was, but there is none between postmodernism and modernism as it is *now*. Thus it is not only postmodernism that is 'after now,' but, equally, modernism itself[8]— or, if you prefer, the *mob* itself has vanished, its being revealed as a mere effect of the metaphysics of presence.[9]

Modernity versus Postmodernity

Unsurprisingly, then, given the paradoxes which seem inevitably to arise whenever attempts are made to distinguish postmodernity from modernity, the thematic differences between modernism and postmodernism appear slight. Modernity itself, in the domains of economics, the sciences, and philosophy, can be regarded as beginning at the time of Descartes, or even earlier (MMM: 273); in any case, there is little doubt that it is well established by the early nineteenth century. Clement Greenberg, for example, dates modernism from the time of *The Critique of Pure Reason*:

> I identify Modernism with the intensification (...) of this self-critical tendency that begins with the philosopher Kant. Because he was the first to criticize the means itself of criticism, I identify Kant as the first real Modernist (...) Modernism criticizes from the inside, through the procedures themselves of that which is criticized. (cited in Melville, 1986: 4)

If modernity is the cultural dominant of the early nineteenth century, then we seem to have ample warrant for the assertion that we are no longer modern: any comparison of the arts, sciences, economies and modes of thought of that era with those of today reveals myriad profound transformations. But the notion that we have undergone a second fundamental modification, one which irrevocably separates us from Baudelaire and Eliot, Picasso, Stravinsky, Bergson and Husserl, that we have experienced an epistemic mutation of the kind which inaugurated modernity itself, seems difficult to sustain. Instead, we are struck by the marked thematic similarities between the thought and artistic production of the era of high modernism and that of today. Partisans of the theory of the fundamental break are therefore faced with the necessity of explaining these obvious similarities between modernism and its successor. As Jameson puts it, "many of the basic postmodern features— self-consciousness,

decentering, reflexivity, textualisation— look suspiciously indistinguishable
from the old modern ones" (1991: 397). To Jameson's list of shared
characteristics, we could add that distinctively postmodern sense of the
decisive break itself. For Virginia Woolf "(o)n or about December 1910
human nature changed"; for D.H. Lawrence, it was in 1915 that "the old
world ended."[10]

In the assertion that we are no longer modern an essentially similar
notion of fundamental rupture reappears; the belief that we have once again
experienced one of those

> cataclysmic upheavals of culture, those fundamental convulsions of the creative human
> spirit that seem to topple even the most solid and substantial of our beliefs and
> assumptions, leave great areas of the past in ruins (noble ruins, we tell ourselves for
> reassurance), question an entire civilisation or culture and stimulate frenzied rebuilding.
> (Bradbury and McFarlane, 1983: 19)

To be sure, this description of epistemic mutation, which dates originally
from 1976— only three years before Lyotard's book brought the term
'postmodern' to the attention of a wide audience— is already dated, arguably
was so even at the time it was written. We no longer appeal quite so
unselfconsciously to "the creative human spirit", nor, according to Lyotard,
do we feel the need to reassure ourselves of the worth of our earlier failures.
We have certainly changed. But that is not the issue. The question we must
confront— to return to our starting point— is this: is this change really of
such a magnitude that contextualization is no longer possible, so that we
must start anew, and create a new tradition in which original work in
philosophy will now take its place? Are the philosophers of the first half of
the twentieth century now as alien to us as are the mediaeval schoolmen?
This, I take it, is ultimately the implication of the assertion that thought has
entered a new epoch.

The impression that thought must, if not actually begin anew, then at
least abandon as reference points the thinkers of just a few decades ago, is
reinforced by a reading of the polemics of the major theorists of the
postmodern, especially when we focus upon the targets of these polemics.
We have characterized postmodernism primarily by two features: the
rejection of totalization and of humanism. One needs only to mention these
features for the targets of the rejection to become apparent: the thinkers
and modes of thought the postmodernists essentially define themselves
against are those which were dominant in France immediately after the war
and which aimed to combine a subject-centered existentialism—
characterized above all by the themes of anguish, abandonment, and
individual freedom— with a relentlessly totalizing Marxism, itself aiming to

overcome the alienation of the subject of history. Paradoxically, both strands of this philosophy have their origins in a select group of German philosophers who, as also somehow precursors of the postmodern, have largely escaped the blanket rejection of out-dated systems. For Derrida, it is "the schemas of the anthropologistic misinterpretation" which "govern the rejection of Hegel, Husserl, and Heidegger into the shadows of humanist metaphysics" (Derrida, 1982b: 119), not the essential lineaments of their thought. Who is guilty of perpetrating this misinterpretation? Derrida's target is clear, signalled from the first page of "The Ends of Man", where, second among three long quotes which precede the text proper, we read the following extract from *Being and Nothingness*:

> Ontology (...) has merely enabled us to determine the ultimate ends of human reality, its fundamental possibilities, and the value which haunts it. (BN: 784)

For Derrida, not only is Sartre's emphasis on the subject responsible for the continuing modernity of French philosophy, while Germany forged ahead into the postmodern, but Sartre also bears the blame for the "misinterpretation" in France of the new German thinkers:

> Even if one does not wish to summarize Sartre's thought under the slogan 'existentialism is a humanism,' it must be recognized that in *Being and Nothingness, The Sketch of a Theory of the Emotions*, etc., the major concept, the theme of the last analysis, the irreducible horizon and origin is what was then called 'human reality.' As is well known, this is a translation of Heideggerian *Dasein*. A monstrous translation in many respects, but so much the more significant. That this translation proposed by Corbin was adopted at the time, and that by means of Sartre's authority it reigned, gives us much to think about the reading or the nonreading of Heidegger during this period, and about what was at stake in reading or not reading him in this way. (Derrida, 1982b: 115)[11]

Certainly, Derrida admits, the notion of "human reality" was intended "to suspend all the presuppositions which had always constituted the concept of the unity of man." To this extent, it tends in the direction of Heidegger's project (which itself failed in the task it had set itself of overcoming metaphysics). Nevertheless, we must recognize that in Sartre's work "the unity of man is never examined in and of itself" (1982b: 115). Existentialism *is* a humanism, and Sartre's thought falls squarely within the modern, metaphysical, tradition:

> The example of the Sartrean project remarkably verifies Heidegger's proposition according to which 'every humanism remains metaphysical,' metaphysics being the other name of ontotheology. (1982b: 116)[12]

What is lacking from Sartre's work, in Derrida's opinion, is a "history of concepts (...) For example, the history of the concept of man is never examined" (116).[13] Presumably, then, Derrida believes that the way to overcoming metaphysics lies along the path of such a history. Heidegger himself, as Derrida notes, offers a first sketch of this history (128). But the project of writing the history of the concept 'Man' is associated above all with the author of the third of the quotes which begin Derrida's essay, Foucault:

> As the archaeology of our thought easily shows, man is an invention of recent date. And one perhaps nearing its end. (OT: 387)

Perhaps Derrida does not mean to suggest that Foucault's thought contains the definitive overcoming of the anthropologism of Sartre. Perhaps, indeed, Derrida has Foucault in mind when he criticizes some of "those who denounce humanism at the same time as metaphysics" for consigning Hegel, Husserl and Heidegger to the scrap-heap of metaphysical humanism (119). *The Order of Things*, from which the Foucault quote comes, has, after all, been seen by some commentators as containing a repudiation of Heidegger.[14] On the other hand, Derrida obviously believes that a symptomatic gulf separates the humanism of Sartre from the antihumanism of Foucault. It cannot be by accident that the quote Derrida has chosen as the final epigraph to his essay refers precisely to that history of the concept of 'Man' Derrida claims is lacking from Sartre.[15]

By his juxtaposition of these two names, then, Derrida indicates that the mutation undergone by French thought over the last thirty years, which has provided the theoretical underpinnings for so much of what goes by the name of 'postmodernism', is expressed in the movement from Sartre to Foucault.[16]

Derrida's point is well taken: the gap between these thinkers does seem to be able to stand in for a much broader shift in the modes of thought which have dominated recent philosophy.[17] On the one hand, Sartre presents us with the archetypal engaged intellectual; on the other, Foucault with the proclamation of the era of the specific intellectual. One the one hand, the philosopher of freedom, on the other the archaeologist revealing the historical structures of knowledge; the one insistent that "Existentialism is a Humanism", the other declaring that "it is no longer possible to think in our day other than in the void left by man's disappearance" (OT: 341-2); the ontologist versus the historian, the Marxist versus the postmodernist.[18] And the juxtaposition of these two names is hardly unique to Derrida. It has in fact become almost a cliché of work on Foucault: one begins by sketching the philosophical environment in which Foucault came to maturity in order to illustrate the themes and modes against which he revolted. To cite one example among many:

> Only twenty-three years separate the philosophical charter of existentialism from *The Order of Things*; however, one feels confusedly that what separates Sartre and Foucault is not simply an existential option, but a different conception of the very essence of philosophy. (Palmier, 1969: XIII)

Rather than continue in the tradition which Sartre had seen as his, that of revealing what is "essential concerning the world and life, morality and the other, God, politics, and history", Foucault has undertaken on a "much more modest task: a kind of diagnostic of the present." Modern *hubris* versus postmodern humility: for many this sums up the difference, not only between two thinkers, but between two incommensurable modes of thought (Flynn, 1997: 247-8).

A substantive comparison, however, is almost never attempted.[19] Yet, despite their "different conception of the very essence of philosophy", the gulf across which thought supposedly cannot leap, it is just such a comparison that I intend to undertake here. The differences which separate Sartre and Foucault have been emphasised often enough,[20] but I wish to examine their possible affinities. Not in order to show that Foucault lacks originality, that Sartre had already made him obsolete before he had a written a word. Nor to assert Sartre's 'superiority' over Foucault: Heidegger's warning against too facile a declaration of a thinker's lack of originality is well taken:

> what is gained by establishing that a thought is, for example, 'already' to be found in Leibniz, or even 'already' in Plato? What use is this information, if it leave Leibniz' and Plato's thought in the same obscurity as the thought that such historical references are supposed to have cleared up? (Heidegger, 1985: 79)[21]

In any case, Foucault's work can stand up for itself against any such attack. But the comparison can be justified, nevertheless, precisely because of the remarkable thematic similarities between at least some characteristically modern and postmodern styles of thought. It is true that the "war on totality", as Lyotard describes it, appears to have been declared only relatively recently to be a central element of philosophy. But it is there, in embryonic form at least, in the relentlessly decentering operations which have been underway, as has so often been noted, since Copernicus. Moreover, the attack on the philosophical primacy of the subject is fully developed in a number of 'modern' thinkers. If the period in which we find ourselves is 'after now', then in some sense that 'now' and that 'after' must coexist. That is why, in spite of the untraversable chasm which, it is claimed, separates modernity and postmodernity, it is necessary to explicate both in order to understand either.

I began my examination of the rejection of contextualization in postmodernism with a quotation from Lyotard, in which he seems to be advocating just such a new start. And there can be little doubt that some of the impetus for this rejection comes from his programmatic essay. If we were to give precedence to narrative forms of knowledge while eschewing the grand narratives, as Lyotard suggests, then we would lose our sense of historical periodization:

> as meter takes precedence over accent in the production of sound (spoken or not), time ceases to be a support for memory to become an immemorial beating that, in the absence of a noticeable separation between periods, prevents them being numbered and consigns them to oblivion. (Lyotard, 1984: 22)

In this form of narrative we can recognise "the mark of that strange temporalization that jars the golden rule of our knowledge: 'never forget'" (22).

By referring to our supposed need to put "the hands of the clock (...) back to zero", Lyotard thus recalls his earlier call to consign history to oblivion. But this time, he does so only in order to reject it: if postmodernism proclaims its radical break with all that has gone before, it will merely follow the same pattern as modernism. In so doing, it will risk repeating much more:

> We now suspect that this 'rupture' is in fact a way of forgetting or repressing the past, that is to say, repeating it and not surpassing it. (Lyotard, 1992a: 90)

By citing this article of Lyotard, I do not intend to establish the postmodernist credentials of what follows; it is not even clear whether Lyotard himself should still be referred to as 'postmodern' at all, now that he no longer appears to believe in the existence of any radical rupture between modernity and postmodernity. It is precisely this rupture that is in question, at least in the domain of theoretical production (and in the belief that this domain will in some way reflect the conditions in the broader cultural, social, and economic arenas). But Lyotard's warning must be heeded, most of all by those who would assert that Enlightenment rationality led to the Gulag and to Auschwitz. This is what, ultimately, is at stake: we dare not repeat the history of the twentieth-century, for we can no longer rely on the second performance occurring as farce. For just that reason, in full awareness of the problems and possible dangers which lie in the experience of reason in modernity, we must examine whether the way forward might not lie, in part at least, in the way back; in a critical examination of the continuities as well as the discontinuities between our thought and the thought which preceded it. For Lyotard, such an examination must take the form of an investigation of the presuppositions of our modernity, a work which takes seriously its responsibility to analyze our period and its assumptions:

> If we abandon that responsibility, we will surely be condemned to repeat, without any displacement, the West's 'modern neurosis'—its schizophrenia, paranoia, etc., the source of the misfortunes we have known for two centuries. (1992a: 93)

TWO

The Nineteenth-Century Man Versus The Magic Lantern

for a little while longer the dead act as if they were living. A little while— one year, ten years, maybe even fifty, but in any case a *finite* period— and then they're buried a second time (...). (A)s long as his books provoke anger, embarrassment, shame, hatred, love— even if he is no longer anything but a shade— he shall live! Afterward, the deluge.

— Sartre, "We Write for Our own Time."

We have noted that the confrontation between Foucault and Sartre has become something of a commonplace in the critical literature on Foucault: one begins by sketching the intellectual milieu in which he was educated, a milieu dominated by phenomenology and marxism, in order to stress the rupture his work represented.[1] This is sometimes explicitly presented as a passage from the modern to the postmodern:

> It is doubtless too early to assess the break introduced by Michel Foucault (...) in a philosophic landscape previously dominated by Sartre and by what Sartre called the unsurpassable philosophy of our time, Marxism. From the outset, starting with *The History of Madness* (1961), Michel Foucault situates himself elsewhere. (Foucault, 1994a: 314)

Now this article, from the monumental *Dictionnaire des philosophes*, highlights a fact of the first importance for any attempt to compare Foucault and Sartre; that is, that both thinkers reject any suggestion that a substantive basis for such comparison exists. For while the *Dictionnaire des philosophes* entry is signed "Maurice Florence", it was in fact written by Foucault. Thus it presents us with Foucault himself endorsing the view that his work represented a "break" with Sartre, that their respective bodies of work were separated by fundamental and irreconcilable differences.

Foucault expressed this opinion, not only in this very late article, but throughout his career. In fact, following the unexpected success of *The Order of Things* in 1966, and spurred on by the French semi-intellectual media, Foucault and Sartre entered into something of a debate on the direction of contemporary thought.[2] Like most such 'debates' in which Sartre engaged, it was for the most part one-sided, consisting mainly of more or less vitriolic attacks by Foucault on Sartre's work. Around 1950, Foucault suggests, he and his generation had become postmodern— or, if not exactly postmodern, then at least post *Les temps modernes*:

> In a very sudden manner, and without apparent reason, we noticed around fifteen years ago that we were very far from the generation of Sartre, of Merleau-Ponty— the generation of *Les Temps Modernes*— who had been our law for thought and our model for existing. (Foucault, 1966a: 14)

The notion that Sartre represents a *passé* modernism is even more forcefully expressed in another interview published just two months later, albeit this time with a differently dated break between the modern and the postmodern:

> *La critique de la raison dialectique* is the magnificent and pathetic effort of a nineteenth-century man to conceive of the twentieth century. In this sense, Sartre is the last Hegelian, and even, I would say, the last Marxist.[3]

In the words of his interlocutor in another interview, dating from 1969, "Sartre would simply be one of the end points of this transcendental philosophy that is falling apart"; to which words Foucault simply responded "That's right" (1996e: 60).

But more usually, Foucault located the break that separated him from Sartre much later, around 1950, as in the *La quinzaine littéraire* interview. Interview after interview repeated the same narrative, a story which ends with the dispersal of modern, totalizing thought and its replacement by a postmodern "diagnostics":

> I belong to a generation of people for whom the horizon of reflection was defined by Husserl in a general way, Sartre more precisely and Merleau-Ponty even more precisely. It's clear that around 1950-55, for reasons that are equally political, ideological and scientific, and very difficult to straighten out, this horizon toppled for us. Suddenly it vanished and we found ourselves before a sort of great empty space inside which developments became much less ambitious, much more limited and regional. (1996d: 55)

Sartre's texts, and even his political activities, "mark an epoch", but "many today work in another direction" (1968a: 21). His generation had a passion for life, politics and existence, but "we have discovered something else, an other passion: the passion for the concept and for what I shall call the 'system'" (1966a: 14). In short, whatever the value and intrinsic interest of Sartre's work, 'we' have left it behind.

What was it about the work of the earlier thinker which made it so incompatible with Foucault's? According to the latter, it was ultimately Sartre's humanism. In Sartre's thought, the entity which he called the for-itself, which is meant to signify that region of being which is consciousness but which Sartre rarely distinguished very rigorously from the empirical individual, gave meaning to the world it encountered. Thus, his version of phenomenology

> placed the bare event before or to the side of meaning— the rock of facticity, the mute inertia of occurrence— and then submitted it to the active process of meaning, to its digging or elaboration. (Foucault, 1977d: 175)

In other words, Sartre's words, the for-itself gives meaning to the in-itself. Foucault criticizes this aspect of Sartre's thought for its idealist tendencies: phenomenology, conceived in this way, cannot properly "grasp the event" (176) because for it the meaning of the event is not inherent in it, but, on the contrary, comes to it from outside, from consciousness.

But this does not explain why the break between Sartre's and Foucault's generation should have occurred around 1950. After all, idealism has been confronting realism for many centuries. It is Foucault's second objection which demonstrates why the philosophy of meaning has no place in postmodern thought:

> The point of rupture is situated the day when Lévi-Strauss, for societies, and Lacan, for the unconscious, showed us that '*meaning*' was probably only a sort of surface effect, a shimmering, a foam, and that what traverses us profoundly, what precedes us, sustains us in time and in space, was the *system* (1966a: 14)

Sartre's subject-centered humanism attempted to explain effects of meaning in terms of a meaning-giving for-itself. But Lacan and Lévi-Strauss had demonstrated that meaning *precedes* us. It is thus that structuralism rejoins Heidegger in proclaiming postmodernism. Just as for Heidegger, "man" is "bespoken by language" (1971e: 192), so for Lacan it is "the structures, the very system of language— and not the subject— which speaks" (1966a: 14).

The break between modernism and postmodernism is thus centered around language. It is the rupture between a form of thought in which the sovereign subject animates its words with exactly that meaning it intends, and one which sees the subject itself as essentially a function of language.

This narrative, which equates postmodernism with a linguistic turn, has proven durable. In 1983, Foucault was still telling essentially the same story concerning the rupture in French thought. The "critical point" in this narrative was "Merleau-Ponty's encounter with language":

the problem of language appeared and it was clear that phenomenology was no match for structural analysis in accounting for the effects of meaning that could be produced by a structure of the linguistic type, in which the subject (in the phenomenological sense) did not intervene to confer meaning. (1988c: 21)

Thus we can sum up the gap between our two thinkers as follows: Sartre's is a humanist discourse, in which consciousness confers meaning on the world; Foucault's a post-humanist, which investigates the way in which the subject-effect is created.

But before we so neatly package our thinkers, we should note that this is not how Sartre saw matters. Although the 'debate' between the two was largely one-sided, Sartre did respond in one interview to the polemic directed against him. To the structuralist critique in general (and Foucault's was by no means the only, nor even the best known, structuralist condemnation of Sartre's social theory) Sartre reiterated his belief that, although structures exist in the social world, it is humanity which lies at their source. Thus Sartre replied on the ground Foucault had chosen for his critique, that of language:

> In nature you will not find oppositions such as those described by the linguist (...) If you admit the existence of such a system, you must also admit that language exists only as spoken, that is, in action (...) Structures impose themselves on us only to the extent that they are made by others. (Sartre, 1971: 111)

Against the analyses of structure proposed by Althusser and Foucault (114), against the proclamation of the death of man by Lacan and Foucault (113), Sartre continues to defend a mode of thought which, while rejecting "a substantial I", insists nevertheless that "(w)hat is essential is not that man is made", not the structures which precede 'him', "but *that he makes that which makes him*" (115) and can therefore always transcend this constitutive structure. Sartre's thought thus remains defiantly subject-centered.

But Sartre also counterattacks on a different ground: not that of language and meaning, but that of history, Marxism and the dialectic. It is here that Foucault comes into Sartre's line of fire in his own right. When Sartre accuses structuralism of "the denial of history", it is to *The Order of Things* that he turns as the paradigmatic example:

> Foucault does not tell us what would be most interesting: how each thought is constructed out of these conditions, or how men pass from one thought to another. To do that, he would have to interpose praxis, therefore history: and that is precisely what he denies (...) he replaces cinema with a magic lantern, movement by a succession of immobilities. (110)

In Sartre's eyes, *The Order of Things* presents "an eclectic synthesis in which Robbe-Grillet, structuralism, linguistics, Lacan and *Tel Quel* are systemically utilized to demonstrate the impossibility of historical reflection" (110). Behind this attack on history, Sartre detects Foucault's ultimate target; that is, Marxism. *The Order of Things* is thus a war-machine, a weapon deployed by reactionary forces in the service of the current social order. Foucault's structuralism is "the latest barrier that the bourgeoisie once again can erect against Marx" (110).

Sartre's extraordinary claims provoked an equally vehement response from Foucault, most notably in an interview published as "Foucault Responds to Sartre." Foucault subsequently claimed (and his interviewer verified) that his remarks on Sartre "were explanations given *off the record* in order to vindicate— in private— my refusal to respond to certain questions" (1968a: 21). Thus his comments had been published without permission (and in fact the radio interview for which the discussion was intended was broadcast with the portions on Sartre omitted). Nevertheless, Foucault's remarks are worth quoting at length, if only because the *prima facie* evidence upon which to compare the two thinkers— their recorded thoughts upon one another's work— is so scarce:

> First, Sartre is a man with too much important work to do (...) to have the time to read my book. In fact, he hasn't read it. Consequently, what he says about it can't seem very pertinent to me. (1996d: 54)

More consequentially, Foucault responds to Sartre's charge that he denies history:

> No historian has ever reproached me for this. There is a sort of myth of History for philosophers (...) For philosophers, History is a kind of grand and extensive continuity where the liberty of individuals and economic and social determinations come to be intertwined (...) this philosophical myth that I am accused of having murdered, well, I would be delighted if I have killed it, since that was exactly what I wanted to do. But not at all history in general. (41)

Explicitly, Foucault was rarely to return to Sartre in his subsequent writings. But in his "mise au point", he noted that over the last eighteen months he had been working "to respond to some questions which have been put to me (...) to some objections which have been formulated— and amongst them those of Sartre" (1968a: 21). This work was *The Archaeology of Knowledge*, and in it the traces left by Sartre's "objections" are clear.

The *Archaeology* reprises, for example, the theme of the philosophical myth of history, which Foucault links with subject-centered philosophy:

> Continuous history is the indispensable correlative of the founding function of the subject: the guarantee that everything that has eluded him may be restored to him (...) Making historical analysis the discourse of the continuous and making human

consciousness the original subject of all historical development and all action are the two sides of the same mode of thought. (AK: 12)

Thus, against Sartre's assertion (the reference to Sartre is implicit here, revealed in the use of the term "project") that structures are human constructs, Foucault insists on the impossibility of ever

reanimating through the project, the work of meaning, or the movement of totalisation, the interplay of material determinations, rules of practice, unconscious systems, rigorous but unreflected relations, correlations that elude all lived experience. (AK: 14)

Later in the *Archaeology* Foucault returns to Sartre, but so obliquely that the reference seems never to have been detected previously. That the target is Sartre is revealed by Foucault's reprise of the former's "magic lantern" image.[4] Foucault sketches an imaginary objection to his work, that "Archaeology (...) seems to treat history only to freeze it":

Discourse is snatched from the law of development and established in a discontinuous atemporality. It is immobilized in fragments: precarious splinters of eternity. But there is nothing one can do about it: several eternities succeeding one another, a play of fixed images disappearing in turn, do not constitute either movement, time, or history. (166-7)

To this objection, Foucault replies that: "Archaeology does not set out to treat as simultaneous what is given as successive", but merely "suspends (...) the theme that succession is an absolute" (169). By this suspension Foucault hopes to capture the event of change in itself, in a singularity that "no teleology would reduce in advance" (203).

Subsequent to *The Archaeology of Knowledge*, references to Sartre become fewer and fewer, although on the whole no more positive.[5] This, no doubt, is due in part to the fact that the two philosphers began to work together in political activities. Foucault, at first grudgingly, then more willingly, accepted Sartre as a partner in the protests he led against racism, against violations of human rights in the prison system, against injustices wherever he saw them. In order not to sour their personal relationship, then, Foucault desisted from unfavorable comments on Sartre's humanism. One could speculate, too, that he no longer felt the need to make a name for himself by attacking the towering figure Sartre represented on the French intellectual scene. Foucault himself was soon to be proclaimed "the new Sartre."[6]

As for Sartre, he was never to repeat the vitriolic attack on Foucault. In his published writings I have been able to locate only three references to Foucault subsequent to his 1966 "Replies." In a 1972 lecture entitled "Justice and the State", Sartre enlists Foucault's aid in establishing three separate conceptions. The first concerns popular justice:

> Michel Foucault (...) says that popular justice does not depend on any absolute principle: If a *damage* is done to it, it *demands compensation.* (1977a: 175)

The second, the role of the state:

> To cite Foucault again, its role since the eighteenth century has been to set up two categories of the masses in opposition to each other. (175)

The third, ironically, concerns the meaning of the physical layout of the courtroom:

> Foucault remarks that the topographical analysis of a courtroom (...) is enough to indicate that the judge belongs to another species. (189)

This third citation is ironic precisely because Foucault's original comment had been made in the course of an explicit critique of Sartre. Foucault's concern, in claiming that the "spatial arrangement of the court (...) implies an ideology" (1972a: 8), was to criticize the 'people's court' at Lens which Sartre had helped to set up. Although Sartre's name is not explicitly mentioned by Foucault, there could have been little doubt as to his target, especially when he adds:

> When, into the bargain, the people's court is organised or presided over by intellectuals (...) the whole thing is infused with idealism. (1980a: 30)

Either Sartre was prepared to overlook Foucault's criticism, or, in a for him very rare show of intellectual humility, he accepted Foucault's appraisal with good grace. Whatever the case, he did not feel it necessary to criticize in turn. But when, only a few months later, he was explicitly interrogated on Foucault's criticism of the people's court, Sartre was quick to the offensive:

> We do not agree, the Maos and I on one side, with him on the other. We consider that the people are perfectly capable of creating a court of justice (...) Justice implies first a huge movement that overturns institutions. But if, in the course of this great movement, the form of revolutionary justice appears, that is, if people are asked in the name of justice what prejudices they have been subjected to, I can't see that whether people are sitting behind a table or not causes any harm.[7]

Nevertheless, this disagreement is of a different order to the barbs launched in 1966. Gone are the fundamental disputes, the tone of denunciation, the attacks *ad hominem.* Instead, Sartre alerts us to a disagreement between comrades working towards the same, revolutionary, goal. Foucault might be "the one who is radical", but at least he errs on the right side.

Sartre mentions Foucault only once more in his published work, in his discussions with Philippe Gavi and Pierre Victor published as *On a raison de se révolter.* Here Foucault is explicitly referred to as an ally in political struggle and as an intellectual of comparable stature to Sartre himself. Because of his advanced years, Sartre says, he can no longer play as active a role as he would like in direct political action:

> I cannot last the distance at demonstrations because I have a bad leg (...) From this point of view, Foucault is better placed than me. It's not that want to cede him my place. (Sartre, et. al., 1974f: 73)

On the surface, Sartre's regret is at Foucault's taking his place at a certain number of demonstrations. But it takes little stretching of the imagination to find in Sartre's complaint a recognition that his position as the leading intellectual and militant of his time is under threat from Foucault.

An Unacceptable Comparison

As we have seen, despite their rapprochement, Foucault was vehement in his rejection of the idea that his thought owed anything to Sartre. Daniel Defert reports that, when Foucault was asked whether he would attend Sartre's funeral, "his response was blunt: 'Why, I owe him nothing'" (Defert, 1990: 1201).[8] On other occasions, however, Foucault spoke of Sartre's "influence" upon him, even if only to assert the necessity he had felt to escape from it:

> When I was a student in the 1950s, I read Husserl, Sartre, Merleau-Ponty. When you feel an overwhelming influence, you try to open a window. (Foucault, 1988b: 12-3)

One might well imagine that some traces of such an "overwhelming influence" must remain, no matter how successful Foucault was in freeing himself from it. In any case, we do have some *prima facie* evidence of how unfavourably Foucault might have reacted to my attempt to compare them:

> I think that Sartre's immense oeuvre, and his political action, mark an epoch (...) I will never accept a comparison— even for the sake of opposing them— of my little enterprise of historical and methodological spadework with an oevure like his. (1968a: 21)

It is worth noting that here Foucault manages to combine an almost obsequious politeness with the suggestion that his work belongs to another epoch than that "marked" by Sartre's.

As to how Sartre might have reacted to the comparison, we have another incident reported by Defert to guide us:

> When someone asked Sartre about Foucault, he cut him short: "There's nothing to say, we do things together." (Defert, 1990: 1206)

In order to compare Sartre and Foucault, it is thus necessary to go against the express wishes of each; to say things about which there is nothing to say; to compare bodies of work separated by the chasm of incommensurable epochs. Nevertheless, I claim Foucauldian warrant for what follows. As Foucault says in relation to a return to Greek thought, those forms of thought which say

> 'See, in such and such a philosopher something has been forgotten' are not very interesting. We cannot derive much from them. This does not mean that contact with such and such a philosopher cannot produce something but we would have to understand that this thing is new. (ECS: 15)

That is what I aim to produce through the comparison of Sartre with Foucault: not the assertion that Foucault has 'forgotten' an essential insight of Sartre's; not the claim that Foucault has compensated for the deficiencies in Sartre's thought; but something which is neither in Foucault's thought, nor Sartre's, nor, strictly speaking, in a synthesis of the two: something new.

Remarks on Methodology

In order to forestall misunderstanding, let me say a few words about what the following chapters attempt to provide, and, equally, what they do not. Sartre and Foucault each wrote a prodigious number of texts, ranging from philosophy to literary criticism, from introductions and prefaces to other people's books to journalism and political statements in response to contemporary events. The sheer size of Sartre's output in particular puts me in a peculiarly Sartrean position: it is necessary to choose. I have thus left out, for the most part at least, Sartre's earliest writings. Quite simply, they do not seem to me to have the interest of the later work, and are too marked by the flaws I will identify in *Being and Nothingness*, the earliest work I will consider at any length.[9]

Since my selection from Sartre is so partial, I will make no attempt at what might be called a total interpretation of his work: many of the points I make with reference to Sartre's texts could very well be contested using other texts. In fact, his work does not seem to me to form a coherent whole, not even were one to take a synchronic slice from the *oeuvre*.[10] That does not mean that I will be presenting Sartre's thought at random, taking from him whatever suits me, with no regard to systematicity. I will attempt to present what I take to be the most valuable aspects of Sartre's thought, which aspects *do* form an internally coherent whole.[11] At times, this even necessitates something of a 'splintering' of the one text; particularly with some of the posthumous writings, which were unpublished presumably in part because they do not form coherent entities. But such a splintering applies to all Sartre's longer works to some extent. As Le Doeuff says, "books have their own destiny and the most usual of these is to be fragmented" (1991: 56).

With Foucault, by contrast, I will be much more concerned to offer a total interpretation. I deal with every major text to some degree, the only exceptions being two very early works, his introduction to Ludwig Binswanger's "Dream and Existence", and his first book, *Maladie mentale et personnalité*, both from 1954. These are excluded because Foucault had not as yet developed an original problematic, and for the related reason that both texts are heavily and explicitly marked by a version of existentialism, albeit of a more Heideggerian than Sartrean kind.[12] They are thus excluded for much the same reason as *The Idiot of the Family*: it is sometimes more interesting and productive to compare thinkers where they are furthest apart, than where they are closest. By situating myself in the gap between two thinkers who, after all, undertake completely different sorts of enterprises, I hope to show both that there are a certain number of consonances between them, and that a sympathetic reading of Sartre can shed light upon certain difficulties in Foucault's work, either by clearing them up or by showing them to be intractable. This is a reading, then, not so much of Foucault's work and of Sartre's, but of Foucault's work in the light of certain aspects of Sartre's. At the conclusion, however, I hope there will emerge not just another interpretation of Foucault, but also that, by a movement of reflux, a new Sartre will be made available for thought. In any case, I will have shown (and the future perfect is not incidental) that Sartre, as much as Foucault, is still capable of provoking "anger, embarrassment, shame, hatred, love." In that sense at least, both are still our contemporaries: they accompany us, follow us, maybe even guide us, as we forge ahead into unknown territory into which they are forbidden to enter.

THREE

Heidegger And The Postmodern

> I was surprised when two of my friends in Berkeley wrote something about me and said that Heidegger was influential. Of course it was quite true, but no one in France has ever perceived it. When I was a student in 1950s, I read Husserl, Sartre, Merleau-Ponty. When you feel an overwhelming influence, you try to open a window.
>
> — Foucault, "Truth, Power, Self"

A rationale for the Foucault/Sartre comparison thus established, I wish to make a brief detour through the work of Heidegger. This detour is necessary to the extent that the proposed comparison revolves around the central issue of postmodernism: Heidegger, more than any other philosopher, has widei̇ ɔeen proclaimed as the precursor of the postmodern.[1] And if the postmodern is thinking in the future perfect, then Heidegger must indeed be considered postmodern, for it was he who proclaimed that it is the "*perfect* tense *a priori*" which characterizes the kind of Being belonging to Dasein" (BT: 117). That is, Dasein is 'always-already' in the world, always already committed to projects, meanings, language.[2] As Krell puts it, Heidegger's analysis "is perfect. Or at least *of* the perfect" (1987: 114).

Moreover, an examination of Heidegger's influence is especially pressing in the case of our thinkers, since Heidegger's writings inspired so much of post-war French thought, from *Being and Nothingness* at least to the coming to prominence of Jacques Derrida and his epigones. As Ferry and Renaut put it:

> French intellectual history (...) has been dominated since 1945 more or less surreptitiously, by a critique of the modern world and of the values of formal democracy, a critique inspired mainly by Marx and Heidegger, successively, and sometimes simultaneously. (Ferry and Renaut, 1990: xi)

If any confirmation of the dominance of Heideggerianism were needed, it was surely provided by the controversy surrounding the recent re-examination of Heidegger's involvement with National Socialism, the extent to which this rocked the French intellectual world, and the need many of its leading lights felt to address the question of Heidegger's silence. As Lyotard has said: "The Heidegger affair is a 'French' affair" (Lyotard, 1990: 4).[3]

That Heidegger stands at the center of Sartre's work cannot be doubted. Sartre himself acknowledged the magnitude of his debt. Heidegger's work, he wrote:

> supervened to teach me authenticity and historicity just at the very moment when war was about to make these notions indispensable to me. If I try to imagine what I'd have made of my thought without those tools, I am gripped by a retrospective fear. (Sartre, 1983b: 182)

But the post-structuralist generation has accused Sartre of popularization and distortion of Heidegger. They see the hegemony of Sartre's interpretation as a barrier to a proper understanding of the German's work. I have already referred to Derrida's criticism of Sartre for the adoption of Corbin's "monstrous translation" of *Dasein* as "human reality." It is this same charge of distortion Derrida has in mind when he speaks of the necessity of freeing himself "from Sartre's and Merleau-Ponty's understanding of Heidegger and Husserl" (Derrida, 1990: 145). Precisely the same accusation has been levelled at Sartre by Foucault himself: just as "the romantcis have guarded us from Hölderlin, Valéry from Rilke or from Trakl, Proust from Joyce", so Sartre "has well protected us against Heidegger" (1966b: 3).

Foucault's Debt to Heidegger

Foucault's own relation to Heidegger has been the subject of some investigation, no doubt prompted by his admission in a late interview that for him Heidegger "has always been the essential philosopher":

> My entire philosophical development was determined by my reading of Heidegger. I nevertheless recognize that Nietzsche outweighed him. I do not know Heidegger well enough: I hardly know *Being and Time* nor what has been published recently. My knowledge of Nietzsche certainly is better than my knowledge of Heidegger. Nevertheless, these are the two fundamental experiences I have had. It is possible that if I had not read Heidegger, I would not have read Nietzsche. I had tried to read Nietzsche in the fifties but Nietzsche alone did not appeal to me - whereas Nietzsche and Heidegger: that was a philosophical shock! (Foucault, 1988e: 250)

Unfortunately, the work addressing Foucault's reception of Heidegger is rarely very extensive, and most concentrates upon either Foucault's critique of Heidegger in *The Order of Things*, or Foucault's relationship to the early Heidegger, or what has been called his "early Heideggerian stage" (During, 1992: 7), extending no later than *Madness and Civilisation*. Thus the full extent to which Foucault's 1960's work is indebted to post-*Kehre* Heidegger is still little appreciated. As recently as 1988 Lebrun felt himself able to assert that "*Les mots et les choses* owes nothing to Heidegger."[4] Hubert Dreyfus's contribution to the conference at which Lebrun had made this comment "provoked quite vehement reactions, all of which questioned the grounds on which he drew the parallel between Foucault and Heidegger."[5] Even Jacques Derrida, regarded by some as Heidegger's most gifted interpreter, has felt able to accuse Foucault of having "never confronted (Heidegger) and, if one may so, never explained himself on his relation to him." This avoidance Derrida apparently interprets as a significant lacuna at the heart of Foucault's philosophy (Derrida, 1989b: 17).[6] Despite the volume of work dealing with the two thinkers, the real extent of Foucault's debt to Heidegger has yet to be clarified.

A book can, and no doubt soon will, be devoted to what Ijsseling calls the "*traces* of Heidegger" in Foucault (Ijsseling, 1986: 414). In this chapter I intend to show how Foucault's ideas regarding language, history, and being were developed through a reading of Heidegger's essays on *Die Sprache*. The analysis will be sketched out only to the degree I believe necessary to situate Foucault in relation to Sartre's own reception of Heidegger.

The thread that ties Foucault's work together into a fragmented whole is his examination, from 1954 and *Maladie mentale et personnalité* to 1984 and *The Care of the Self*, of the institutional and practical conditions of possibility of knowledge. Thus, if one attempts to classify his enterprise, epistemology appears to be the traditional philosophical category to which it comes closest. Now, there is some evidence that this is not Foucault's own interpretation of his work, at least at the time of *The Order of Things*. Rather, he regarded himself as an ontologist, and the ontology he expounds was, in its essential respects, drawn from Heidegger.[7] The foundation of each episteme, the principle that causes it to be incompatible with those which preceded it and those which will follow, is the being of the elements within it. In the change from one episteme to another:

> the mode of being of things, and of the order that divided them up before presenting them to the understanding, was profoundly altered. (OT: xii)

Clearly, this form of thought operates at the boundary between epistemology and ontology, for it is concerned both with "the mode of being of things" and with the manner in which they are presented to the understanding. Foucault's enterprise is better thought as ontology than epistemology, nevertheless, for he appears to refer both knowledge and its objects back to a more archaic level defining the mode of being of both:

what we must grasp and attempt to reconstitute are the modifications that affected knowledge itself, at that archaic level which makes possible both knowledge itself and the mode of being of what is to be known. (OT: 54)

The notion that history consists essentially in a succession of discontinuous unities which define the mode of being of the entities within them is not original to Foucault, but is, in broad outline, drawn from Heidegger (Habermas, 1987: 266).[8]

According to Heidegger, it is art that establishes the mode of being of the entities found within a particular *episteme*:

Always when that which is as a whole demands, as what is, itself, a grounding in openness, art attains to its historical nature as foundation. This foundation happened in the West for the first time in Greece. What was in the future to be called Being was set into work, setting the standard. The realm of beings thus opened up was then transformed into a being in the sense of God's creation. This happened in the Middle Ages. This kind of being was again transformed at the beginning and in the course of the modern age. Beings became objects that could be controlled and seen through by calculation. At each time a new and essential world arose. (Heidegger, 1971a: 76-7)

This "radical change (...) of the lighting of the Being of beings" is, for Heidegger, "*a stretch of the way of actual history* (...) a history that always concerns the openness of Being— or nothing at all" (MMM: 280).

Heidegger's use of the terms "lighting of the Being of beings" and "the openness of Being", or, more usually, "clearing" (all of which translate the German *Lichtung*), might suggest that he thinks of the change from episteme to episteme as involving no more than a change in *Dasein's* comportment toward an unchanging substratum of Being. Such a conception is not entirely absent from Heidegger, as we shall see. But within the epistemes themselves, Heidegger asserts that what is involved is a change in being, not merely in our access to, or knowledge of, things unknowable in themselves. As Clark notes, "Heidegger grants an ontological function to language" (Clark, 1986: 1006). This is most clearly expressed in the lectures published as "The Nature of Language" (Heidegger, 1982c). There (as in "Words", included in the same volume) he examines a late poem of Stefan George, which, according to Heidegger, "points to the relation of word and thing" (73) (perhaps giving us a clue as to the source of the title of *Les Mots et les choses*). The poem ends with a line expressing that relationship:

Where word breaks off no thing may be.

Heidegger interprets this to mean that "no thing *is* where the word, that is, the name is lacking. The word alone gives being to the thing" (62). The famous proposition, first advanced in the "Letter on Humanism", that "language is the house of Being" Heidegger now reinterprets to mean that "the being of anything that is resides in the word" (63).

Now, the totality of Being revealed through the language of a historical epoch represents, for Heidegger, that epoch's understanding of Being. Hence the importance of ontology, the privileged discourse which describes, not Being as it is (for the question of Being has long been 'covered over'), but the being of the beings of a particular epoch. Ontology, then, despite its name, concerns not the ontological, but the ontic:

> Metaphysics grounds an age, in that through a specific interpretation of what is and through a specific comprehension of truth it gives to that age the basis upon which it is essentially formed. (AWP: 115)

Each age thus presents a self-enclosed unity, grounded upon an interpretation of being. In "The Age of the World Picture" (1977b), Heidegger distinguishes three such ages, or what Foucault was to call *epistemes* (a word Heidegger himself uses, to refer not to such epochs in general, but to the Greek age in which it originated), the Greek, the medieval, and the modern. Clearly, the Foucault of *The Order of Things* is not simply elaborating upon and providing evidence for Heidegger's already developed narrative of history. *The Order of Things* could better be described as a critique of Heidegger's overly reductionist division, but one advanced from within a generally Heideggerian perspective. Heidegger characterises the Middle Ages as the epoch in which

> that which is, is the *ens creatum*, that which is created by the personal Creator-God as the highest cause. Here, to be in being means to belong within a specific rank of the order of what has been created— a rank appointed from the beginning— and as thus caused, to correspond to the cause of creation. (AWP: 130)

Foucault too refers to "this immense, taut, and vibrating chain, this rope of 'convenience'" (OT: 16), in his characterization of the sixteenth century. In fact, there is no reason to believe that he would have objected to Heidegger's description, although he might have wished to modify it in certain respects, principally by stressing the related but separate matter of the importance of resemblance to this episteme. Furthermore, whereas Heidegger describes this era as the "Middle Ages", Foucault appears to limit it to the Renaissance (Heidegger associates the Greek episteme with the pre-Socratics and dates the medieval episteme from Aristotle to Descartes; at least, so it appears from his remark that "the much-cited medieval Schoolman Roger Bacon remains merely a successor to Aristotle" (122)).

It is with the interpretation of post-Renaissance knowledge/being configurations that Heidegger and Foucault really part ways. Both date what

Foucault calls the Classical age from much the same time: for Foucault, "Don Quixote's adventures form the boundary" (OT: 46); for Heidegger, Descartes' work is symptomatic of the change, although only as "substantially participating" in a movement, already then a century old, of "reflection upon the fundamental meaning" of the mathematical" (MMM: 275).[9] Foucault also follows Heidegger's interpretation of the meaning of the *mathesis* that dominates Classical thought:

> the relation of all knowledge to the mathesis is posited as the possibility of establishing an ordered succession between things, even non-measurable ones (...) this relation to the mathesis as a general science of order does not signify that knowledge is absorbed into mathematics, or that the latter becomes the foundation for all possible knowledge. (OT: 57)

For Heidegger, the mathematical is the projection in which

> is posited that which things are taken as, what and how they are to be evaluated before hand (...) the mathematical projection is the anticipation of the essence of things, of bodies; thus the basic blueprint of the structure of every thing and its relation to every other thing is sketched in advance. (MMM: 268)[10]

Unlike Foucault, however, Heidegger asserts that an understanding of being which is still with us was established in Descartes's period; one wherein the human being becomes subject and the world becomes object:

> Until Descartes every thing at hand for itself was a 'subject' but now the 'I' becomes the special subject, that with regard to which all the remaining things first determine themselves as such. Because— mathematically— they first receive their thingness only through the founding relation to the highest principle and its 'subject' (I), they are essentially such as stand as something else in relation to the 'subject,' which lie over against it as *objectum*. The things themselves become 'objects.' (MMM: 280)

In the process, "the very essence of man itself changes (...). But this is possible only when the comprehension of what is as a whole changes" (AWP: 128).

In *The Order of Things*, Foucault implicitly, and almost without mentioning Heidegger's name, argues that in this interpretation the German had conflated two epistemes, two epochs of the history of Being. The order in which Descartes worked was not the episteme of 'Man', but rather that of representation. Foucault's picture of the Classical age is thus radically different from that of Heidegger:[11]

> In Classical thought, the personage for whom the representation exists, and who represents himself within it, recognising himself therein as an image or reflection, he who ties together all the interlacing threads of the 'representation in the form of a picture or table'— he is never to be found in that table itself. Before the end of the eighteenth century, *man* did not exist. (OT: 308)

Rather, it is with the collapse of the episteme of representation that the subject of whom Heidegger speaks, the one to whom all being is referred, enters the picture. It is with Kant, and not Descartes that the transcendental/empirical doublet comes to characterize Western thought.

The Problems of Modernity: Heidegger's Diagnosis

It is clear that Foucault's analysis of the 'history of being' represents an advance on Heidegger's, in that it presents a much more refined, less unwieldy and less reductionist model, in which, for example, the essence of the modern age is no longer seen as the logical outgrowth of Platonism. That said, it is also clear that Foucault finds more in Heidegger's work to agree with, to develop and to elaborate than to criticize (Ijsseling, 1986: 419-20). In particular, Foucault is essentially in agreement with Heidegger as to what lies at the root of the problems of modernity, and, although he ignores or criticizes much of Heidegger's solution to this problem, his own solution develops from scattered hints in Heidegger. The problem, as Foucault and Heidegger both see it, is objectification, which for both also entails subjectification. For Heidegger, in the era ruled by the essence of technology, the former "world content of things" becomes "the object character of technological dominion." As a result, "the humanness of man and the thingness of things dissolve into the calculated market value" (Heidegger, 1971b: 114-5). The final consequence of this interpretation of being is the turning of everything that presences into the "standing-reserve":

> Everywhere everything is ordered to stand by, to be immediately at hand, indeed to stand there just so that it may be on call for a further ordering. Whatever is ordered about in this way has its own standing. We call it the standing-reserve. (QCT: 17)

Hubert Dreyfus is basically correct when he asserts that Heidegger is concerned to show how our technological interpretation of Being "distorts our understanding of *things*", whereas Foucault "is not interested in how *things* show up but exclusively in people's actions" (Dreyfus, 1992: 86, 81). But Dreyfus overstates his case. I hope I have already shown that the Foucault of *The Order of Things* was indeed interested in *things*.[12] As for Heidegger, while it is true that he believed the technological understanding of being represented an assault upon beings, which "already had annihilated things as things long before the atom bomb exploded" (Heidegger, 1971c: 170), the conclusions he drew from this were much the same as Foucault's.

The interpretation of being that transforms things into objects and people into subjects ends by converting both into standing-reserve:

> As soon as what is unconcealed no longer concerns man even as object, but does so, rather, exclusively as standing-reserve, and man in the midst of objectlessness is nothing but the orderer of the standing-reserve, then he comes to the very brink of a precipitous fall; that is, he comes to the point where he himself will have to be taken as standing-reserve. (QCT: 26-7)

The consequence of this transformation is strikingly similar to Foucault's notion of the disciplined society. It is to this transformation that Heidegger traces "the current talk about human resources, about the supply of patients for a clinic" (QCT: 18). On similar grounds to those developed in *Madness and Civilisation*, Heidegger objects to the attempt to capture "human existence (...) in the objectness belonging to psychiatry" (Heidegger, 1977e: 174).

Foucault as 'Young Heideggerian'

The similarities between Heidegger and Foucault are here so great that, notwithstanding the latter's well known critique of this "magical" notion (AK: 21), we must conclude that the German's work had indeed exerted a considerable *influence* upon Foucault.[13] But these similarities should not be allowed to obscure the equally great differences, which show the extent to which Heidegger's ideas, far from being *only*, "a sublimated philosophical version (...) of the political or ethical principles which determined the philosopher's support for Nazism" (Bourdieu, 1991: 3-4), are actually amenable to employment within what can only be described as a 'left-wing' context.[14]

The essential difference lies in the two philosophers' analyses of modernity, and of the functioning of the disciplinary society.[15] For Heidegger, the modern era is one of reduction, of levelling and of uniformity, an epoch in which:

> everything becomes equal and indifferent in consequence of the one will intent upon the uniformly calculated availability of the whole earth. (Heidegger, 1977c: 105)

In Heidegger's hatred of mass-production, the average and the everyday, Pierre Bourdieu detects an equation in which authenticity and inauthenticity equals the "opposition between the 'elite' and the 'masses'" and in Heidegger's "contempt for all forces which 'level down' (...) a particular disgust for egalitarian ideologies" (Bourdieu, 1991: 79).[16] Modernity erases distinctions of rank; through its paradimatic political form— democracy— it threatens to subject us all to the rule of the hated ordinary people.

Despite the profound influence the German exterted upon him, the political import of modernity for Foucault was almost precisely the opposite of that which Heidegger saw in it. For him, the problem with discipline is not that it levels; but that it *individualizes*:[17]

> The problem in the past for the one who wrote was to tear himself out of the anonymity of everything; nowadays, it's to succeed in effacing one's own name and of coming to lodge one's voice in this great anonymous murmur of discourses held today. (Foucault, 1996c: 28)

Foucault's most extensive exposition of this theme, prior to its full development in the genealogical texts of the 1970s, occurs in *The Birth of the Clinic*, where, however, he is content to allow the political implications to remain unstated. In clinical practice, as opposed to the medicine of species, "in which the individual could receive no positive status" (BC: 15),

> (t)he gaze is no longer reductive, it is, rather, that which establishes the individual in his irreducible quality. And thus it becomes possible to organise a rational language around it. The *object* of discourse may equally well be a *subject*, without the figures of objectivity being in any way altered. It is this *formal* reorganisation, *in depth*, rather than the abandonment of theories and old systems, that made *clinical experience* possible; it lifted the old Aristotelian prohibition: once could at last hold a scientifically structured discourse about an individual. (xiv)

Here, as for the Heidegger of *Being and Time*, the individual is constituted only by a knowledge that detours through the experience of death (During, 1992: 50):

> the perception of death (...) is constitutive of singularity; it is in that perception of death that the individual finds himself, escaping from a monotonous, average life; in the slow, half-subterranean, but already visible approach of death, the dull, common life becomes an individuality at last. (171)[18]

Given Foucault's negative evaluation of individualization, should we construe this registering of individualizing knowledge's necessary passage through death as a criticism of Heidegger?[19] Answering in the affirmative is made difficult by Foucault's own seeming valorization of death in the works of this period, where he found in it, not the source of individuation, but the consummation of subjectivity. For Foucault, being-toward-death plays the role of a limit-experience wherein the individual dissolves into the oceanic. Death marks the limit of human experience, beyond which there is the void:

> literature, first with surrealism (...) then, more and more purely, with Kafka, Bataille and Blanchot, posited itself as experience: as experience of death (and in the element of death), of unthinkable thought (and in its inaccessible presence), of repetition (of

original innocence, always there at the nearest and yet always the most distant limit of language) of experience as finitude. (OT: 383-4)

Like the exploration of language, of the unconscious, of sexuality and of the structures which overhang us and mark our limits and our finitude, so the experience of death can mark the boundary between transitory (both historically and biologically) subjectivity and that which was, is, and will be, to which we can only gesture, the unrepresentable which Heidegger calls Being.

Thus if a criticism of Heidegger is intended, it is one launched from an essentially Heideggerian perspective (Clifford, 1990: 117). Foucault exploits an ambiguity in Heidegger's privileging of death, to bend Heidegger's philosophy to his own purpose. The death towards which authentic *Dasein* must be in anticipation, *Dasein*'s "ownmost possibility", which, "individualizes Dasein down to itself" (BT: 308), is ontologically indistinguishable from the death of any other individual, from any other death that was or will be. The possibility of dying in which *Dasein* finds its individuality is the one possibility which is both certain and certain for all equally.[20] Foucault, then, has as much warrant to seek in death a dissolution of individuality as Heidegger had to find in it the ontological possibility of apartness.

Despite his emphasis upon authenticity, which he was never able finally to relinquish, other elements of Heidegger's thought point toward the lack of importance of individual humanity. Heidegger never renounces entirely the idea that only the authentic individual could understand Being, and that, in Foucault's terms, individual action could bring about a change in the episteme— even if that action consisted only in waiting. At the same time, however, and often in the same texts wherein it is difficult not to detect the hope that the individual can make a difference, Heidegger repeatedly expressed his conviction that "merely human meditations and endeavours" cannot "bring about a direct change in the present state of the world" (Heidegger, 1990: 57). Our current understanding of being, like its predecessors and those which will follow it, is not the result of human actions, but a dispensation from Being:

> the unconcealment itself, within which ordering unfolds, is never a human handiwork, any more than is the realm through which man is already passing every time he as a subject relates to an object. (QCT: 18)

No more than human activity created our technological age can 'merely' human doing bring it to an end. Thus, as Heidegger says: "Only a god can still save us" (1990: 57).

There exists, then, a contradiction between Heidegger's refusal to abandon the concept of authenticity and his conception of human activity as determined by outside forces. On the one hand, Heidegger asserts that our conception of being is dictated to us by Being; on the other he appears to suggest that the thinker can have access to Being in itself. Thus, thinking must "prepare (build) for the coming to presence of Being that abode in the midst of whatever is into which Being brings itself and its essence to utterance in language" (Heidegger, 1977h: 40). Being is manifest, in its withdrawal, in the clearing in which whatever is presences. In the turning away from self-assertion, this "clearing belonging to the essence of Being suddenly clears itself and lights up (...) the truth of Being flashes, the essence of Being clears and lights itself up" (1977h: 44). Not only is the clearing seen *as* a clearing, that is, as a historical dispensation of being, as the gift from Being which determines everything that presences, but Being itself is glimpsed. Beneath the historically relative, changeable if not arbitrary, understanding of what is, there lies Being in its truth. Beneath the cobblestones, the Being.[21]

Being and the Self: Parallel Confusions

A parallel confusion exists in Foucault's work from the period when Heidegger's influence upon him is strongest. As we have seen, Foucault too has a concept of the understanding of being which underlies that which presences in every epoch of history, forming, for him, the foundation of the episteme. But at the same time, he too suggests that beneath the relative there lies the absolute. And, although Foucault rejects the stance Heidegger prescribes for the intellectual in order to allow unconcealedness as such to be thought, that is, the attitude of letting be or of waiting, he too, like Heidegger, believes that Being can be gestured towards or hinted at by the attempt to explore the limits of humanity: through the exploration of language in literature, through the experience of death, of repetition and of sexuality.

For Heidegger, the first two of these markers of our finitude, and perhaps the third too, play a comparable role of signifying that which necessarily escapes signification, thus gesturing beyond its borders to a region which, while unthinkable, is not unexperiencable. Thus, for Heidegger, "Death is the shrine of Nothing", which "harbours within itself the presencing of Being" (1971c: 178-9). And art, the "linguistic work" especially (1971a: 73), is, in its highest essence (though all too often not in practice), a revealing of the clearing, and thus potentially both an antidote to the exclusiveness of the technological interpretation of what is, and a pointer towards Being. As Heidegger puts it in "The Question Concerning Technology", if art is "granted (the) highest possibility of its essence in the midst of the extreme danger", it "may expressly foster the growth of the saving power, may awaken and found anew our look into that which grants and our trust in it" (QCT: 35).

For Foucault, the meaning of the experience of death and that of language as language are exactly the same as for Heidegger: on the one hand, they point to the relative nature of our episteme, on the other to the absolute which underlies it. On the one hand, literature might shatter "all the familiar landmarks of my thought", relativizing our episteme merely by showing us the possibility of thinking otherwise: "the exotic charm of another system of thought" demonstrates "the limitation of our own" (OT: XV). On the other hand, literature can manifest "the living being of language (...) this raw being that had been forgotten since the sixteenth century" (OT: 44):

> Writing, in our day, has moved infinitely closer to its source, to this disquieting sound which announces from the depth of language— once we attend to it— the source against which we seek refuge and towards which we address ourselves. (1977c: 60)

Foucault even links death with language in a typically Heideggerian move. Just as the German asserts the importance of "the essential relation between death and language" (Heidegger, 1982c: 107), where authentic poetry is the "singing of death" (1982a: 187), so Foucault finds in "the zone shared by language and death, the place where language discovers its being in the crossing of its limits" (1977b: 48).

Representing the Unrepresentable

We see, therefore, that we must modify our earlier characterization of Foucault's thought as occupying the boundary between ontology and epistemology, since this form of his thought exists side-by-side with an ontology that does indeed posit a thing in-itself, and moreover, one to which access *is* possible. It is in his attempt to reach this *Ding-an-sich* that there arises the first of Foucault's two major problems at this stage of his development, that to which Derrida famously pointed in his essay on *Histoire de la folie*. If one believes that there is indeed an *unrepresentable* thing-in-itself which surrounds us on all sides, then one must give up the attempt to represent it. That is, if Foucault wishes to point to the experience of madness as it is, before it is tamed by the representation current at any given time, and if at the same time discursive language is necessarily a betrayal of this essential unreason, then he cannot hope to write a reasoned history thereof, employing the very language which subjugates it. Thus, Foucault's attempt to put the language of reason on trial in the name of what lies outside it "may be impossible, for by the simple fact of their articulation the proceedings and the verdict unceasingly reiterate the crime" (Derrida, 1978a: 35).[22]

Foucault reacts to this criticism with an increasingly tortuous prose style. If he cannot speak in the voice of unreason itself, of "all that which is able to render the profound presence of unreason (*déraison*) irreducible" (HF: 462), then he can at least gesture towards that absence at the heart of his work by employing a 'poetic', rather than a rational, discourse. This, too, is a move indebted, indirectly, to Heidegger. At the time of writing *Histoire de la folie*, Foucault largely accepted Heidegger's assessment of Descartes' status as the first to articulate the new understanding of being. According to Foucault's reading of the *Meditations*, to which Derrida so strongly objected, Descartes can safely dismiss the possibility that he might be mad, because the very procedure of radical scepticism itself excludes the possibility of madness: "the *will* (*volonté*) to doubt already excludes the involuntary enchantments of unreason" (HF: 157). Just as Heidegger detects the roots of our current interpretation of being in Descartes's change of the meaning of the word "subject", from "every thing at hand for itself" to the "I" (MMM: 280), so Foucault finds in Descartes's inoculation of himself against madness the possibility of taking unreason as an object. For Foucault, the "objectivity that we recognize in the forms of mental illness (...) gives itself, precisely, only to someone who is protected from it. Knowledge of madness supposes, on the part of those who possess it (...) a certain manner of not being mad" (HF: 480). Literature, on the other hand, does not define itself exclusively against unreason. For literature, "the lunatic (*fou*) gives herself as object of knowledge (connaisssance) (...) and as theme of recognition (reconnaissance)" (538). "Reflection" sees only the Other; literature the Same and the Other. Hence the importance Foucault assigns to the literary experience of madness (as well as of death, sexuality and repetition). "Discursive language" is

> ineffectual when asked to maintain the presence of these figures (...) as if it were forced to yield its voice so that they may continue to find their words, to yield to these extreme forms of language in which Bataille, Blanchot, and Klossowski have made their home. (Foucault, 1977b: 38)[23]

The result is a hybrid discourse, which cannot make up its mind whether to be judged by the standards of literature or by those of philosophy. Of course, this is not necessarily a weakness from the point of view of transgressive literature— merely from that of traditional philosophy. Once Foucault gives up the claim to bring madness as it is to presence, he is still able, theoretically at least, to gesture towards its absence. I point to the problem only as the sign and the site of a tension in Foucault's work, between a literature of transgression and a rational discourse which claims effects of truth for itself. This tension, it might be argued, is the source of the peculiar power of Foucault's texts at this stage of his career.

Foucault's Mad Thought

The second problem is internal to Foucault's work, and it suggests that this tension might have been felt by him as such. Throughout the writings of this period, Foucault attempts to combine a deeply felt nominalism[24] and relativism with a notion of an ontologically real outside, a natural order. The signs of this tension are already clearly evident in *Mental Illness and Psychology* (1987a). Even in this very early work Foucault had begun to develop a positive conception of power. He opposes his own conception of mental illness to those held by Durkheim and Ruth Benedict. According to Durkheim, behaviors that are classified as pathological are those that depart from the average. In Benedict's work, "each culture chooses certain of the possibilities that form the anthropological constellation of man" (MIP: 61) to be its space of normalcy, whilst "those whose natural reflexes fall within an arc of behavior which does not exist in their civilisation" are the ill. Thus, in both conceptions mental illness is defined negatively, "in relation to an average, a norm", that is, to that which it is not. For both thinkers, the ill are those whose behaviours, while not being "in themselves morbid", depart from the standards a culture sets for itself (62). According to Foucault, this model suffers from a "cultural illusion", stemming from the fact that "our society does not wish to recognize itself in the ill individual whom it locks up or rejects; as it diagnoses the illness, it excludes the patient" (63). In these theories of the origin of the pathological, then, Durkheim and Benedict assume that the term "deviancy" refers to the behavior of a number of individuals who just happen to act in a manner that is not condoned by a particular society. They miss the fact that the pathological, just as much as the normal, is a construct, that "a society expresses itself positively in the mental illnesses manifested by its members" (MIP: 63). Thus, the mad, the abnormal, the criminal and the deviant are not on the outside of a culture, no matter "whether it places them at the center of its religious life (...) or whether it seeks to expatriate them by placing them outside social life" (63). This is so because, as Foucault was to write much later:

> power *is* 'always already there' (...) one is never 'outside' it (...) there are no 'margins' for those who break with the system to gambol in. (1980f: 141)

Thus, Foucault concludes, "if one is to avoid resorting to (...) mythical explanations":

> one must not regard these various aspects of mental illness as ontological forms. In fact, it is only in history that one can discover the sole concrete a priori from which mental illness draws, with the empty opening up of its possibility, its necessary figures. (MIP: 85)

Yet, in this very same work, Foucault also feels able to advocate an attempt "to study madness as an overall structure— madness freed and disalienated, restored in some sense to its original language" (76).[25]

The marks of this confusion remain with Foucault at least until *The Archaeology of Knowledge*.[26] Despite his early and continuing efforts to historicize power, at times his conception of madness seems to differ in no essential way from those advanced by Benedict and Durkheim.[27] In the 1964 essay included as the first appendix to the revised edition of *Histoire de la folie*, for example, he seems to conceive of behavior as forming a continuum, a certain portion of which is selected by a culture as its norm. Thus, he can look forward to a day when:

> Artaud will belong to the foundation of our language, not to its rupture; the neuroses will belong among the constitutive forms (and not the deviations) of our society. Everything we experience today in the mode of a limit, or as foreign, or as intolerable will have returned to the serenity of the positive. And whatever currently designates this exteriority to us may well one day designate us. (Foucault, 1995: 290)

In other words, the spotlight which illuminates what Heidegger might have called the clearing of normalcy will have changed position, a different part of the continuum will have been designated as the inside of culture, and it is our clearing which will then constitute the *déraisonnable*.

The result of such a conception is the paradoxical trivialization of experiences which point to the 'outside'; paradoxical because it is in avoiding that relativism which arises from asserting that there is nothing outside the creations of power that Foucault is led to a relativism which arises from the assertion of an unbroken continuum of behaviors, none of which can be said to have any ontological or ethical priority. It is necessary that a culture select a certain part of this continuum for its clearing, just as it is necessary that there will be people who do not conform to the criteria of normalcy. Thus: "To say that madness is disappearing today (...) is not to say that the general form of transgression (...) is also disappearing", for "There is not a single culture in the world where everything is permitted" (Foucault, 1995: 293). Just as the clearing will change, so a new 'outside' will come to be defined, occupied, not by new behaviors, but by old ones given a new significance. What is more, it is not even clear that transgression is as much of a "passage to the outside" (Foucault, 1987b: 12) as Foucault claims. For it is transgression itself which creates the limit as limit; "it incessantly sets up as the law the limit it transgresses" (1977b: 51):

> The limit and transgression depend on each other for whatever density of being they possess: a limit could not exist if it were absolutely uncrossable and, reciprocally, transgression would be pointless if it merely crossed a limit composed of illusions and shadows. (1977b: 35)

This least limiting of limits has no existence outside of the act which transgresses and is experienced, apparently, as the no more than slight resistance felt when "language (...) says what cannot be said" (51). This is in line with Foucault's conception of behaviors as forming an unbroken continuity: there will *necessarily* be people whose acts fall outside of the acceptable, who say things that "cannot" be said.

This conception is to be found side by side with others which point to a more positive conception of power. In *Histoire de la folie* itself, Foucault observes that as the practice of internment

> changes its features (...) madness (*la folie*) changes in turn (...) By a recurrence which is strange only if one supposes that madness preexists the practices which designate it and which concern it, its situation becomes its nature. (458)

In *The Order of Things*, the tension finds expression in the distance between the two figures presiding over Foucault's project, Mallarmé and Nietzsche. The contradiction between Foucault's attempts to think *Being* and the realization that there is nothing outside *being* is isomorphic with the difference between "the great task to which Mallarmé dedicated himself (...) that of enclosing all possible discourse within the fragile density of the word", and Nietzsche's investigation, not of the being of language, but of "who was being designated, or rather *who was speaking* when one said *Agathos* to designate oneself and *Deilos* to designate others." Foucault continues:

> To the Nietzschean question: 'Who is speaking?', Mallarmé replies— and constantly reverts to that reply— by saying that what is speaking is, in its solitude, in its fragile vibration, in its nothingness, the word itself— not the meaning of the word, but its enigmatic and precarious being (...) It is quite possible that all those questions now confronting our curiosity (What is language? What is a sign? What is unspoken in the world, in our gestures, in the whole enigmatic heraldry of our behavior, our dreams, our sickness— does all that speak, and if so in what language and in obedience to what

grammar? Is everything significant (...) What relation is there between language and being (...) What, then, is (...) 'literature' (...))— it is quite possible that all these questions are presented today in the distance that was never crossed between Nietzsche's question and Mallarmé's reply. (OT: 305-6)

The opposition between Nietzsche and Mallarmé, as expressed here, is equivalent to that between genealogy and transgressive thought, between a conception of power as positive and the attempt to speak in the voice of the other, between a completely historicized investigation of concrete power relations and a Heideggerian investigation into the being of language.[28]

In these two opposite modes of contesting that which is, we are justified in glimpsing the outline of the "two strategies" Derrida tells us are available to deconstruction:

a. To attempt an exit and a deconstruction without changing terrain, by repeating what is implicit in the founding concepts and the original problematic (...) Here one risks ceaselessly confirming (...) at an always more certain depth, that which one allegedly deconstructs (...)

b. To decide to change terrain, in a discontinuous and irruptive fashion (...) by affirming an absolute break and difference (...but) the simple practice of language ceaselessly reinstates the new terrain on the oldest ground (...) (Derrida, 1982b: 135)

"It goes without saying", Derrida adds, "that the choice between these two forms of deconstruction cannot be simple and unique. A new writing must weave and interlace these two motifs of deconstruction." Perhaps this is the solution Foucault proposed to himself: he would oppose the episteme both by showing its contingency and by appealing to the essence it supposedly repressed, thereby working both within and outside its boundaries. In the end, however, he was forced to choose, and he chose the way of genealogy— of Nietzsche, rather than Mallarmé. He made that choice, we may surmise, both because of the logical incompatibility of a positive conception of power and a belief in deep truths and because of his growing realization that such anti-repressive discourses were easily colonized by the powers to which they wish to stand opposed.[29]

This is not say that Foucault abandoned Heidegger altogether. As Dreyfus (1984; 1987; 1992) and Sawicki (1987) have each separately shown, Foucault remained Heideggerian at least insofar as he continued to analyze and resist the calculative thinking which arises from the constitution of subjectivity and its correlative representation of everything that presences in objectivity. In this sense, in fact, his entire career could be described as profoundly Heideggerian. But rather than accept Heidegger's assertion that the clearing is a gift, a dispensation of Being, and that therefore the problem is to think the outside rather than to remain in the clearing, Foucault came to see that the 'outside', as much as the sanctioned, is a *construction* of the episteme, that there cannot therefore be any question of a passage to an outside in its wild state. Foucault would continue the task Heidegger had set for himself as early as *Being and Time*, that of the "destruction of the history of ontology" (BT: 44), but in a more concrete manner than Heidegger was ever able to achieve. For it was only once Foucault had abandoned Heidegger's negative theology, in favor of an investigation of the real practices of power, that the way became clear for him to construct a truly *political* form of thought.

FOUR

Modernity— The Dead-End Of Philosophy?

The ambiguity of the human condition: a synthesis that cannot take place

— Sartre, *Notebooks for an Ethics*.

In chapter nine of *The Order of Things*, Foucault identifies three aporias, three points at which thought, in its struggle to advance, finds itself thrown from one pole of an alternative to the other, seemingly without hope of resolution, each of which arises, he claims, inevitably in a modern thought dominated by the philosophy of "man." If we are to characterize Foucault's work as postmodern, it is thus necessary to show how, if at all, his work overcomes these "doubles", and how his still modernist opponents fall into them.

Although Foucault identifies Kant as marking "the threshold of our modernity" (OT: 242), his concrete analyses of the doubles of modernity point to a Cartesian origin, consonant with Heidegger's own location of the beginning of "our" epoch. The doubles seem to arise from Descartes' attempt to discover an indubitable foundation for knowledge. From the moment Descartes established this foundation in the *cogito*, modern thought has been faced with the necessity of attempting to resolve the empirical/transcendental double: how, from the starting point of apodictic consciousness, can we assure ourselves of the reality of external, merely empirical, matter? From this moment on, philosophy is faced with three choices: to reduce the empirical to the transcendental (idealism); to reduce the transcendental to the empirical (materialism, empiricism); or to refer both the transcendental and the empirical to an ontologically more fundamental level of being— God or Spirit. All three alternatives seem to present insurmountable problems. If we reduce matter to thought, we are unable to account for own ability to be wrong about the world, to make hypotheses about it which are then verified or falsified. If we reduce thought to matter, we seem unable to account for our own ability to think, for our apparent experience of freedom. And if we refer both poles to a more primal level, we seem to be in the realm of pure speculation. Kant's decisive contribution to the form of modernity, then, is not in founding the transcendental/empirical double, but in giving it its contemporary shape, by reducing the duality to the single pole of the transcendental. From that moment on, the subject is posited as the source and foundation of all knowledge, knowledge which, paradoxically, seems to arise from the empirical world before it can be referred to the subject. That is, it is by analysis of our knowledge of the world that one can define the categories which shape it, and thus determine what we can legitimately know:

> Man, in the analytic of finitude, is a strange empirico-transcendental doublet, since he is a being such that knowledge will be attained in him of what renders all knowledge possible (...) it is a question of revealing the conditions of knowledge on the basis of the empirical contents given in it. (OT: 318-319)

Hence the transcendental/empirical double leads to a form of thought which constantly oscillates between two poles. From the empirical pole of concrete knowledge, we are referred to the constitutive power of the subject, but this power is empty in itself and seems to need independent matter to rescue it from abstraction. Kant posited an unknowable thing-in-itself as guarantee that knowledge is actually knowledge *of* something, but once again this leads to the realm of speculation: by definition, there can be no phenomenal evidence for an unknowable noumenon.

The very name of the second double, the cogito/unthought, also points to a Cartesian heritage. This double arises from the attempt to bring the empirical, the unthought, under the control of the transcendental, the cogito. For it soon becomes clear that the division between the two realms of being is not absolute: the transcendental is inherently shaped and determined by the empirical, just as much as it shapes in its turn:

> If man is indeed (...) that paradoxical figure in which the empirical contents necessarily release, of themselves, the conditions that have made them possible, then man cannot posit himself in the immediate and sovereign transparency of a *cogito*; nor, on the other hand, can he inhabit the objective inertia of something that, by rights, does not and never can lead to self-consciousness. (OT: 322)

The paradigmatic examples of the unthought in modern philosophy are language and the unconscious; both necessarily shape the very thought that would try to bring them under its sovereignty. It is for this reason that modern thought is "both knowledge and a modification of what it knows":

> whatever it touches it immediately causes to move: it cannot discover the unthought, or at least move towards it, without immediately bringing the unthought nearer to itself—

or even, perhaps, without pushing it further away, and in any case without causing man's own being to undergo a change by that very fact. (327)

Thus modern thought is faced with a task that is necessarily "outlined in the paradoxical form of the endless" (314); the conditions it sets out to investigate no longer apply, or apply in a different manner, at the end of the investigation, and the new situation, no less than the former, requires investigation.

The final double, that of the retreat and return of the origin, raises the historical and epistemological question of the beginning. "Origin", in this context, may refer either to the founding act or event of history, or to the foundation which makes knowledge possible, or, perhaps most usually, to the single event which makes possible both knowledge and history— the self-estrangement of Spirit. Once philosophy is set upon a Cartesian path where only apodictic knowledge counts as knowledge at all, the specification of this origin becomes of primary importance: the origin, too, is an unthought which must be appropriated if the subject is to be able to bring that which determines it from the outside under its control. The problem faced by all attempts to specify the origin is its seemingly inevitable and infinite retreat: what could possibly serve as an origin for us which would not itself be located in a history already underway? The origin cannot be located *in* history, but must be an event simultaneously *outside* history and yet the first event *of history*— the origin "must be both internal and foreign to it" (329). But with the death of God— the rejection of the theological notion of the *ens causa sui* as speculative metaphysics— the origin seems destined to retreat indefinitely: "It is always against a background of the already begun that man is able to reflect on what may serve for him as origin" (330). Faced with this inevitable retreat into the past, modern philosophy looks elsewhere for what may serve it as origin. With Hegel and Marx, Foucault argues, it finds it in the future: the origin becomes that which once was and will be again when alienation, or history, is ended. It seems, however, that the flow of history is destined to continue unabated; the once-and-future origin appears to recede into the distant future as quickly as into the past.

Past the Modern Impasse

It is not immediately clear from a reading of *The Order of Things* and Foucault's other works of his archaeological period what could constitute a successful attempt at an escape from the doubles of modern thought. Perhaps Foucault would argue that this is an inevitable lacuna, given his apparent perception of his own work as occupying a position on the border between modernity and a new episteme. I take it, however, that 'postmodern' thought would not finally resolve any of the contradictions inherent in modern thought. Instead, the removal of 'Man', that "strange empirico-transcendental doublet" (318), from the center of thought would entail that these problems would simply cease to occupy thinkers: "The true contestation of positivism and eschatology" would take as its starting point the question "does man really exist?" (322). Postmodern philosophy, perhaps by no longer regarding only apodictic knowledge as admissible, would reconcile itself to the inevitability of the unthought, to the impossibility of appropriating the origin. Thus Hoy writes that "Heidegger, *the prophet* of the postmodern, is reconciled to the inevitability of the unthought" (Hoy, 1988: 18). Yet a number of writers have asserted that chapter nine of *The Order of Things*, the very chapter Ijsseling says "would not exist if all (the) Heideggerian words were erased" (Ijsseling, 1986: 417), was partly or largely directed against the Heidegger of *Being and Time*. That is, in his analysis of the three aporias of modern thought, "it is primarily Heidegger that Foucault has in mind" (Hill, 1989: 334).

The Existential Exit

It must be recognized that both Heidegger and Sartre identify at least one of the doubles of modernity, the transcendental/empirical double, and develop their philosophies as explicit attempts to overcome it. Thus, in *Being and Time*, Heidegger attempts to show that "if we posit an 'I' or subject as that which is proximally given, we shall completely miss the phenomenal content of Dasein" (72). In this interpretation of 'man' as a present-at-hand entity, "the question of his Being has remained forgotten" (75). To the traditional account of the human being as a knowing subject constituting the world, or being constituted by it— that is, to the reduction of the empirical pole to the transcendental, or of the transcendental to the empirical— Heidegger opposes Being-in-the-world, wherein both poles are seen as abstractions from a primary "*unitary* phenomenon" (78). In words that closely parallel those Foucault would write four decades later, Heidegger warns that "ontological foundations can never be disclosed by subsequent hypotheses derived from empirical material, but that they are always 'there' already" (75). It is in the always-already nature of existence that Heidegger hopes to find the exit from the doubles of modernity, and from modern philosophy itself.

Sartre, explicitly following Heidegger, also apparently intends to overcome the ontological dualism of the transcendental/empirical double. Consciousness, he tells us:

> is an abstraction since it conceals within itself an ontological source in the region of the in-itself, and conversely the phenomenon is likewise an abstraction since it must 'appear' to consciousness. The concrete can only be the synthetic totality of which consciousness, like the phenomenon, constitutes only moments. The concrete is man within the world in that specific union of man with the world which Heidegger, for example, calls 'being-in-the-world.' (BN: 34)

In both thinkers' early major work, it is relatively easy to show that, their initial intention notwithstanding, they each fall back into versions of the analytic of finitude. In *Being and Time*, for example, and despite Heidegger's assertion that being-in-the-world is a "unitary phenomenon", the meaning of entities in the world is referred ultimately to *Dasein* as constituting subject. In the experience of anxiety, *Dasein* reveals the world as essentially other than *Dasein*:

> In anxiety what is environmentally ready-to-hand sinks away, and so, in general, do entities within-the-world. The 'world' can offer nothing more, and neither can the Dasein-with of Others. (BT: 232)

Anxiety thus individualizes *Dasein*, revealing it as constituent subject in a meaningless world. What remains is "Nothing" (Heidegger, 1975a: 249). Thus, Hill concludes, Heidegger, as Foucault reads him, is caught in the transcendental/empirical double. *Dasein*, as the being which provides "the ontico-ontological condition for the possibility of any ontologies" (BT: 34), is both "an 'ontic' fact to be studied empirically, and yet the transcendental condition for all 'ontic' knowledge" (Hill, 1989: 337). Heidegger merely replaces Kant's categories with the existentials of *Dasein*. *Dasein* remains, then, a "strange empirico-transcendental doublet."

The Heideggerian Overcoming

But if Foucault does primarily have Heidegger in mind in his characterization of modern thought, this could well be construed as loyalty to, rather than betrayal of, the older thinker. For in criticizing *Being and Time* as overly subjectivistic despite its stated intentions, Foucault follows Heidegger's own later self-interpretation. In his famous reply to Sartre's *Existentialism is a Humanism*, and in an attempt to distance himself from what he saw as Sartre's own subjectivism, Heidegger writes that: "The adequate execution and completion of this other thinking that abandons subjectivity is surely made more difficult by the fact that in the publication of *Being and Time* the third division of the third part, 'Time and Being,' was held back. Here everything is reversed. The section in question was held back because thinking failed in the adequate saying of this turning" (1977a: 207-8). In his later writings, Heidegger continued his effort to overcome the thinking of *Dasein* as subjectivity, to build on the foundations of being-in-the-world he had laid in his first major work. We may, therefore, see Foucault's own work as made possible by the very mode of thought he criticizes (Clifford, 1990: 109).

But Foucault's critique of the retreat and return of the origin *is* directed at Heidegger, and explicitly so (Habermas, 1987, 266-7). It is, says Foucault, in "the experience of Hölderlin, Nietzsche, and Heidegger", that "the return is posited only in the extreme recession of the origin" (OT: 334). In the work of these three thinkers, and in Heidegger's later work to a greater extent than in *Being and Time*, the origin is that which will be, as much as that which was.

The Origin of the Problem

The later Heidegger, as Fell notes, subscribes to a notion of two beginnings (Fell, 1979). For Fell, these are the beginning which creates the opening of historicity, the event of the forgetting of Being, and "'the other beginning'— a future and merely possible terminus toward whose realization his thinking is underway" (Fell, 1979: 246). In fact, it is possible to argue that Heidegger delineates *three* beginnings, each in close relationship with the others; to the two Fell analyses, we can add the 'always already' and, in Heidegger's terms, "remaining" beginning which is the fourfold play of 'earth', 'sky', 'divinities' and 'mortals.' It is this 'fourfold', rather than the projections of *Dasein*, which for the later Heidegger is constitutive of the world:

> earth and sky, divinities and mortals dwell *together all at once*. These four, at one because of what they themselves are, belong together. Preceding everything that is present, they are enfolded into a single fourfold. (Heidegger, 1971c: 173)

Heidegger's thinking thus remains transcendental in the weak sense that the world is constituted, but at the same time seems able to escape the transcendental/empirical double by virtue of the fact that the constituting force is no longer an empirical given within the very world it constitutes. In fact, this 'unthought' *underlying* the empirical cannot in any way be analyzed. Rather than continue in the modern task of attempting to clarify the origin,

Heidegger asserts that this origin, that which allows us to think and to take something as our as object, can never itself be an object. Instead, the fourfold is the way in which Being 'worlds' the world, and this opening is withdrawn from us, not by accident or through some oversight of ours, but necessarily. It is withdrawn because it must necessarily efface itself to allow the world to appear in the space it opens: it is "the opening of presence concealing itself, the opening of a self-concealing sheltering" (1977i: 391). It follows, not only that it cannot be objectified as one more empirical entity among others, but also that it cannot be traced to an assignable origin:

> We will want to know at once when that event took place (...) the problems which here lie in wait come rushing at us when we add still further: that which really gives us food for thought did not turn away from man at some time or other which can be fixed in history— no, what really must be thought keeps itself turned away since the beginning. (1977f: 348-9)

That which grants presence as a gift to mortals, that in which mortals participate essentially, but can neither control nor even ascertain the extent of their own contribution, is the "mystery" before which we can only stand in awe.

It appears, then, that Heidegger escapes all the doubles of modernity. He makes no attempt to bring the unthought into the light of the *cogito*, since he realises that the *cogito* is founded upon the unthought in such a way that it can have no access to it; it can only be invoked. The transcendental is not for him an empirically occurring object within the world; instead it is that which grants world. And the origin is not some distant event in the past; it is the 'always already' event of the fourfold and of language (Fell, 1979: 257-8).[1] But when Heidegger claims that the origin has turned away from us "since the beginning", he trades on the notions of two different beginnings. One such is the always already beginning which cannot be dated, since there is nothing which precedes it. The other is the origin of our history. At some time in our distant past, mortals were aware of the first beginning as that which withdraws, but subsequently this beginning has been forgotten, resulting in the inauguration of the history of the West as the story of metaphysics' vain effort to locate its own ground. The actual date of this beginning is located by Heidegger at some time in classical Greece. In "The Origin of the Work of Art", the forgetting of the opening takes place with the translation of Greek philosophy into Latin:

> Beneath the seemingly literal and thus faithful translation there is concealed (...) a *translation of Greek experience into a different way of thinking. Roman thought takes over the Greek words without a corresponding, equally authentic experience of what they say, without the*

Greek word. The rootlessness of Western thought begins with this translation. (1971a: 23)

Much later, in "The End of Philosophy and the Task of Thinking", the beginning is located *within* Greek thought, in Plato:

> Throughout the whole history of philosophy, Plato's thinking remains decisive in changing forms. Metaphysics is Platonism. (1977i: 375)

Later Heidegger backed away from this notion that the origin of history could be located at some relatively precise point, without, however, ever abandoning it completely. His task, as he saw it, was "to think what the Greeks have thought in an even more Greek manner" (1982b: 39), for while "pre-Platonic thinking (...) does indeed name Being itself (...) it does not think presencing specifically as presencing, from out of its truth." Thus the origin cannot be located even with the pre-Socratics: "The history of Being begins, and indeed necessarily, *with the forgetting of Being*" (1977c: 109).[2] But *there is* an origin, for the Greeks remain closer to it than any other epoch in recorded history.

Thus the origin retreats into the more and more distant past—unsurprisingly, since it is the origin which allows there to *be* a past. Heidegger might have concluded from this that the origin, like the background which allows beings to come to presence, is essentially unthinkable. Yet it remains the task of his philosophy to think the origin. Since it cannot be reached by remembering Greek thought, Heidegger will think still more originally than the Greeks and allow the origin to return in the future.

This is to be accomplished by "turning" away from the rule of technology, which dictates our present thinking of being as present-at-hand. Our age is ungrounded, claims Heidegger, it:

> hangs in the abyss. Assuming that a turn still remains open for this destitute time at all, it comes some day only (...) if it turns away from the abyss. In the age of the world's night, the abyss must be experienced and endured. But for this it is necessary that there be those who reach into the abyss. (1971b: 92)

Despite Heidegger's suggestion that the turning of the origin away *from us* (and not we from the origin) is inevitable and unsurmountable, he sets out precisely to surmount it: by *our* turning we will retrieve the lost origin. Thus he enjoins us to "prepare (build) for the coming to presence of Being that abode in the midst of whatever is into which Being brings itself and its essence to utterance in language" (1977h: 40). The origin withdraws from the beginning, he has told us; now that beginning is interpreted as merely the beginning of the epoch of metaphysics. Thus the origin cannot be captured in the reasoned language of this fallen world, but may be retrieved ("repeated") in a thinking which will at the same time inaugurate the era of higher reason.[3] Therefore, the "surmounting" of "the coming to presence of technology (...) comes to pass out of the arrival of another destining, a destining that does not allow itself either to be logically and historiographically predicted or to be metaphysically construed as a sequence belonging to a process of history." This 'destining' is not *in* history, since it is the arrival of the origin whose retreat founded history. And its advent, far from being mythical or distant, may, on the contrary, be very near: "Perhaps we stand already in the shadow cast ahead by the advent of *this* turning", Heidegger speculates.

This much to be hoped for turning is *both* "the abiding turn, back to where we already are" (1982c: 85)— the recognition of the always already— and the reappearance at some date in the future of the lost origin from a distant time. The two are, of course, inextricably linked. It is through the recognition of where we already— and always— are that the past origin may return: "there is a turn with mortals when these find their way to their own nature" (1971b: 93).

Despite the fact that this turn is, in part, a call for us to recognize our mortality, our finitude and our place in the fourfold, we cannot dismiss Heidegger's promise of the return as mere rhetoric, making the two returns completely assimilable. For it is not enough for mortals simply to become what they are. The same tension which pervades Heidegger's philosophy, between an affirmation of the commonplace as the real locus of being, and an ethical voluntarism which finds expression in the notion of authenticity, is carried over into the question of beginnings. It is the poet and the thinker "who reach into the abyss" (1971b: 92), who are "the most daring" (118). To be sure, it is of the "nature" of all "mortals" to "reach into the abyss sooner than the heavenly powers" (93). But only a special few, those who are set apart, are able to conform to this nature. "Man" is "the one who by his nature has language and constantly ventures it", but "the more venturesome (...) are sayers to a greater degree" (137).

Just as the ones who affirm the commonplace cannot themselves be common, so the place that is affirmed cannot just be any place, but must conform to the fourfold. Such a place is the "old wooden bridge" across the Rhine, "that joined bank with bank for hundreds of years", to which Heidegger referred in "The Question Concerning Technology" (16). Such a bridge "*gathers* to itself in *its own way* earth and sky, divinities and mortals" (1971d: 153), just as the jug, in "The Thing", in its own way, gathers the fourfold, just as *all* things, in their own way, gather the fourfold. Evidence for this lies in "the Old High German word *thing*", which means "a gathering, and specifically a gathering to deliberate on a matter under discussion" (1971c: 174). In "The Thing", Heidegger helpfully provides a list of such *things*:

> the jug and the bench, the footbridge and the plough. But tree and pond, too, brook and hill, are things, each in its own way. Things, each thinging from time to time in its own way, are heron and roe, deer, horse and bull. Things, each thinging and staying in its own way, are mirror and clasp, book and picture, crown and cross. (1971c: 182)

Mortals too are properly mortals when they are in conformity with the fourfold. To be in conformity here is to dwell:

> Dwelling, as preserving, keeps the fourfold in that with which mortals stay: in things (...) Dwelling preserves the fourfold by bringing the presencing of the fourfold into things. (1971d: 151)

> Mortals dwell in that they receive the sky as sky. They leave to the sun and the moon their journey, to the stars their courses, to the seasons their blessing and their inclemency; they do not turn night into day nor day into harassed unrest. (1971d: 150)

To dwell, then, is to be in conformity with nature. Whereas "technological production (...) levels every *ordo*, every rank, down to the uniformity of production" (1971b: 117), dwelling is in conformity with the order ordained by Being.

It has become clear that the commonplace, in which mortals may dwell in conformity with their nature, and in which things gather the fourfold, is not just anywhere. It is in nineteenth century rural Germany. Heidegger cannot appeal to a natural order of being, to which we must conform if the origin is to return, for the landscape he describes is not 'natural', in the sense that it does not occur without human intervention, It is thoroughly formed, shaped, ordered. To be sure, neither Being nor the thing occurs without mortals, just as "the very *nature* (...) of language *needs and uses* the speaking of mortals in order to sound as the peal of stillness for the hearing of mortals" (1971e: 208). But just as authentic language is in conformity with natural order, and does not "drift away into the more obvious meanings of words" or "succumb to the danger of commonness" (1977f: 365), so the commonplace must be in conformity with nature. The point, however, is that *there is no 'natural' way, no one authentic way, for "earth" and "mortals" to be together.* For one born in Messkirch in the second half of the nineteenth century, perhaps a landscape of ploughs and field paths might well seem the authentic way for nature to be.[4] But if one is born elsewhere, then nature might seem to manifest itself most primordially in terraced rice-paddies. And if one is born into a society in which individuals have the mobility to experience other environments, exposure and access to a great deal of information concerning other places, and in which the environment is largely a built one, then one may be in a position to realize that there is no primordial way for humanity and nature to occur together at all.[5] Thus, just as Heidegger attempts simultaneously to grant to language an ontological power, and yet to affirm that beneath the human world is Being, so he attempts to affirm the commonplace while warning of the dangers of "floundering in commonness" (1977f: 365). In keeping with this confusion, there are two origins: one 'always already' and one that was and that is to come. But we cannot retrieve the second origin by affirming the first, for they are of a different order. One "origin' consists of the background practices which shape the subject and the world, and which can never be entirely illuminated by the cogito, simply because it is the foundation of the cogito. The other is entirely mythical, and all efforts at retrieving it quickly reveal themselves as equally mythical.[6]

FIVE

Beyond The Doubles

We spent our time fleeing from the objective into the subjective and from the subjective into objectivity. This game of hide-and-seek will end only when we have the courage to go to the limits of ourselves in both directions at once.

— Sartre, *Saint Genet*

It might be suspected, from the internal connections which exist between Heidegger's failure to escape the analytic of finitude and his notions of language and Being, that Foucault, too, despite his accurate diagnosis of the doubles of modernity, might fall into those very same doubles. In fact, while the Foucault of *The Order of Things*— who lacks even the limited means Heidegger retains from phenomenology to affirm the *true* commonplace— threatens at times to lapse back into the doubles, in *The Archaeology of Knowledge* he appears to have freed himself from them completely. The question we must ask, however: at what cost is this 'postmodern' philosophy achieved?

Foucault believes he can avoid the doubles of modernity by decentering the subject. Rather than argue that that empirico-transcendental doublet, the constituting-constituted subject, is the source of meaning and being, Foucault follows the structuralists in asserting that the subject, like its world, its language and its social systems, is constituted by codes or rules that lie outside it:

> The fundamental codes of a culture— those governing its language, its schemas of perception, its exchanges, its techniques, its values, the hierarchy of its practices— establish for every man, from the very first, the empirical orders with which he will be dealing and within which he will be at home. (OT: XX)

Instead of retelling the philosophical narrative leading to the discovery, with Kant, of the human being as transcendental constitutor, Foucault tells a very different story, in which, through a play of rules and forces beyond the intentional control of the subject, the Kantian subject is born at the end of the eighteenth century:

> Before the end of the eighteenth century, *man* did not exist (...) He is a quite recent
> creature, which the demiurge of knowledge fabricated with his own hands less than
> two hundred years ago: but he has grown old so quickly that it has been only too easy
> to imagine that he had been waiting for thousands of years in the darkness for that
> moment of illumination in which he would finally be known. (OT: 308)

The importance, as far as the analytic of finitude is concerned, of this new
centering upon structuring codes as the condition of both knowledge and
being lies in its *a priori* disqualification of the question of the origin. Codes,
like language, upon which their analysis is based, are 'always already.' No
matter where we look to find their founding moment, we find only an
already meaningful reality— necessarily, for the analysis of origins and
causes *implies* meaning— that is to say, an already structured, coded, reality.
To be sure, some structuralists and quasi-structuralists, such as Chomsky,
make the further move of attempting to explain these codes themselves,
tracing them back to the subject and giving them the status of invariant
structures of the human mind. But Foucault rejects this lapse into
transcendental philosophy. It is this rejection which lies at the heart of his
much criticized refusal to explain historical change. Foucault will halt at the
level of meaningless rules and the description of the discontinuous epochs
they structure, for to attempt to trace the formation of one *episteme* out of
another, to reconstitute the system of causes that makes the death of a
system of empiricity and the birth of a new one intelligible, would be to
cause the origin to retreat into the past without coming any closer to its
source. He would be forced to explain modernity in terms of the Classical
Age, the Classical Age in terms of the Renaissance, and so on, until the
origin retreated beyond retrieval into prerecorded history, leaving the
historian in the realm of speculation. Such an analysis, Foucault believes, is
the inevitable correlative of a philosophy of the constituting subject:

> Continuous history is the indispensable correlative of the founding function of the
> subject; the guarantee that everything that has eluded him may be restored to him; the
> certainty that time will disperse nothing without restoring it in a reconstituted unity; the
> promise that one day the subject— in the form of historical consciousness— will once
> again be able to appropriate, to bring back under his sway, all those things that are kept a
> distance by difference, and find in them what might be called his abode. (AK: 12)

It is clear that the methodology Foucault applies in *The Order of Things*, and
explicitly formulates in *The Archaeology of Knowledge*,[1] is in part an attempt to
avoid the problem of origin raised by *Histoire de la Folie*. For what Derrida had
criticized in that work, three years before Foucault would formulate his
critique of the doubles of modernity in *The Order of Things*, was neither more
nor less than a (necessarily) failed attempt to capture the origin. In *Histoire de*

la Folie, Foucault attempts to trace the division reason/madness back to an original unity. Foucault's insurmountable problem, of course, is that it is from *within* reason that he speaks. The question he must therefore answer is by what right he assumes a transcendental position beyond the division between madness and reason, from which to speak of madness and for madness without reducing it to reason. Either "the archaeology of silence" is "the *repetition* (...) of the act perpetrated against madness", placing reason on trial for crimes against madness in which "the proceedings and the verdict unceasingly reiterate the crime" Derrida, 1978a: 35); or Foucault must draw "his language from the wellspring of a reason more profound than the reason which issued forth during the classical age" (36), that is, a reason not divided against itself:

> Because the silence whose archaeology is to be undertaken is not an original muteness or nondiscourse, but a subsequent silence, a discourse arrested by *command*, the issue therefore is to reach the origin of the protectionism imposed by a reason that insists upon being sheltered (...) from within a logos that preceded the split of reason and madness. (38)

But where is Foucault to find such a source of higher reason? On the one hand, Foucault appears to follow Heidegger in finding it in Greece, for "the Greek Logos had no contrary." Yet this originary Logos is already divided against itself in Socrates' "reassuring dialectic" (MC: xiii). As Derrida notes, if Socratic dialectic is reassuring, then it cannot *precede* the origin.[2] Foucault cannot locate the division between madness and reason in the Classical Age, because reason was already divided by the time of Socrates. The origin retreats into the distant past.

Thus, Derrida concludes, Foucault must give up the attempt to reach the origin, to locate the point at which madness itself spoke in its own voice, to "write the history of the origin of history" (Derrida, 1978a: 43). "Language itself", claims Derrida, "must simultaneously in fact and in principle escape madness (...) this (...) is an essential and universal necessity from which no discourse can escape" (53). We cannot hope to write, or even think, the history of what might have preceded reasoned history and the history of reason. Foucault's entire enterprise is exposed as essentially metaphysical:

> The attempt to write the history of the decision, division, difference runs the risk of construing the division as an event or a structure subsequent to the unity of an original presence, thereby confirming metaphysics in its fundamental operation. (40)

Far from contesting modern philosophy, then, Foucault in *Histoire de la Folie* merely retells its characteristic story of a fall from original grace. He escapes from the transcendental/empirical double, not by studying his own empirical, constituting reason, but by the illegitimate means of placing himself in the transcendental position of a higher reason for whose origin he cannot account.

Having realized the futility of this quest for the origin, the archaeological Foucault places more emphasis on the conception of language as a positive, constitutive, power, at the expense of his negative theology. By the time of *The Archaeology of Knowledge*, he explicitly criticizes *Madness and Civilisation's* "history of the referent" (47):

> It would certainly be a mistake to try to discover what could have been said of madness at a particular time by interrogating the being of madness itself, its secret content, its silent, self-enclosed truth; mental illness was constituted by all that was said in all the statements that named it, divided it up, described it, explained it, traced its developments, indicated its various correlations, judged it, and possibly gave it speech by articulating, in its name, discourses that were taken as its own. (AK: 32)

I have already shown that, in *The Order of Things*, Foucault does not consistently apply this positive conception of language, at times appealing to the referent beneath the discourses, and implying an unacknowledged and unjustified transcendental viewpoint. In the *Archaeology*, however, there is no trace remaining of this earlier, 'poetic' Foucault.[3]

Instead the new, self-described positivist, Foucault will content himself with the description of discursive formations as they appear on their surface, without reference to origin, value, truth, or meaning, thus producing what Dreyfus and Rabinow call "A Phenomenology to End All Phenomenologies" (Dreyfus and Rabinow, 1983: 44). To describe history as it appears, in its discontinuity, without attempting to refer it to an origin, whether in history or in a constituting subject, and thus without reducing the *originality of the new*—this is Foucault's aim, expressed in his denunciation of the wish he attributes to the traditional historian:

> that it should never be possible to assign, in the order of discourse, the irruption of a real event; that beyond any apparent beginning, there is always a secret origin— so secret and so fundamental that it can never be quite grasped in itself. Thus one is led inevitably (...) towards an ever-receding point that is never itself present in any history (...) from this point all beginnings can never be more than recommencements or occultation (in one and the same gesture, this *and* that). (AK: 25)

Throughout the *Archaeology*, Foucault never wavers from his determination to treat discourse as it appears. But having thus dispensed with the retreat and return of the origin double, by adopting a position as unassailable as it is unsatisfying, Foucault immediately finds himself in difficulties once again. These arise from the status of the regularities he detects in discourse. Archaeology seeks to describe "a group of rules proper to discursive practice. These rules define not the dumb existence of a reality, nor the canonical use of a vocabulary, but the ordering of objects" (AK: 48-9). What, then, is the source of this order? Foucault rejects the two traditional alternatives: order is neither the product of the constituting subject nor is it simply there, to be found in the objects among which that subject lives. That is, Foucault rejects both the transcendental and the empirical options as exclusive alternatives. He notes, however, that there is experiential evidence for both interpretations:

> Order is, at one and the same time, that which is given in things as their inner law (...) and also that which has no existence except in the grid created by a glance, an examination, a language. (OT: xx)

How is it that order is both a given *and* constituted? Foucault is not here affirming a dialectic of subject and object. Rather he refers both back to a prior level, the level of language and of codes:

> We wish to (...) dispense with 'things.' To 'depresentify' them (...) To substitute for the enigmatic treasure of 'things' anterior to discourse, the regular formation of objects that emerge only in discourse. (AK: 47)

Together with 'things', Foucault will dispense with the transcendental subject. However, this still leaves unanswered the question of what the source of this order might be. If we accept Foucault's assertion that the fundamental ground of meaning and being is not the subject, but the underlying codes, the historical *a priori* of an *episteme*, then why shouldn't this *a priori* itself be conceived of as an "empirico-transcendental doublet", as mysterious as the subject in post-Kantian thought? Foucault's reply, I think, would be twofold. First, the *a priori* is not itself a doublet, since it is not an empirical given: the codes which govern knowledge and the experience of empiricities cannot themselves be an empirical object *in* the world. If they were, they would be in the position of governing their own givenness.

Now, it is precisely these ambiguous entities, rules which regulate themselves, which Dreyfus and Rabinow believe they detect in *The Archaeology of Knowledge*. Since "it seems clear that the regularities he describes are not simply accidental ordering (...) but that they must be evidence of some underlying systematic regulation", and since Foucault disallows the notion that nondiscursive practices govern the formation of these rules, then Foucault "must locate the productive power revealed by discursive practices in the regularity of these same practices. The result is the strange notion of regularities which regulate themselves" (Dreyfus and Rabinow, 1983: 84).

Thus, Dreyfus and Rabinow conclude, "Foucault's methodological problems bear a suspicious similarity to the tensions he finds in the anthropological doubles" (91). They quote *The Order of Things*, substituting "Archaeological discourse", for "Man":

> (Archaeological discourse), in the analytic of finitude, is a strange empirico-transcendental doublet, since (it) is a being such that knowledge will be attained in (it) of what renders all knowledge possible. (92)[4]

In fact this criticism misses its target. What Dreyfus and Rabinow ambiguously call "archaeological discourse" *cannot* be an empirico-transcendental doublet in the same way as the philosophical subject, simply because the two poles are separated. The empiro-transcendental doublet is pressing in post-Kantian philosophy because it is the subject itself which reveals the constutive conditions of knowledge, the categories of the transcendental subject. But on Foucault's view, it is not the discourse itself which does the knowing. While the discursive formation may play the transcendental role of constitutor of empiricities, it does not itself occur empirically. Thus we are not caught in the endless aporia where each pole refers us back to the other as its truth and its essence.

Yet how can Foucault succeed in keeping the two poles apart, in relegating order entirely to the transcendental plane, if this order is itself the object of Foucault's discourse? Once again, Foucault is consistent on this point. He does *not* take his own archive as an object of discourse:

> it is not possible for us to describe our own archive, since it is from within these rules that we speak (...) It emerges in fragments, regions, and levels, more fully, no doubt, and with greater sharpness, the greater the time that separates us from it. (AK: 130)[5]

Once again, that is, the transcendental and the empirical poles are kept rigorously apart: the archaeologist is able to adopt a transcendental position to the archives of the past quite simply because they no longer govern our knowledge.[6] Thus the subject who analyzes an archive archaeologically is not the subject who is shaped by the discourse analyzed: "Man disappears in philosophy, not as an object of knowledge but as subject of freedom and existence" (1996d: 52-3).

This still leaves unanswered the question of the source of the orders Foucault describes. I said above that Foucault had two possible responses to the question whether the discursive formation is itself an empirico-transcendental doublet. One is to insist that the two poles are kept separate in his thought: the transcendental order never occurs empirically. But Foucault has another, simpler, response available to him: that he does not wish to explain the source of order at all. Just as he has systematically refused to raise the question of the origin of the historical periods he discusses, he will refuse to speculate as to the source of the apparently meaningful orders which define those periods. In a move strictly analogous to the Heideggerian endeavour to reveal Being beneath the ontic givens of the world, Foucault wishes merely to point to the fact that order *is*. Just as Being is for Heidegger the essential mystery, before which we can only stand in awed silence, so for the Foucault of *The Archaeology of Knowledge*, order cannot be explained, only revealed as what Heidegger might have called the "groundless ground." Just as for Heidegger metaphysics, "insofar as it always represents only beings as beings, does not recall Being itself" (Heidegger, 1975b: 266), for Being is what withdraws to allow beings to come to presence, so for Foucault the statement is the true ground of possibility of discourse—which means of all empirically given objects (Deleuze, 1988: 18). The statement:

> has this quasi-invisibility of the 'there is', which is effaced in the very thing of which one can say: 'there is this or that thing.' (AK: 111)

For Heidegger, since it is able to conceive only of beings and never of Being, metaphysics looks for the ground of beings in a higher being, and so misses its own ground: "Being is the nearest. Yet the near remains farthest from man. Man at first clings always and only to beings" (1977a: 210-11). So for Foucault the statement "is like the over-familiar that constantly eludes one" (AK: 111); "other analyses of language" miss it, their own ground, simply because it is too close for them to see:

> The fact that, each time, it is indispensable if an analysis is to take place deprives it of all relevance for the analysis itself. (AK: 112)

Thus Foucault does not try to explain the source of the orders he describes. He only seeks to "reveal the fact (...) there is *language*" (AK: 111), "the fact, in short, that order *exists*" (OT: xx).

Foucault thus undertakes "the project of a *pure description of discursive events*" (AK: 27). He will not seek to explain, to trace a series of causes and effects, to analyze the internal coherence of a discourse, or even to establish its meaning. He has, it appears, thus managed to escape from all the doubles of modernity. He does not raise the question of origin, and need not, for he studies synchronous systems, not history as a process of change. He keeps the transcendental and the empirical poles of analysis meticulously separate from each other.[7] He need not raise the question of the unthought in his thought, since it is not the system underlying his own thought that he studies. To be sure, *The Order of Things* less clearly escapes from the doubles it analyzes. In particular, Foucault is ambiguous on the extent to which he

describes his own discursive formation in that book: he seems at the same
time to place the postmodern era in the future, and to speak from what
"may perhaps be the space of contemporary thought" (263). But even here,
Foucault's discourse switches to the conditional mode as he approaches our
present, and recognizes that he can answer "those who wish to still talk
about man (...) only with a philosophical laugh— which means, to a certain
extent, a silent one" (OT: 343). This laughter is necessarily silent, because
we cannot articulate our own archive, cannot formulate reasoned arguments
as to why one episteme has disappeared and another taken its place.[8]

Overcoming Relevance

But the cost of achieving this almost flawless thought has been a high one.
Foucault still believes his archaeology to be "valid for our diagnosis"
because it points to "the border of time that surrounds our presence, which
overhangs it, and which indicates it in its otherness; it is that which, outside
ourselves, delimits us" (AK: 130). Thus, the act of describing the archive
which immediately precedes our own:

> deprives us of our continuities; it dissipates that temporal identity in which we are
> pleased to look at ourselves when we wish to exorcize the discontinuities of history; it
> breaks the thread of transcendental teleologies; and where anthropological thought
> once questioned man's being or subjectivity, it now bursts open upon the other, and
> the outside (...) It establishes that we are difference. (AK: 131)

The fundamental value of archaeological thought, then, is that it relativizes
and destabilizes the present. We can no longer regard our own world as the
predetermined outcome of past history, nor as a 'natural', unalterable
inevitability. For this reason alone, archaeology is indeed an enterprise
worth carrying out; it is an enterprise with potential *political* force.[9] Once it
has been carried through, however, as in *The Order of Things*, with *The
Archaeology of Knowledge* serving to correct the inconsistencies which remain
in the former work, there no longer seems anything left to accomplish. It is
hardly worth demonstrating once more that "we are difference." Once
"deprived of our continuities", we must wait for them to be restored before
they can be shattered yet again. The archaeologist is banned from talking
about our own period: that way the transcendental/empirical double lies.
Nor can Foucault speculate upon the form of a future *episteme*: his own
theory forecloses upon the possibility that change is in any sense a
predictable outcome of the present or the past. For a discourse which
wishes to avoid being "outlined in the paradoxical form of the endless"
(OT: 314), it appears that nothing more remains to be done, other than to

wait for a new episteme to be established, and then, if it allows archaeological discourse, to relativize it in its turn. More importantly, although archaeological discourse has a political effect, it is an entirely negative one. It tells us nothing about our present, about where change could come from, and why change is desirable— only that it is possible. Small wonder, then, that Foucault published no major work for six years after *The Archaeology of Knowledge*, and that when he did, that new work substantially revised, not to say rejected, large parts of his archaeological theory.

A Third Way?

Heidegger's attempt to come to terms with the doubles of the analytic of finitude while remaining both politically and philosophically relevant lead him back into these doubles but, as it were, blindly. He situated himself securely in the doubles of modernity while believing himself to speak from somewhere entirely other. Foucault, on the other hand, had been able largely to purge his discourse of the doubles, but at the expense of relevance. Perhaps, then, what is needed is a third way. The outline of such a way is present, I believe, in the work of Jean-Paul Sartre.

Conventional philosophical wisdom would no doubt find this a surprising, even outrageous, claim. Few philosophers are as fundamentally modern as Sartre, it will be said.[10] Furthermore, Sartre, as he himself tells us, is a humanist, and as we know from Heidegger, "every humanism is either grounded in a metaphysics or is itself made to be the ground of one" (Heidegger, 1977a: 202).[11] Finally, and this should put an end to any further discussion of the matter, Sartre, as he is fond of telling us, finds "the sole point of departure is the interiority of the *cogito*" (BN: 329).[12] *Everything*, in the end, is referred to the subject. As Theunissen puts it, despite the fact that being-in-itself characterises "the transphenomenal being of the intended object", since "being-for-itself is (...) intentionality itself, it acquires an essential precedence over being-in-itself" (Theunissen, 1984: 206). Thus Sartre's thought fall squarely within the ambit of the analytic of finitude: his for-itself seems to be a transcendental subject, which will lead inevitability to the transcendental/empirical doublet and probably to the cogito/unthought doublet as well. Worse still, he makes the for-itself its own origin:

> Each for-itself continuously repeats its origin— each act of consciousness repeats the ceremony of its birth by an ever renewed negation of Being. (Fell, 1979: 211)

Certainly, there is good reason to believe Foucault himself would have been rather surprised by the claim that it is Sartre, and not Heidegger, the structuralists or the poststructuralists, who is most able to free himself from the modern doubles. Indeed, Sartre's thought often seems to be Foucault's implicit target when he criticizes "modern thought." As Flynn, remarks "it is against phenomenology that Foucault thinks" (Flynn, B.C., 1978: 203).[13] While in the archaeological work Foucault goes out of his way to avoid what he calls "transcendental narcissism", by refusing to abrogate to archaeology the sole right to truth, he makes one significant exception to this methodological pluralism:

> I should not like the effort I have made in one direction to be taken as a rejection of any other possible approach. Discourse in general, and scientific discourse in particular, is so complex a reality that we not only can, but should, approach it at different levels and with different methods. If there is one approach I do reject, however, it is that (one might call it, broadly speaking, the phenomenological approach) which gives absolute priority to the observing subject, which attributes a constituent role to an act, which places its own point of view at the origin of all historicity— which, in short, leads to a transcendental consciousness. (OT: xiv)

The analyses of modernity in both Foucault's major books of this period contain a sustained attack on phenomenology. According to Foucault, phenomenology attempts to give empirical content transcendental value, or at least to displace it in the direction of a constituent subjectivity, thus giving rise

> at least silently, to an anthropology— that is, to a mode of thought in which the rightful limitations of acquired knowledge (and consequently of all empirical knowledge) are at the same time the concrete forms of existence, precisely as they are given in that same empirical knowledge. (248)

So Husserl remains essentially trapped within the tradition of Kant. This is why phenomenology, which attempts, by restoring "the forgotten dimension of the transcendental", to establish itself "as a radical contestation of positivism and eschatology" (320), remains part of the very same archaeological network as that which it wishes to contest. As Foucault puts it in *The Birth of the Clinic*, the figures phenomenology opposed to positivism were:

> already present in its underlying structures: the original powers of the perceived and its correlation with language in the original forms of experience, the organisation of objectivity on the basis of sign values, the secretly linguistic structure of the datum, the constitutive character of corporal spatiality, the importance of finitude in the relation of man with truth, and in the foundation of this relation, all this was involved in the genesis of positivism. Involved, but forgotten to its advantage. So much so that contemporary

thought, believing that it has escaped it since the end of the nineteenth century, has merely rediscovered, little by little, that which made it possible. (BC: 199)

Phenomenology is a more dangerous, because dissimulated, version of positivism, differing only from that which it claims to oppose in so far as it is explicit in referring the being of the empirical world it describes to the constituent subject. Phenomenology is thus, like all modern philosophies, "a discourse of mixed nature", for it refers its starting point in the world of actual experience to the subject as that world's foundation, while that the subject in turn is referred to the world as its intentional object. Far from being a contestation of post-Kantian thought:

> This analysis (...) is doing no more (...) than fulfilling with greater care the hasty demands laid down when the attempt was made to make the empirical, in man, stand for the transcendental. (OT: 320)

In Foucault's view, Husserl's disciples fall into two camps, depending upon whether they place the emphasis on the transcendental or the empirical pole of the doublet. But this either/or necessarily becomes a both/and, as the phenomenologist is led from objects to the thinking subject, from thought to what the thought is about:

> The phenomenological project continually resolves itself (...) into a description— empirical despite itself— of actual experience, and into an ontology of the unthought that automatically short-circuits the primacy of the 'I think.' (OT: 326)

No Exit

An examination of the most important work of Sartre's early period does little to contradict this assessment. Sartre's is a "discourse of a mixed nature" from first to last: the transcendental/empirical doublet occurs at several crucial points in his thought, and at several different levels. Sartre is no crass idealist. In fact, the attraction for him of phenomenology lies in its affirmation of the independent existence of the in-itself:

> The appearance does not hide the essence, it reveals it; it *is* the essence. The essence of an existent is (...) the manifest law which presides over the succession of its appearances. (BN: 5)

The fact that the existent is revealed as it is in its appearances means that its being is not relative to the for-itself. Thus:

> the existent in fact can not be reduced to a *finite* series of manifestations (...) the sole fact of there being a subject implies the possibility of multiplying the points of view. (BN: 5)

And "the series of its appearances is bound by a principle which does not depend upon my whim." How an existent appears to us is dependent upon its being as a transcendent object, not upon the being of the intending subject.

Conversely, because the for-itself *is* intentional, it is essentially dependent on the in-itself:

> The for-itself is outside itself in the in-itself since it causes itself to be defined by what it is not; the first bond between the in-itself and the for-itself is therefore a bond of being. (245)

But this is "a bond of being" without reciprocity. For "while the For-itself *lacks* the In-itself, the In-itself does not *lack* the For-itself" (145n.). While existents can be considered abstract "in so far as they cannot exist as phenomena without *appearing* to a consciousness",

> nevertheless the being of phenomena as in an in-itself which is what it is can not be considered as an abstraction. In order to be, it needs only itself; it refers only to itself. (239)

However, while Sartre affirms the existence of being-in-itself independent of consciousness of that being, the *meaning* of the in-itself is essentially relative to the for-itself: "(W)e choose the world, not in its contexture as in-itself but in its meaning" (596). Although the for-itself is not free simply to confer any meaning whatsoever upon any situation in which it finds itself, nevertheless any and all meanings of the in-itself are meanings conferred upon it by the for-itself, and for the for-itself. Thus, while it is necessary that I

> *play at being* a café waiter in order to be one, still it would be in vain for me to play at being a diplomat or a sailor, for I would not be one (...) this impalpable difference which distinguishes the drama of realization from drama pure and simple is what causes the for-itself, while choosing the *meaning* of its situation and while constituting itself as the foundation of itself in situation, *not to choose* its position. (131)

We must, therefore, distinguish between two related but analytically separable regions of being. There is being-in-itself, which simply *is* without meaning or possibility, and the world, whose being is relative both to being-in-itself and to the being of the for-itself insofar as the for-itself chooses its meaning.

This same structure is repeated at the level of the for-itself itself. Again there are two regions of being, called by Sartre non-thetic consciousness and the ego or the 'I':

> I am alone and on the level of a non-thetic self- consciousness. This means first of all that there is no self to inhabit my consciousness, nothing therefore to which I can refer

my acts in order to qualify them. They are in no way *known*; I *am my acts* and hence they carry in themselves their whole justification. I am a pure consciousness *of* things. (BN: 347)

But when I assume a reflective attitude toward myself, or with the advent of another for-itself, and thus the irruption of my being-for-others, a self comes to inhabit my consciousness. "I now exist as *myself* for my unreflective consciousness":

> Now the unreflective consciousness is consciousness *of* the world. Therefore for the unreflective consciousness the self exists on the level of objects in the world (...) Only the reflective consciousness has the self directly for an object. (349)

Thus the for-itself is divided, like the in-itself, into two regions of being: a thematically unknowable, unobjectifiable, being-for-itself, and the ego, being-for-itself insofar as it is an object for itself. Just as the being of the existent cannot be reduced to a finite series of manifestations, so:

> the consciousness which I have of the 'I' never exhausts it, and consciousness is not what causes it to come into existence; the 'I' is always given as having been there before consciousness— and at the same time as possessing depths which have to be revealed gradually. Thus the Ego appears to consciousness as a transcendent in-itself, as an existent in the human world, not as *of the nature of* consciousness. (156)

It is already apparent that Sartre's for-itself is indeed an "empirico-transcendental doublet" (Hendley, 1991: 195; Kemp, 1984: 99), simultaneously being-in-the-world which is "thrown", thus not of its own choosing, and source of the meaning, not only of its own being, but of the world. On this analysis, the aporias of the analytic of finitude seem inevtiable. The human sciences are forced, when analyzing language for example, into a perpetual oscillation from the empirical pole (for language is simply given to us, predates us, anticipates and preforms our thoughts and our efforts to express them) to the transcendental (since language appears as an instrument for use, meaningless and silent until it is animated by the intentional expression of the subject) and back again. In much the same way, Sartre finds the meaning of the world inexplicable without reference both to the meaning-conferring powers of the for-itself and the brute being of the in-itself, both of which, as is indicated by Sartre's example of the waiter who cannot be a diplomat, are given in an already social world. Meaning is thus always *both* freely conferred upon the world by the for-itself, *and* simply given without the for-itself's wanting or choosing it, and both irreducibly.

In Sartre's later works, as I shall show, meaning is increasingly simply encountered in the world by the for-itself. But the fact remains that there is meaning only on condition that the world has been made meaningful by subjects: Sartre's subject will remain an empirico-transcendental doublet from first to last. In a conversation with Simone de Beauvoir, late in his life, Sartre describes the concept of the subject to which he came in *Being and Nothingness*: "He was a curious thing, a man. He was both a being lost in the world and consequently surrounded by it on all sides— imprisoned in the world, as it were— and at the same time he was a being who could synthesize the world and see it as his object, he being over against the world and outside. He was no longer in it; he was outside. It's this binding together of without and within that constitutes man" (Sartre, 1984: 435). No more accurate a description of the empirico-transcendental doublet could be imagined. And it was to this conception that Sartre still held, at this late stage of his career.

According to Foucault's analysis, phenomenology tends to emphasize either the empirical or the transcendental side of this equation, but is unable to avoid referring to both. This tension between the two poles of being makes phenomenology, along with all other modern modes of thought, inherently unstable. Is Sartre aware of the tension produced by the radical hiatus he explicitly introduces between the two regions of being? Let us examine one of Sartre's phenomenological descriptions. In *Being and Nothingness*, Sartre presents us with a "homosexual" who, while "avowing each and every particular misdeed (*sic*) which he has committed", refuses to consider himself a homosexual. His friend, the "champion of sincerity", asks of him only that he admits to being a homosexual. "Who is in bad faith?", Sartre asks.

On the one hand, Sartre suggests, the homosexual's attitude "includes an undeniable comprehension of truth." He is right in believing that "a homosexual is not a homosexual as this table is a table", that is, that a for-itself can never be simply an in-itself, a pure and simple thing. On the other hand, if he declares to himself that he is not a homosexual in the sense that "this table *is not* an inkwell", he is in bad faith.

What of the man's friend? If he demands of him that he recognizes his essence *as* homosexual, then he is equally in bad faith:

> a statement such as, 'He's just a pederast,' (...) removes a disturbing freedom from a trait and (...) aims at henceforth constituting all the acts of the Other as consequences following strictly from his essence. (BN: 108)

While the homosexual appeals to his irreducible transcendence in order to claim that he is not a homosexual, the champion of sincerity points to his equally undeniable facticity. Both are equally in bad faith, for both attempt to reduce the phenomenon of being to only one of its two irreducible poles.

Thus, the homosexual may validly deny his homosexuality, but only if he understands that denial to mean "I am not what I am." That is:

> (t)o the extent that a pattern of conduct is defined as the conduct of pederast and to the extent that I have adopted this conduct, I am a pederast. But to the extent that human reality can not be finally defined by patterns of conduct, I am not one. (BN: 108)

Good faith consists in the effort to affirm both our empirical, 'factical' being-in-the-world, and our transcendence of that world, without attempting to reduce either pole to the other. The human being "is at once a *facticity* and a *transcendence*":

> These two aspects of human reality are and ought to be capable of a valid coordination. But bad faith does not wish either to coordinate them or to surmount them in a synthesis. (98)

Sartre's use of the term 'synthesis' may be misleading, since the syntheses he produces are of a very special, non-Hegelian, kind. In fact, the Sartrean dialectic—and not only in *Being and Nothingness*, but in all his work—results not so much in a synthesis as a circle, in which each term is seen as abstract, or, as Sartre would say, *unselbständig*, without its dialectical opposite, and yet neither can they be sublated into a higher level concept which would preserve both (Howells, 1992: 342). Thus the ceaseless oscillation between the transcendental and the empirical poles of being, which Foucault claims to detect in all modern modes of thought, occurs in Sartre not as the unintended result of a transcendental or realist a philosophy which, despite itself, cannot avoid implicit reference to the repressed pole, but instead as an essential and acknowledged constituent of his thought (Knee, 1990: 121).[14]

The notion of synthesis also occupies an important place in Sartre's thinking about origins. In *Being and Nothingness* Sartre presents two answers to the fundamental question of metaphysics. To the question, "why is it that *there is* being", Sartre gives the answer, "because the for-itself is such that there is being" (788). But by 'being' Sartre here means not unqualified being-in-itself, but the being of the existent which occurs in a meaningful world, which meaning Sartre has consistently referred to the for-itself. Thus the sentence immediately following that quoted above runs: "The character of a *phenomenon* comes to being through the for-itself."

Next Sartre presents a hypothesis as to the origin of the for-itself. Ontology teaches us, Sartre says, that "*everything takes place as if* the in-itself in a project to found itself gave itself the modification of the for-itself" (789-90). Such a hypothesis, Sartre notes, is contradictory, since it is through the for-itself that the possibility of a foundation comes to the world. In order to be a project of founding itself, the in-itself would of necessity have to be originally a presence to itself— *i.e.*, it would have to be already consciousness. (789)

The value of this speculation, then, would consist only in its offering us "the possibility (...) of unifying the *givens* of ontology." Such conjectures "will remain hypotheses since we cannot expect either further validation or invalidation" (790).

Thus, despite a residual desire to complete his system with metaphysical hypotheses which he knows can only ever be pure speculation, Sartre accepts the conclusion Foucault will come to twenty-five years later; that origins are forever out of reach, ungraspable by any form of thought which owes to them its very existence. The response of most thinkers to this realization, as Foucault has pointed out, is to reverse the quest for the origin, to make the origin that which, in our distant future, we advance towards. Sartre too projects the origin into the future: the hypothetical project he attributes to the in-itself, that of giving itself the modification of the for-itself in order to found itself, is taken up as a goal by the for-itself. The ultimate goal the Sartrean subject seeks is the synthesis of the for-itself with the in-itself:

> The fundamental value which presides over this project is exactly the in-itself-for-itself; that is, the ideal of a consciousness which would be the foundation of its own being-in-itself by the pure consciousness which it would have of itself. It is this ideal which can be called God. Thus the best way to conceive of the fundamental project of human reality is to say that man is the being whose project is to be God. (723-4)

This synthesis, as Sartre indicates by utilizing the term 'God', is impossible: "The idea of God is contradictory." Thus, Sartre famously concludes: "Man is a useless passion" (784).

Thus 'origin' for Sartre has two meanings. It refers both to the strictly unknowable event by which there is being, and to the regulative principle we are forced to posit as the goal of being. In either case, the origin is forever out of reach, and explicitly held by Sartre to be so.

What of Foucault's third double, that of the cogito/unthought? Again, it is easy to show how Foucault's analysis applies to Sartre's thought. As a phenomenologist, Sartre wishes to affirm being-in-the-world as the unthought which silently rules over our thought and our projects. It is in terms of our situation that we choose ourselves. To think the unthought is to realize that this situation is what it is by reference both to the for-itself and to the in-itself as unqualifiable existent. It is thus to assume the situation "with the proud consciousness of being the author of it" (707-8). On the other hand:

the *situation*, the common product of the contingency of the in-itself and of freedom, is an ambiguous phenomenon in which it is impossible for the for-itself to distinguish the contribution of freedom from that of the brute existent. In fact, just as freedom is an escape from a contingency which it has to be in order to escape it, so the situation is the free coordination and the free qualification of a brute given which does not allow itself to be qualified in any way at all. (627)

Thus the for-itself is in the position of having to assume responsibility, as if it were the author, for a situation for which it knows it is only partially responsible, and for which the extent of its *actual* authorship is, on principle, unknowable— for the simple reason that we cannot subtract our meanings from the existent and still be able to know that existent. Certainly we can, indeed must, explore the character of our situation— we can, for example, discover whether or not this rock is climbable. The fact we then discover about the rock is objective, in the sense that we are not responsible for the degree of its susceptibility to our project. However, we must recognize that this fact we have discovered is at the same time relative to us, in that a rock is only climbable or not climbable for a for-itself which projects the project of climbing it. More fundamentally, as Sartre points out at the beginning of *Being and Nothingness*, the existent is not exhausted by any (necessarily) finite series of manifestations: "it would require an infinite process to inventory the total contents of a thing" (11). We come to know the existent the better the longer we examine it, but its total being remains necessarily beyond our grasp. The attempt to know either the existent or the situation is thus "outlined in the paradoxical form of the endless", (OT: 314). It remains the endlessly retreating horizon of absolute knowledge.

In exhibiting the applicability to *Being and Nothingness* of Foucault's appraisal of the analytic of finitude, I have, I hope, also outlined Sartre's possible responses to Foucault's criticism. Yes, Sartre's thought oscillates continually between the transcendental and the empirical poles of being. Yes, Sartre's attempt to think the unthought is a process without possible end. Yes, Sartre finds it necessary to posit an origin toward which the for-itself constantly advances, without ever coming any the nearer to it. Yet Sartre enters into all these doubles lucidly. He wishes to maintain them *as* contradictory poles, with no possibility of reconciliation. Only by thinking both poles simultaneously is it possible to develop a mode of thought which could make a difference to our way of being. That this is so is indicated by Foucault's inability to produce a truly political style of thought while simultaneously maintaining a radical separation between the transcendental and the empirical poles. If we are to attempt to cultivate a style of thought of any use in our current situation, showing how and why it could be enhanced or altered, it is necessary to take ourselves as our own objects.

Since we are then situated firmly in the *same* archive as our object, we must jump feet first into the doubles; there must be an unthought without possibility of total clarity; there must be a being— each one of us— which, while empirically occurring in the world, assumes a transcendental position with regard to itself. And the analysis this being performs upon itself will never be 'disinterested', but will always be for the sake of certain goals.[15]

This is not to say that Sartre's thinking in *Being and Nothingness* is without problems. Far from it. It can easily be shown that, at this stage of his development, he fails to maintain a balance between the poles of being. As has been shown many times, and as Sartre himself would later recognize, in *Being and Nothingness* he overstresses the transcendental pole. This stress on the transcendental recurs at all levels in *Being and Nothingness*. We may take Sartre's assertion that "there is no situation in which the for-itself would be *more free* than in others (...) the slave in chains is as free as his master" (702-3) as symbolic of such overemphasis. Essentially, Sartre's attempt to hold to both the facticity and the transcendence of the for-itself fails when he refuses to recognize that materiality can constitute a genuine limitation to the freedom of the for-itself. However, that Sartre does not manage to pull off the balancing act does not invalidate the attempt. At the very least, we are now able to affirm that a form of thought which aims to make a difference to our present world *must* attempt to maintain its transcendence over that world while affirming its inevitable involvement therein. Perhaps, then, the relationship between modern and postmodern types of thought is more complex than Foucault had imagined at the time of writing *The Archaeology of Knowledge*. Perhaps it is not a simple matter of a before and an after. Perhaps postmodern thought will reject not simply modernist problematics, but also the characteristic modernist tendency to attempt radical breaks and new beginnings.[16] It might well affirm the very aporias of modern philosophy as the (currently) unsurpassable horizon for thought, and set itself resolutely *into* those aporias, rather than attempting to resolve or shatter them in the modernist manner. This is in line with our initial interpretation of postmodern thought as the attempt, not to reconcile the doubles, but to be reconciled to their inevitability[17]— although *not* in line with Foucault's attempt to achieve such a reconciliation through the rejection of the questions they raise. In retrospect, then, modernity might turn out to *have been* the past *of* the postmodern age, rather than simply the epoch preceding it. Perhaps, then, the relationship between modernity and postmodernity is not that between two discontinuous epistemes, but of the kind indicated by the word 'postmodern' itself: after now.[18]

SIX

The Gaze

Were I to fix the date of completion of the carceral system (...) the date I would choose would be the 22 January 1840, the date of the official opening of Mettray. Or better still, perhaps, that glorious day, unremarked and unrecorded, when a child in Mettray remarked as he lay dying: 'What a pity I left the colony so soon' (...) This marked the death of the first penitentiary saint

— *Discipline and Punish*: 293

Perhaps we should see in this passage from *Discipline and Punish* an implicit reference to that other "penitentiary saint", Jean Genet. For Genet too was a product of Mettray, "the model in which are concentrated all the coercive technologies of behaviour" (DP: 293). And of all Sartre's many books, none could have interested Foucault more than *Saint Genet*. In the figure of Genet are combined several of Foucault's most enduring interests: the outsider, the homosexual, the convict. Coincidentally, Foucault made the acquaintance of Sartre and of Genet, "the hagiographer and the saint", as Claude Mauriac described them (1976: 291), at the same time, in 1971. Foucault and Genet took part together in demonstrations against racism, and, significantly, for prison reform.[1] Moreover, *Discipline and Punish* represents Foucault's most extended treatment of one of the central themes of *Saint Genet*, in fact one of Sartre's most characteristic (and controversial) topics: the gaze.

The gaze, for Sartre, is that which brings objectivity to the world and to particular objects within it: "Objectivity = the world seen by another who holds the key to it" (NE: 8). In so saying, he appears to follow the Husserlian contention that the objective world implies an Other. But Sartre gives the link between objectivity and the Other a distinctive twist. If objectivity implies the possibility of different points of view on the same thing, then it follows that the thing offers a different face to the Other, that the world has a different signification for the Other which, by definition, is irrealizable for me. Even if I were to look at the world from the spatial position the Other occupies, I could not look at it with their subjectivity.

Moreover, since we have defined objectivity as 'showing another face to Others', we cannot ignore this subjectivity as though it were, so to speak, merely subjective. It is constitutive of objectivity: the face that the object turns toward the Other is an aspect of its truth. Thus the Other appears in my world first as:

> the permanent flight of things toward a goal which I apprehend as an object at a certain distance from me but which escapes me inasmuch as it unfolds about itself its own distances (...) The grass is something qualified; it is *this* green grass which exists for the Other (...) This green turns toward the Other a face which escapes me (...) suddenly an object appears that has stolen the world from me (...) it appears that the world has a kind of drain hole in the middle of its being and that it is perpetually flowing off through this hole. (BN: 343)

It is this peculiarly negative reading of objectivity which is distinctive in Sartre's thought at this early stage of his career: "the original fault (*faute*): objectivity as a sign of oppression and as oppression" (NE: 8).

But there is more. Thus far Sartre has limited his description to the effects of the Other's gaze upon objects of my world. Objectivity is the flow of my world toward Others who are themselves objects within my world. My world is stolen from me, but "*the Other* is still an object *for me* (...) hence the disintegration of my universe is contained within the limits of the same universe" (BN: 343). When the Other looks at me, however, everything changes: a new object is born in the world, and that object is me.

To follow Sartre's logic here, it is necessary to give a brief description of the Sartrean subject. The for-itself is not simply the centered, Cartesian subject "devoid of any internal alterity" (LaCapra, 1978: 24) most commentaries have described it as being. Far from being centered, or unproblematically present to itself (and despite the fact that it can be *defined* as presence to itself),[2] Sartre's subject is described "as being what is not and not being what it is" (BN: 28).[3] That is, its essence ("everything in the human being which we can indicate by the words— that *is*" (BN: 72)) lies in its past, and by this very fact the subject— which is a project towards a future— is separated from its being by a nothingness, its freedom. It is not what it is. Or as Sartre puts it elsewhere, human beings are their past in the mode of having to be it, for "it is that in terms of which they make themselves what they are" (BN: 173). On the other hand, the for-itself, as project towards... is *already* what it is *not yet*:

> I am indeed already there in the future; it is for the sake of that being which I will be there at the turning of the path that I now exert all my strength, and in this sense there is already a relation between my future being and my present being. But a nothingness has slipped into the heart of this relation; I *am* not the self which I will be. First I am not that self because time separates me from it. Secondly, I am not that self because

what I am is not the foundation of what I will be. Finally I am not that self because no actual existent can determine strictly what I am going to be. Yet as I am already what I will be (otherwise I would not be interested in any one being more than another), *I am the self which I will be in the mode of not being it.* (BN: 68)

Caught between a past which it is, without being it any longer, and a future which it is not yet, the for-itself is nothing, nothing but a wrenching away of itself from being. Consciousness is centered only to the extent to which nothingness can be said to be centered. It exists only as intentionality, as awareness of something other than itself:

consciousness has no 'inside.' It is just this being beyond itself, this absolute flight, this refusal to be a substance which makes it a consciousness. Imagine for a moment a connected series of bursts which tear us out of ourselves, which do not even allow to an 'ourselves' the leisure of composing ourselves behind them, but which instead throw us beyond them into the dry dust of the world (...) you will then grasp the profound meaning of the discovery which Husserl expresses in his famous phrase, "All consciousness is consciousness *of* something." (Sartre, 1970: 5)

The for-itself *is* not, it will be. And since *what* it will be will never coincide with its present, it will be its future only in the mode of having been it: it will have been. The for-itself exists in the perpetual future-perfect. The for-itself is a project towards its future. Insofar as it can be said to be, it is only as the objectivation of its acts upon the world: "one creates oneself in creating the thing and in the same way as one creates it" (NE: 131). Or, more simply: "my work is me" (NE: 125). The self is not within consciousness, it is outside, in the world.

Once this is grasped, we are in a position to understand Sartre's distinctively negative reading of the Other. The for-itself by itself exists as nothing but consciousness of an existent in the world:

I am alone and on the level of a non-thetic self-consciousness. This means first of all that there is no self to inhabit my consciousness, nothing therefore to which I can refer my acts in order to qualify them. They are in no way *known*; I *am my acts* and hence they carry in themselves their whole justification. I am a pure consciousness *of* things (...) No transcending view comes to confer upon my acts the character of a *given* on which a judgement can be brought to bear (...) my attitude (...) has no 'outside.' (BN: 348)

At this level, the for-itself has a self only to the extent to which it reflects upon itself. When it turns its attention towards itself, a self exists for reflective consciousness. The reflecting consciousness is separated from itself by the infinitesimal nothingness which allows it to take itself as an object: the self exists for-itself as an object in the world. But it is not yet objective: it refers only to myself, and, although it gives itself "as possessing depths which have to be revealed gradually" (BN: 156), it exists only insofar as I sustain it in being. The self exists, therefore, as a "quasi object" (NE: 11). With the advent of the Other, however, my self becomes objective, just as the existent in the world gains the dimension of objectivity through the presence of Others. Whereas previously the presence of the Other had stolen a dimension of the world from me, now her look gives birth to an aspect of *myself* which is by definition unknowable by me. Henceforth, *I* am the object of which the Other holds the key.

This, of course, is the dimension of self Sartre calls being-for-others: my being in the dimension of the Other, yet inescapably mine. I must interiorize this being just as I must my past. It, too, is what I am in the mode of having to be it: "I recognize that I *am* as the Other sees me (...) Thus the Other has not only revealed to me what I was; he has established me in a new type of being" (BN: 302). This new type of being cannot be existed. It is what I have to be in the mode of being it:

> my transcendence becomes for whoever makes himself a witness of it (...) a given-transcendence; that is, it acquires a nature by the sole fact that the *Other* confers on it an outside (...) If there is an Other (...) I have an outside, I have a *nature*. My original fall is the existence of the Other. (BN: 352)

Nature, essence, being— all those ontological categories which for Sartre represent the opposite of freedom— come to inhabit the for-itself due to the simple presence of the Other. But there is yet one more twist to be given to the knife which the gaze of the Other represents for Sartre. Thus far we have described the "haemorrhage" of my world that occurs when the Other looks at it, and the creation of myself under the Other's gaze. This last can occur, however, when the Other looks not only at me directly, but also at myself as I exist in the world; i.e., myself as objectified in acts. What distinguishes the indirect and the direct look from each other is that, in the latter, my being an object is not simply an additional aspect of my being; it exists, temporarily, as the sole manner in which I am. When the Other looks at me, I exist as object for a subjectivity that transcends me. The Other ceases to be an object in my world and I become one in theirs:

> my relation to an object or the potentiality of an object decomposes under the Other's look and appears to me in the world as my possibility of utilizing the object, but only as this possibility on principle escapes me; that is, in so far as it is surpassed by the Other toward his own possibilities. (BN: 353)

I am a transcendence transcended. I can, of course, look at the Other in turn, and transcend their transcendence of my transcendence. But in that case I exist as a subject for an Other-object. The relation subject/object is infinitely reversible, but can take only the forms object/subject (I exist as transcended for a transcendence) and subject/object (I exist as a transcendence for a transcended transcendence). The encounter of two subjectivities, or intersubjectivity, never takes place:

> Hence *on the same plane* I am a specific object and a free subject, but never both at once, and always the one haunted by the Other. (NE: 94)

This subject/object polarity has led some commentators to conclude that Sartre's work represents "the most completely elaborated denial of true intersubjectivity that has ever appeared in philosophy" (Owens, 1970: 10). Sartrean intersubjectivity is often summed up with a line from *No Exit*: "Hell is other people" (1955: 47; translation modified).[4] And support for that statement is hardly lacking in the philosophical works:

> The essence of the relations between consciousnesses is not the *Mitsein*; it is conflict. (BN: 555)

> Nothing— not even wild beasts or microbes— could be more terrifying for man than a species which is intelligent, carnivorous and cruel, and which can understand and outwit human intelligence, and whose aim is precisely the destruction of man. This, however, is obviously our own species as perceived in others by each of its members in the context of scarcity. (CDR: 132)

Strictly speaking, then, to say that 'man is a wolf to man' falls well short of the terrible reality.

Sartre might reply to the accusation that in his philosophy "the subject's basic position (is) that of ontological loneliness" (Owens, 1970: 9); by arguing that he means to suggest only that *harmonious* relationships between people are impossible, that, precisely, the relation between two for-itselfs is one of conflict, not that there exists no relation at all. In *Existentialism is a Humanism*, however, Sartre goes even further. A student comes to Sartre, seeking advice. But, says Sartre, his choice of adviser is already a choice of the advice he is to receive: he could have sought a priest. And if he had, he would have had to further refine his choice: a collaborationist or a resistance priest? By coming to him, Sartre's student has chosen to be told: "You are free, therefore choose— that is to say, invent" (EH: 356). A subject can always learn from an object; in fact, the structure of objectivity implies an infinity of possible points of view on the object and therefore an inexhaustible depth to it. But the for-itself, it seems, can do no more than receive confirmation from another for-itself of the choice it has already made— in this case, the choice not to receive advice. A more profoundly solipsistic view is hard to imagine.

Now, it should immediately be clear that the world of the for-itself, in which the upsurge of the Other represents an ontological fall from some mythical state of grace, is completely alien to the thoroughly historicized and material world of *Discipline and Punish*. It is at this level that we encounter the most formidable obstacle to any attempt, not only to effect a rapprochement between Foucault and Sartre, but even simply to compare them. Throughout his works, even when his subject matter is concrete, Sartre works at a level of abstraction and generality alien to Foucault. We will find no assertions in Foucault that the gaze is ontologically alienating, nor any discussion of the dimensions of being of the subject. Yet, through Foucault's concrete analyses, a picture begins to emerge which reveals some striking similarities between the Sartrean analysis of the gaze and the Foucauldian panoptic society.[5]

For Foucault as much as for Sartre, objectivation is our original fall, and this fall occurs by the agency of the Other's gaze. From Foucault's very first works, it is the gaze that establishes "the distance that constitutes all objective analysis" (MIP: 46). I will presently show how the objectification/observation theme is present in Foucault's first major work, *Histoire de la folie*. But first I wish to turn to Foucault's most extended treatment of the gaze prior to *Discipline and Punish*, that in *The Birth of the Clinic*, the book he described as "about space, about language, and about death; it is about the act of seeing, the gaze" (BC: ix).

As with much else in Foucault, *The Birth of the Clinic* is concerned with the formation of that singular object of knowledge that is also its subject: 'man.' And in this book he shows— if I may use a visual metaphor to describe a book which demonstrates the connection between seeing and knowing— that the constitution of this object is accomplished by the gaze:

> The gaze is (...) that which establishes the individual in his irreducible quality. And thus it becomes possible to organize a rational language around it. The *object* of discourse may equally well be a *subject*, without the figures of objectivity being in any way altered. It is this *formal* reorganisation, *in depth*, rather than the abandonment of theories and old systems, that made *clinical experience* possible; it lifted the old Aristotelian prohibition: one could at last hold a scientifically structured discourse about an individual. (xiv)

Not that the individual is constituted as object of medical knowledge by the mere fact of being looked at by the doctor; if that were so, 'man' would date back well beyond Aristotle. The eye that constitutes the object of knowledge is a particular eye, the "already encoded eye" (OT: xxi) of which Foucault speaks in *The Order of Things*. This eye sees its object in terms of certain pre-theoretical presuppositions, or, more accurately, it is given objects in terms of an historical *a priori*:

> It was not, therefore, the conception of disease that changed first and later the way in which it was recognized; nor was it the signaletic system that was changed first and then the theory; but together, and at a deeper level, the relation between the disease

and this gaze to which it offers itself and which at the same time it constitutes. At this level there was no distinction to be made between theory and experience, methods and results; one had to read the deep structures of visibility in which field and gaze are bound together by *codes of knowledge*. (BC: 90)

Thus, *The Birth of the Clinic* tells the story of how "the relation between the visible and the invisible—which is necessary to all concrete knowledge—changed its structure" (xii), how new objects came to light, simultaneously and indissolubly for the gaze and for knowledge. But Foucault's history is not a neutral chronicle of how, in a particular domain at a particular time, new objects came to replace old—tempted though he was sometimes to present it thus. The story has a moral charge. These are not just new objects, but a new type of object, the object that is also a subject. And its appearance was not confined to the domain of medicine: it is a symbol for a new way of thinking about human being which was to have profound and far-reaching effects.

In the first place, it must be recognized that the transformation in medicine forms part of a general shift in *episteme*. Not for nothing does Foucault concentrate his analyses in almost all of his books on the so-called 'Classical Age' and the transition to the modern. These are the years of the birth of modernity, and modernity brings new subject/object relations:

The cosmological values implicit in the *Aufklärung* are still at work here. The medical gaze, whose powers were beginning to be recognized, had not yet been given its technological structure in the clinical organization; it was only one segment of the dialectic of the *Lumières* transported into the doctor's eye. (BC: 51-2)

The words traditionally used to describe this period— *Lumières*, *Aufklärung*, Enlightenment— all clearly express the connection between visibility and the new epoch. The Enlightenment is not yet the birth of 'man', but it does lay the indispensable foundation for his birth.

Man, or as Foucault puts it in *The Birth of the Clinic*, the individual, is born only when the medical gaze on life takes a detour through death. Only when medicine had taken the decisive step of 'opening up a few corpses' could the individual enter scientific discourse:

That which hides and envelops, the curtain of night over truth, is, paradoxically, life; and death, on the contrary, opens up to the light of day the black coffer of the body (...) Nineteenth-century medicine was haunted by that absolute eye that cadaverizes life and rediscovers in the corpse the frail, broken nervure of life. (BC: 166)

This is the birth not simply of the medical individual, but of the subject who is *medicalizable*; not just a mutation in the structure of medical knowledge, but a sign and a constitutive element of the birth of a new object which will make new knowledges possible:

It will no doubt remain a decisive fact about our culture that its first scientific discourse concerning the individual had to pass through this stage of death. Western man could constitute himself in his own eyes as an object of science, he grasped himself within his language, and gave himself, in himself and by himself, a discursive existence, only in the opening created by his own elimination: from the experience of Unreason was born psychology, the very possibility of psychology; from the integration of death into medical thought is born a medicine that is given as a science of the individual. (BC: 197)

With this mutation of the givens of empirical perception, death "became the concrete a priori of medical experience" (BC: 196).

The construction of a body of positive knowledge concerning life by way of a detour through death is significant for the structure of the knowledge thus constituted. For it reinforces and ossifies the subject/object polarity inherent in any relation between two individuals, one of whom possesses a knowledge which the other seeks. Nothing the objects of knowledge can say about their own illness can have any bearing on that knowledge, for the truth of illness can appear only on the foundation of the disappearance of the ill subject. It is with the autopsy, "the triumph of the gaze" (195), that the truth will be validated. From the time that positive knowledge of the subject comes to be founded on its disappearance *as* subject, 'man' is born, the subject of knowledge who is also its object, "but never both at once, and always the one haunted by the Other" (NE: 94).

Pinned by a Look

Foucault brings to the analysis of the gaze a concreteness lacking in Sartre. The gaze is not simply the gaze of an Other; it is the gaze of a doctor, of a warder, of a teacher—in short, a gaze authorized to perform a function. The subject/object relation is a power-relation, and as such it is not infinitely reversible. Even were the gaze not solidified in architectural forms, its object would be in no position to "transcend" its objectivation in turn. Sartre was not, however, to remain trapped in the overly idealistic perspective of *Being and Nothingness. Saint Genet* is still far from being as 'materialistic' as *Birth of the Clinic*: as Sartre himself was later to realize, "the study of the conditioning of Genet at the level of institutions and of history is inadequate—very, very inadequate" (Sartre, 1974e: 43). But it does represent a decisive step towards the concrete. Genet is not simply 'the for-itself', caught in a gaze, and thus able to escape from being-an-object by gazing back. Instead, for him the gaze becomes solidified. Whereas, in *Birth of the Clinic* and more especially in *Discipline and Punish*, Foucault shows how the gaze will become congealed in architecture and in the structures of certain forms of knowledge, Sartre shows in *Saint Genet* how the gaze can take up residence in the subject itself.

The child Genet steals. Prior to the crisis which will install the gaze within him, he resembles the for-itself at the key-hole in *Being and Nothingness*. No self comes to inhabit pre-thetic consciousness:

> An air-tight partition (...) separates his virtues from his pilfering (...) he lives on two levels at the same time. Of course Genet condemns theft! But in the furtive acts he commits when he is all alone he does not recognise the offence which he condemns. (SG: 15)

Inevitably, however, he is caught, trapped by a gaze and named a thief: "Beneath this gaze the child comes to himself. He who was not yet anyone becomes Jean Genet" (17). The gaze of the Other confers objectivity upon the nothingness which is the for-itself: "an action undertaken without reflection (...) has just *become objective*. Genet learns what he *is objectively*" (18). It is at this point that we can appreciate the full weight of Sartre's equation of objectivity and oppression. If the for-itself is that being for which "*existence* comes before *essence*" (EH: 348), then we have here a moment of capital importance; the provision of a being with an essence which is not its past, but its *nature*— the principle behind the least of its actions. Genet is:

> suddenly provided with a monstrous and guilty 'ego' (...) An evil principle dwelt in him unperceived, and now it has been discovered. It is this principle which is the source of everything (...) all the impulses of his heart are equally guilty because all alike express his essence. (18)

In uncritically accepting the adult's judgement upon him, Sartre claims, Genet has consecrated "the priority of the object over the subject" (6). He will later attempt to 'explain' Genet's homosexuality in terms of this priority. But, on Sartre's own terms, it is not necessary to suppose any pathology to explain Genet's plight. All we need to say is that he has now been provided with a nature of which he cannot, by definition, have an intuition— for it is nothing more than his being-for-others— but which he must nevertheless recognize as being his.[6] Genet would be in good faith if he were to say, paraphrasing *Being and Nothingness*; "to the extent that a pattern of conduct is defined as the conduct of a thief, I am a thief." But the morality and the ontology he learns from those around him is not nominalist; it is essentialist. Provided with an essence, the reaction of the young Genet is to attempt first of all to perceive it: "He observes himself, spies on himself" (39). But he can never have any intuition of his being, firstly because it is his being-for-others, and secondly because stealing is condemned by the very morality which has been instilled in him. To encounter the thief in himself, therefore, he would have to come across himself wanting to commit an act he does not wish to commit. When he will finally decide to attempt to coincide with his essence, to be the thief, he will judge the extent to which acts conform to his nature by the degree of revulsion they arouse within him.

To have an intuition of himself as he appears to others, therefore, Genet attempts to become another to himself. He attempts to live on the plane of reflective consciousness. Genet's goal, which he shares with every for-itself, is to be the for-itself-in-itself, to be self-caused. His will be the gaze that constitutes within himself his thief's nature. The project has no more chance of success, of course, than any other attempt to be the foundation of one's own being. Nevertheless, under his gaze his essence will be sustained in being.

Much of Sartre's analysis is patently inadequate. Sartre fails to explain how the designation 'thief' constitutes in Genet a greater objectivity than the being-for-others gives to most other people. And Genet's social position— a foundling, adopted by peasants— hardly intrudes at all. 'Jean Genet', in fact, should be looked upon as the name given by Sartre to an entirely fictional philosophical abstraction— we can hardly even call him a character— by means of which Sartre illustrates some of the theses of *Being and Nothingness* at a greater level of concreteness, but still completely abstractly. If we turn to Foucault's concrete histories of institutions, however, Sartre's analyses will help us to glimpse part of the general philosophical background to Foucault's specific analyses.

A Foucauldian Existentialism?

Foucault was as loath as Sartre to have labels attached to his thought. But if we were to attach such a label, we might define it, paraphrasing *Being and Nothingness* once more, as follows: "to the extent that adherence to the doctrine 'existence precedes essence' is a sufficient condition for being an existentialist, Foucault is an existentialist."[7] As much as Sartre, Foucault believed that subjectivity as a fixed essence was a product of certain practices. This is evidenced not only by his statement that "man is only a recent invention" (OT: xxiii), but also by the persistent yet primarily implicit theme that the forms of subjectivity preceding our *episteme* were less constraining, more fluid, than the subjectivity of the empirico-transcendental doublet. This is true, of course, of *Madness and Civilisation*, which is precisely the story of "reason's subjugation of non-reason" (xi) and therefore of a limitation on the ways in which it is possible to be a subject. It is implicit in later works, too— for example in Foucault's celebration, in *Discipline and Punish*, of "the discourse of an illegality that remained resistant to the coercions and which revealed indiscipline (...) as the affirmation of inalienable rights." Thus Foucault:

> All the illegalities that the court defined as offences the accused reformulated as the affirmation of a living force: the lack of a home as vagabondage, the lack of a master as independence, the lack of work as freedom, the lack of a time-table as the fullness of days and nights. (DP: 290)

Foucault leaves it to *La Phalange* to draw the conclusion that in this little drama are confronted the forces of discipline and an as yet untamed freedom. No doubt, he would reject such analysis as overly simplistic. But his reading of this "exemplary scene" is sufficiently sanctioning to lend support to Deleuze's claim to detect traces of a vitalism in Foucault (Deleuze, 1995: 91).[8]

Even if we reject as residual romanticism Foucault's occasional hints at an earlier, relatively untamed, subjectivity, it remains the case that it is the gaze that fixes the essence of the Foucauldian subject, and this fixing represents a closing off of possibilities. *Discipline and Punish*, like *The Birth of the Clinic*, tells the story of the birth of an object of knowledge who is also a subject; in this case not the medical, but the criminal, subject. This is the subject who is defined, not by having committed an offence against the law (just as the medical subject is not defined simply by being ill), but by two important characteristics: "it is not so much his act as his life that is relevant in characterizing him" (251); and "he is not only the author of his acts (the author responsible in terms of certain criteria of free, conscious will), but is linked to his offence by a whole bundle of complex threads (instincts, drives, tendencies, character)" (253). In other words, the difference between the authors of crime and delinquent subjects lies in the fact that the first are defined by their acts, the second by their criminality. Or, as Sartre might have said, the offender exists, the delinquent subject *is*. It is this constitution of a guilty *nature* that Foucault finds so objectionable in the carceral system.

And the mechanism for this constitution is the gaze.[9] Discipline in general functions by means of surveillance:

> The exercise of discipline presupposes a mechanism that coerces by means of observation; an apparatus in which the techniques that make it possible to see induce effects of power, and in which, conversely, the means of coercion make those on whom they are applied clearly visible. (170-1)

The apparatus of discipline "subjects" individuals to its constraints. Here Foucault plays upon all the ambiguity of both the French and English words subject, *assujettir*— to place under constraint, but also to construct a subject. Discipline is that modality of power which *subjects* by the gaze:

> Disciplinary power (...) imposes on those whom it subjects a principle of compulsory visibility (...) It is the fact of being constantly seen, of being able always to be seen, that maintains the disciplined individual in his subjection. (187)

Discipline is the power which constrains individuals, not only to obey, but to be. Discipline produces the subject, as both subject and object of knowledge: "the individual as effect and object of power, as effect and object of knowledge" (192) is "a reality fabricated by this specific technology of power that I have called 'discipline'" (194).

Reversing the Gaze

We have still to examine two other features of the Sartrean gaze which find an echo in Foucault's work. The first is the principle of reversibility. In Sartre, as we have seen, the gaze of the Other represents my objectivation and is the basis for possible oppression. But the gaze by itself is a sufficient condition neither for oppression, nor even for alienation, which Sartre defines as the precedence of the Other over the Same, and which therefore might be seen as following from the constitution of my objectivity as a permanent and immutable state. But my objectivity is fixed only when I am no longer able to reverse the power relation. Oppression exists, not when there is a power relation between two people or two groups of people, but when this power relation is irreversible and unidirectional in a number of important areas. As Foucault himself put it: "relations of power are not something bad in themselves (...) The problem is rather to know how you are to avoid in these practices— where power cannot not play and where it is not evil in itself—the effects of domination." These effect arise from states in which "the relations of power are fixed in such a way that they are perpetually asymmetrical and the margin of liberty is extremely limited" (ECS: 18, 12). Part of Foucault's definition comes in response to his interlocutor's noting that "You are far removed from Sartre who used to tell us 'Power is evil'." If power is evil in Sartre, it is a necessary evil, for the foundations of oppression and alienation exist wherever two for-themselves encounter each other.[10]

Given that it is not power itself that is evil, but states of domination, Foucault directs his attention toward permanently asymmetrical power relations. And from a very early stage in his work, such relations are constituted by an irreversible gaze. "In classical confinement", Foucault tells us in *Madness and Civilisation*, the madman was indeed observed:

> but such observation did not, basically, involve him; it involved only his monstrous surface, his visible animality; and it included at least one form of reciprocity, since the sane man could read in the madman, as in a mirror, the imminent movement of his downfall. The observation Tuke now instituted as one of the great elements of asylum existence was both deeper and less reciprocal. It pursued in the madman the least perceptible signs of his madness (...) and the madman cannot return this observation in any form, since he is merely observed. (MC: 249)

Psychoanalysis reinforces the non-reciprocity of the relation between reason and unreason, doubling

> the absolute observation of the watcher with the endless monologue of the person watched— thus preserving the old asylum structure of non-reciprocal observation but balancing it, in a non-symmetrical reciprocity, by the new structure of language without response (MC: 250-1).[11]

Another parallel between Foucault's gaze and Sartre's lies in the fact that it, like the gaze which transfixed Genet, is internalizable. Moreover, the mechanism for internalization is linked indissolubly to the unilaterality of the gaze. The Panopticon, Jeremy Bentham's sketch of an ideal prison, serves as the best example here.[12] In order for power to be exerted as economically as possible, and to provoke as little resistance as possible, mechanisms of panoptic surveillance are so constructed as to function continuously but unobtrusively. The Panopticon has as its "major effect":

> to induce in the inmate a state of conscious and permanent visibility that assures the automatic functioning of power. So to arrange things that the surveillance is permanent in its effects, even if it is discontinuous in its action; that the perfection of power should tend to render its actual exercise unnecessary, that this architectural apparatus should be a machine for creating and sustaining a power relation independent of the person who exercises it; in short, that the inmates should be caught up in a power situation of which they are themselves the bearers. (DP: 201)

In order for the functioning of power to be automatic and continuous, the prisoners are to be made their own guards. This is achieved simply by imparting to them the knowledge that they may be observed at any time. If they are aware that surveillance is a perpetual possibility, but are unable to know when, or even if, that possibility will be actualized, the prisoners will be forced to behave at all times as though they are presently under the eye of power:

> He who is subjected to a field of visibility, and who knows it, assumes responsibility for the constraints of power; he makes them play spontaneously on himself; he inscribes in

himself the power relation in which he simultaneously plays both roles; he becomes the
principle of his own subjection. (DP: 202-3)

All that is necessary for the gaze to be internalized is the existence of a state
of absolute non-reciprocity between the observing and the observed
subject. The Panopticon guarantees that non-reciprocity:

> The Panopticon is a machine for dissociating the see/being seen dyad: in the peripheric
> ring, one is totally seen, without ever seeing; in the central tower, one sees everything
> without ever being seen. (DP: 201-2)

In *Madness and Civilisation* we find a movement of internalization of the gaze
even closer to the model presented in *Saint Genet*. Here the support for the
gaze is found, not in architecture, but in the consciousness of the inmate.
The gaze is internalized in the form of guilt. It is on this basis that the
objectification of unreason is possible: "A purely psychological medicine
was made possible only when madness was alienated in guilt" (183). For
Foucault:

> The asylum no longer punished the madman's guilt, it is true; but it did more, it
> organized that guilt; it organized it for the madman as a consciousness of himself, and
> as a non-reciprocal relation to the keeper; it organized it for the man of reason as an
> awareness of the Other (...) by this guilt the madman became an object of punishment
> always vulnerable to himself and to the Other; and, from the acknowledgment of his
> status as object, from the awareness of his guilt, the madman was to return to his
> awareness of himself as a free and responsible subject (...) This movement by which,
> objectifying himself for the Other, the madman thus returned to his liberty, was to be
> found as much in Work as in Observation. (MC: 247)

Madness is now forced to assume responsibility for itself, on the terms
imposed by reason. Observed by the doctor, "pitilessly observed by
himself" (264), the madman knows:

> that he is watched, judged and condemned (...) all this must end in the internalization
> of the juridical instance, and the birth of remorse in the inmate's mind: it is only at this
> point that the judges agree to stop the punishment, certain that it will continue
> indefinitely in the patient's conscience. (MC: 267)

Like Sartre's Genet, Foucault's madman and his delinquent are each
provided with an essence, and that essence is guilty. But 'guilt' as an
existential category can only exist for an Other. Like the category 'thief', it
refers to my outside, not to my consciousness:

> A thief cannot have an intuition of himself *as thief*. The notion of 'thief' is on principle
> incommensurate with the realities of the inner sense. It is of social origin and
> presupposes a prior definition of society (...) There can therefore be no question of a
> mind's *encountering* theft within itself. (SG: 39)

Since the categories of my being-for-others can only be sustained in being by the gaze of Others, it is necessary, if they are to be rendered the permanent essence of my being, for the gaze to be internalized, for the self to become other *for itself*. Like Genet, it is the delinquent or the madman "himself who will be both the court and the accused, the policeman and the thief" (SG: 21). "Je est un autre", writes Sartre, à propos of Genet. This statement is true even for the authentic for-itself. The 'je' is a category for others, and, as such, is other than itself. But Genet, like Foucault's convicts and madmen, is forced to suppose the priority of the Other over self. Though Foucault would never have used the word, his subjected individuals are *alienated*.

This Millenial Yoke of Confession

After *Discipline and Punish*, the thematic of the gaze as the principle of subjectivation is absent from Foucault's work. If we continue to think about the construction of essences in terms of being-for-others, however, it is possible to shed new light on Foucault's next major work, *The History of Sexuality, Volume 1* (*La volonté de savoir*). Despite its nominally forming one third of a 'History of Sexuality', in many ways this book is more profitably be seen as a continuation of the analyses of *Discipline and Punish*, focusing this time on the process— always implicit in the earlier book— whereby, not the delinquent, the madman, or the child, but the 'normal' individual is subjected to a regime of power/knowledge.

The History of Sexuality, Volume 1 tells, once again (and for the last time in Foucault's career), the story of the construction of the modern subject— subject of and to power, object of knowledge. In the modern power/knowledge regime, Foucault suggests, this subject has been led to internalize the ultimate in self-constraining mechanisms, an obligation to confess concerning which the subject believes that nothing less than its freedom is at stake. Sexuality, we are led to think, has been repressed; in order to free ourselves from the insidious effects of this repression, we must speak its truth. The new deployment opposes truth to oppression: to speak the truth of sex is to "speak out against the powers that be" (HSI: 7). But to speak the truth concerning our sex is no easy task. If sex is repressed, then it is impossible for us to free ourselves from this elusive and deep-rooted domination all at once. We must attempt to speak the truth of sex, recognize the signs of repression in our supposed truth, and begin again. For between ourselves and our truth stand the powerful interdictions of our society, internalized in the form of the super-ego. We are, therefore, accomplices in our own repression— or so the story goes. Foucault takes this archetypical hermeneutics of suspicion origin-myth, and turns it back upon itself. Instead of freeing us from our guilt concerning our sexuality, he will free us from our guilt over being guilty concerning sexuality. Foucault's is a meta-hermeneutics of suspicion, for he sees in the repressive hypothesis simply:

> a fable that is indispensable to the endlessly proliferating economy of the discourse on sex. What is peculiar to modern societies, in fact, is not that they consigned sex to a shadow existence, but that they dedicated themselves to speaking of it *ad infinitum*, while exploiting it as *the* secret. (HSI: 35)

Foucault thus sees our fall as having occurred, not when we repressed our sexuality, but when we constituted our sexuality as having-been-repressed. The historical question to ask ourselves, therefore, is not 'When was sex repressed?' (a question usually answered in terms of Christian conceptions of the body) but:

> What paths have brought us to the point where we are 'at fault' with respect to our own sex? (...) How does one account for the displacement which, while claiming to free us from the sinful nature of sex, taxes us with a great historical wrong which consists precisely in imagining that nature to be blameworthy and in drawing disastrous consequences from that belief? (HSI: 9)

For the repressive hypothesis, the belief that our sexuality contains our nature, coupled with the conviction that concerning that nature "we have never said enough" (33), authorizes a more massive, more total and at the same time more precise extension of the mechanisms of subjectification than ever before. The subjectification examined in *Discipline and Punish* functioned as a principle of the individuation of the 'deviant', the departure from the norm: "the child is more individualized than the adult, the patient more than the healthy man, the madman and the delinquent more than the normal and the non-delinquent" (DP: 193). But the deployment of sexuality has the triple effect of relativizing the norm as a cultural construct, of depreciating its value as a sign of health, and, paradoxically, of placing ever greater emphasis on the importance of measuring each individual's relationship to it. It is the apparently normal, 'sane' individual, as much as the criminal or the mad, who must now be examined in order to liberate an overly-repressed sexuality. The psychologization of the individual authorizes access to every space of human life, not just to the hospital and the prison, the school and the workplace, but to the spaces of private life, notably the family home.[13] If the procedures of discipline "lowered the threshold of describable individuality" (DP: 191), then sexuality represents an exponential intensification of this process:

> The deployment (*dispositif*) of sexuality has its reason for being, not in reproducing itself, but in proliferating, innovating, annexing, creating, penetrating bodies in an increasingly detailed way, and in controlling populations in an increasingly comprehensive way. (HSI: 107)

Now, this sexuality concerning which it is so difficult to pronounce the truth is presumed to hold an essential secret concerning our nature. If repression represents culture, civilization, the necessary work of sublimation, then sexuality represents our being, that which is most natural and essential in ourselves— and our individuality may be defined as the intersection of the two. To know ourselves, therefore, is at least in important part to know the truth about our sexuality:

> It is through sex (...) that each individual has to pass in order to have access to his own intelligibility (seeing that it is both the hidden aspect of and the generative principle of meaning), to the whole of his body (since it is a real and threatened part of it, while symbolically constituting the whole), to his identity (since it joins the force of a drive to the singularity of a history). (HSI: 155-6)

But the peculiarity of this 'truth' produced by a subject about that same subject, and with immediate effects upon that subject, is that it is not destined for the speaker. For the privileged mode in which this truth is produced is not merely self-reflection— though this power/knowledge regime produces a reflexive style of thought as its philosophical and literary correlative (HSI: 59-60)— but confession. By its very structure, the technique for the production of truth implies two participants: one who confesses, who speaks the truth, yet cannot comprehend the truth thus articulated; and a listener, who learns the truth from the confession, yet is the only one able to validate its truth, interpret the symbols, perceive the reality through the distortions and finally articulate, not the truth about the subject, but the truth about this truth: "His was a hermeneutic function" (67).

This truth, although deprived of its power and validity without the authentification of the listener, finds its fulfilment, and, as it were, confirmation of that authentification at yet a third level, in the effect it, in its clarified version, is presumed to have upon the subject whose truth it is. Confession is a ritual:

> in which the expression alone, independently of its external consequences, produces intrinsic modifications in the person who articulates it: it exonerates, redeems, and purifies him; it unburdens him of his wrongs, liberates him, and promises him salvation. (62)

Thus the listener combines two figures; the priest who forgives and the master who interprets; "the forgiving master, the judge who condemned or acquitted" and "the master of truth" (67).

Foucault's description of confession is, of course, not neutral but implicitly a critique. And Sartre is similarly critical of the function of the confession in a discourse believed to produce the truth concerning the subject. Moreover, his criticisms are made for precisely the same reasons: that confession produces a truth concerning the subject which is a truth for Others; and that confession produces a Self, an essence which the for-itself does not have to be, but is.

We have already encountered the confession in Sartre's work as an example of bad faith: in the case of the homosexual whose friend, the "champion of sincerity", demands only that he confess, "that the guilty one will recognize himself as guilty" (107), in order to be absolved of his guilt. Confession liberates. If the homosexual will constitute himself as a thing before his friend, and entrust his freedom to him, his friend will return it to him (BN: 108-9). "Confession frees" (HSI: 60). Hence its fascinating attraction. The structure of the confession consists in a recognition of an essential nature in order to constitute the individual as beyond that nature:

> the man who confesses that he is evil has exchanged his disturbing 'freedom-for-evil' for an inanimate character of evil (...) but by the same stroke, he escapes from that *thing*, since it is he who contemplates it (...) He derives a *merit* from his sincerity. (BN: 109)

But essentializing oneself is a dangerous game: we have seen that in the case of Genet. The for-itself is defined by its acts, and the act of giving oneself a nature will have as its inevitable consequence the reduction of the for-itself, for itself and for-others, to that nature. Confession aims to free the individual from an essence, but the effect may well be firmly to cement that individual to its nature.

Through the mechanism of confession, Foucault tells us, the perverse individual is constituted as an example of a species. And one of the most important examples of the new breeds of people was that species known as the homosexual, defined by "nineteenth century psychiatry, jurisprudence, and literature" in all its "species and subspecies" (HSI: 101). My species-being, my belonging to a species, when it is that species known as humanity, is of course a specific mode of being-for-others, that element of my being-for-others I share with all the Others. But it is also strictly equivalent, for Sartre, to the unconscious, for my species is:

perpetually assimilable to an outside of my consciousness and, as I necessarily internalize this outside in thinking of it as *mine*, it is like an unconscious, which is the underlying meaning of my *consciousness*.

In this way, consciousness subtly becomes inessential in my own eyes without my ever being able to grasp the essential. (NE: 95; translation modified)

Since my unconscious, my being-outside-of-myself (within myself),[14] contains my truth *for me*, but is also, by definition, inaccessible to me, then if I am to learn the truth about myself I must place myself under the tutelage of a "master of truth." Truth about the self can only come to the self through the mediation of the other-than-self. Finally, however, it is not so much the method of production of the truth, as the fact that a stable truth about the individual is constituted, which the individual must submit to in order to recover even a partial freedom in relation to it, to which Sartre and Foucault object in the practice of confession. For Foucault this is because such an essence is oppressive in itself, and because it both justifies the extension of power and enables it to circulate:

through progressively finer channels, gaining access to individuals themselves, to their bodies, their gestures and all their daily actions. (1980e: 151)

In Sartre's terms, I need to assume the being-for-others constituted in this manner as a real aspect of my being and make myself responsible for it, but I cannot hope to recover it for myself and place my freedom at its foundation. Sincerity, the form this particular attempt to make myself the for-itself-in-itself assumes, is bad faith.

Thus, I can adopt an authentic attitude towards that aspect of my being which is mine, but which I cannot know, only by attempting to produce myself as I wish to be, not by attempting to reconcile myself to what I already am. "Authenticity reveals that the only meaningful project is that of *doing* (not that of being)" (NE: 475). Foucault suggests a similar conclusion when he criticizes the demand confession places on us to avow our sexual *being*:

It is no longer a question simply of saying what was done— the sexual act— and how it was done; but of reconstituting, in and around the act, the thoughts that recapitulated it, the obsessions that accompanied it, the images, desires, modulations, and quality of the pleasure that animated it. (HSI: 63)

We must, that is, confess everything in the act which could be taken to be a sign of the being it expresses. Authenticity, and more importantly a relation between power and knowledge less susceptible to the institution of states of domination, can thus be achieved by substituting nominalism for essentialism. It seems that Foucault has returned once more to the question he had not so much asked as problematized in *The Order of Things*, the question Kant added, in his *Logic*, to the three already posed in the *Critique of Pure Reason* (What can I know? What should I do? What is it permitted for me to hope?): Was ist der Mensch? (OT: 341). Once again, Foucault does not answer the question, but rather refuses its terms: *Der Mensch ist nicht* (Hacking, 1986: 39). "Man is an invention of recent date. And one perhaps nearing its end" (OT: 387). Or, the for-itself *is* not, it exists.

Trapped in Truth

These many parallels aside, however, Foucault's work raises a difficulty absent in Sartre. He raises the disturbing prospect that truth itself is intrinsically linked to the power it is usually thought to oppose:

> We are subjected to the production of truth through power and we cannot exercise power except through the production of truth (...) we *must* speak the truth; we are constrained or condemned to confess or to discover the truth. (Foucault, 1980c: 93)

We wish to oppose power, but we can no longer oppose it in the name of the truth of ourselves. Our weapons have betrayed us. To put the problem in terms of *The Order of Things*: "Man and the unthought are, at the archaeological level, contemporaries" (OT: 326); in attempting to advance toward the truth of man, one reinforces the episteme which produced him. The problem is raised most acutely in *Discipline and Punish*, à propos of prison reform:

> Prison 'reform' is virtually contemporary with the prison itself. It constitutes, as it were, its programme. From the outset, the prison was caught up in a series of accompanying mechanisms, whose purpose was apparently to correct it, but which seem to form part of its very functioning, so closely have they been bound up with its existence throughout its long history. (DP: 234)

That this reform movement was and is, at least in part, not a cynical exercise in manipulation, but a genuine attempt to correct perceived inefficiencies and inequities we may surmise from the fact that those engaged in its formulation ranged from "the very official *Société pour l'amélioration des prisons*" to "various philanthropic groups" (234) and even groups of former prisoners (235). The criticism, made in good faith, of the functioning of discipline, lead to an intensification of that very discipline, an intensification which justifies itself *in the name of the criticism made of it*. Prison reform is thus "isomorphic, despite its 'idealism', with the disciplinary functioning of the prison" (DP: 271), just as Reich's "'antirepressive' struggle", for all its acknowledged importance, "represented nothing more

(...) than a tactical shift and reversal in the great deployment of sexuality" (HSI: 131).

In this situation, what can be the future for critical thinking? In the name of what, utilizing what instruments, can we criticize the effects of the disciplinary society? On what can Foucault himself ground his own discourse? The truths produced by the current power/knowledge regime seem to be too inextricably bound up with the functioning of discipline to serve as effective support for a critique of this same discipline. New truths, on the other hand— leaving aside for the moment the question how one can produce such new truths as will not be born already compromised by the old, their inevitable point of departure— will be of no more use, for the problem, it appears, lies not so much in the specific nature of the truths as in the fact that they are truths at all. Any truth about the subject we may wish to oppose to the deployment of sexuality is potentially just as subjectifying. The subjectification/objectification couple seems to be intrinsic to the nature of truth itself. Can we, then, oppose discipline in the name of non-truth? Once again the difficulties appear to be manifold and insurmountable. Even if we are able to formulate a non-truth which would not itself claim the status of a new truth, or claim to reject the truth/falsity division altogether, how can we hope to be able to set our non-truth against the fascinating power of a discourse which claims to be true (and whose truth we, by our very rejection of the truth/falsity distinction, appear to have implicitly recognized). If we take this route, nothing less than a complete overthrow of the will-to-truth would be the indispensable precondition of effective criticism.

Foucault had previously believed that man was on the verge of disappearance, and with him would vanish the problem. By the time he publishes *The History of Sexuality, Volume 1*, he seems no longer to be able to detect signs of any such approaching cataclysm, or even of the fundamental change in *episteme* which would dethrone the will-to-truth. Has he, then, produced a new version of the dialectic of Enlightenment? Is the situation such that any attempt to escape from the ever increasingly oppressive domination of power will only intensify its effects? What can be the role of philosophy, "that discourse which *par excellence* is concerned with truth" (1980c: 93), in this situation? Is it destined to become merely a functionary of power? If self-reflection, that style of thought which aims to produce truth about the subject, is shown to be the accomplice of the very domination it condemns, must we abandon the critical project itself? For it is of the essence of this style of thought that criticism cannot exempt itself from this generalized imperative without risking, in the language of the

Enlightenment, the substitution of one form of tyranny for another. Moreover, how are we even to think about the problems which confront us without the central category of the subject? If we abandon the question concerning the subject, must we not also abandon, as Kant implies, the other three questions (and thus epistemology and ethics)? We seem to be faced with the following alternative: either to abandon critique definitively, or to abandon it provisionally, until a new *episteme* brings the possibility of a new mode of thought; resign ourselves to living on the plane of what Sartre calls non-thetic consciousness, or adopt an attitude of Heideggerian *Gelassenheit*. Is quietism, then, the ineluctable consequence of Foucault's self-proclaimedly critical thought? It is to these questions that I wish to turn in the next chapter.

SEVEN

A Daily Labor, Long And Disappointing

We are not lumps of clay, and what is important is not what people make of us but what we ourselves make of what they have made of us.

— Sartre, *Saint Genet*

What role is played by reflection and critique in the early works of Foucault and Sartre? In the case of Sartre, the answer seems clear: Sartre is a rationalist, a self-proclaimed Cartesian. Thus critical reflection by the self upon the self would seem to constitute an important element in both his politics and his ethics— defining the latter, with Foucault, as the relation which the self enters into with itself (1984: 48). And indeed Sartre wishes reflection to play such a role. In one of the few explicit references to political action in *Being and Nothingness* (a book which, we must remember, was first published in occupied France), Sartre tells us that it is reflection which constitutes the indispensable ground for revolution. For:

> In so far as man is immersed in the historical situation, he does not even succeed in conceiving of the failures and lacks in a political organization or determined economy; this is not, as is stupidly said, because he 'is accustomed to it', but because he apprehends it in its plenitude of being and because he can not even imagine that he can exist in it otherwise (...) It is on the day that we can conceive of a different state of affairs that a new light falls on our troubles and our sufferings and we *decide* that these are unbearable. (561)

Thus, the situation itself cannot provide the motive for changing it; it is lived as *natural*. It is only after the workers have reflected upon their situation that they can form the project of changing it, and only subsequent to that reflection will the situation appear intolerable. The condition for all political action is the withdrawal of the subject in relation to their situation, so that this situation may appear as an object for that subject. Such a withdrawal is always possible for Sartre: consciousness, by virtue of its freedom, has "the permanent possibility of effecting a rupture with its own past" (563). Thus, Sartre concludes, "we must recognize that the indispensable and fundamental condition of all action is the freedom of the acting being" (563).

Freedom and the Possibility of Choosing Otherwise

But the difficulties with Sartre's explanation of the possibility of change appear at once. For if, as Sartre argues, it is only subsequent to the project of changing a situation that that situation will appear as needing-to-be-changed, what can possibly motivate a for-itself to formulate such a project of change in the first place? Why change a situation which appears natural? As I have already noted, *Being and Nothingness* is not much concerned with politics. Yet if Sartre's position on the possibility of revolutionary change can be shown to be unsustainable, the ramifications will reach to the heart of Sartre's description of the for-itself. For what is at stake is the very freedom of the Sartrean subject.

For the Sartre of *Being and Nothingness*, the freedom of the for-itself is absolute. In fact, it is only in terms of this freedom that there is a world. The for-itself bestows the meaning constitutive of the world upon brute being in terms of its original, freely chosen project: "We choose the world, not in its contexture as in-itself but in its meaning, by choosing ourselves" (BN: 596). So total is this freedom that the for-itself cannot even begin to engage itself in being unless it first places a limit on that freedom: it places that limit upon itself through its original choice of itself, its project. Before the choice (a 'before' which has the status of an origin myth, a heuristic device, and is meant to refer to a logical, not temporal, genesis), freedom was absolute and unconditioned. After the choice, however, the for-itself is faced with a simple either/or: either to continue to live out its choice of itself and the world, or to reject that choice. Sartre denies that this reduction of alternatives to an either/or involves any limitation of the freedom of the for-itself, since none of my acts are actually determined. No matter how I have acted, I could always have chosen to have acted differently. But let us examine Sartre's presentation of this choice:

> There is no doubt that I could have done otherwise, but that is not the problem. It ought to be formulated rather like this: could I have done otherwise without perceptibly modifying the organic totality of the projects which I am (...) I could have done otherwise. Agreed. But *at what price?* (585)

The price to be paid, of course, is a total renunciation of the project. Sartre is perfectly correct in saying that, in necessitating the for-itself to choose the (single) meaning of the world, he has not limited its freedom. Only the concrete freedom to act within a world deserves to be called freedom, for only such a freedom involves choice between alternatives:

> The structure of the choice necessarily implies that it be a choice in the world. A choice which would be a choice *in terms of nothing*, a choice *against nothing*, would be a choice of nothing and would be annihilated as choice. (BN: 617)

Given, however, that only a choice in the world deserves to be called a choice, how can Sartre be justified in calling the choice *of* that world a choice? The answer is clear: choice and world must arise simultaneously.[1] Yet Sartre has precluded the possibility of such a simultaneity in his assertion of the logical *priority* of the choice upon the world. Thus, it seems the choice of the original project is a choice against the background of nothing; or, to be more specific, a choice by the for-itself which is nothingness, against the background of brute in-itself, as yet without the meaning which could motivate such a choice.

Sartre himself recognizes the possibility of this criticism, and attempts to forestall it. He hopes to rescue choice from incoherence, by interpreting deliberation "in terms of an original choice." Thus:

> as soon as there are cause and motive (...) there is already a positing of ends and consequently a choice. But this does not mean that the profound choice is thereby unconscious. It is simply one with the consciousness which we have of ourselves. This consciousness, as we know, can be only non-positional; it is we-as-consciousness since it is not distinct from our being. And as our being is precisely our original choice, the consciousness (of) the choice is identical with the self-consciousness which we have. (594-5)

Thus we are conscious of choice as choice, as having been made by us, and therefore as able to be changed, Sartre claims. The for-itself has a "pre-ontological comprehension of the meaning of his acts" (591). But this does not solve the problem. It only claims to explain how the choice is able to be changed, not what *makes* it a choice. For once causes and motives exist, the choice has *already* taken place. Sartre's assertion of a simultaneity of choice and world— "One must be conscious in order to choose, and one must choose in order to be conscious" (595)— can only apply in an already meaningful world; that is, *subsequent* to the choice which bestows meaning upon being.

Thus Sartre fails to establish that the original choice deserves to be called a choice, that is, that it is free, for it is a choice *without alternatives*.[2] But his problems do not end there. At this point, it would seem that reflective critique is called upon to intervene: the for-itself was unable to choose its original project; will it now be able to reflect upon that project and freely alter it? As we have already seen, Sartre claims that it can: the for-itself has a pre-ontological comprehension of its choice *as* choice, and thus as able to be changed. But are we indeed conscious of our choice *as a choice?*

> I enjoy a full consciousness of myself and of my fundamental projects, and this time the consciousness is positional (...) But such is the structure of the positional consciousness that I can trace this knowledge back to a subjective apprehension of myself, and it refers me to other objects which I produce or which I dispose of in connection with the order of the preceding without being able to perceive that I am thus more and more sculpturing my figure in the world. (BN: 596-7)

I am aware of my choice, for I read it in my world. *But I cannot perceive that this choice is myself.* The world does not appear to me as having been chosen as me, but as pre-existing me and the choices I have been able to make. The world appears to me to be *natural.* We first noted the importance of reflection in Sartre with regard to the workers' project of revolution. Let us now return to these workers:

> Their misfortunes do not appear to them 'habitual' but rather *natural*; they *are*, that is all (...) they are integrated by the worker with his being. He suffers without considering his suffering and without conferring value upon it (...) Therefore this suffering can not be in itself a *motive* for his acts. Quite the contrary, it is after he has formed the project of changing his situation that it will appear intolerable to him. This means that he will have had to give himself room, to withdraw in relation to it. (561-2)

Just as the workers' world appears to them as natural, as having to be lived, so the world of all for-themselves appears as untranscendable to them. The for-itself may give meaning to the world, but subsequent to that gift, it is limited to reading that meaning in the world as having always-already been there. It is necessary to withdraw in relation to the world in order to form the project of changing it, but the motive for such withdrawal will only exist *after* it has already been accomplished.

Given all these difficulties, I do not see what resources Sartre has to explain how the project of altering the world might arise. For the sake of continuing the discussion, however, let us grant that despite all the obstacles placed before the for-itself, it somehow conceives of the project of rejecting its initial choice. It performs a reflective withdrawal in relation to the world, and it realizes that the meanings of the world stem from it. Well and good: it will now freely choose other meanings for that world, in absolute sovereignty. But what other meanings? What can possibly motivate the for-itself in such a situation to choose one set of meanings, rather than another? For, as Sartre has told us, causes and motives imply a choice that has *already* been made:

a voluntary deliberation is always a deception. How can I evaluate causes and motives on which I myself confer their value before all deliberation and by the very choice which I make of myself? (BN: 581)

This means, first of all, that there is no choice possible within the boundaries of a single project. I act, either in accordance with my project and with the values I have already conferred upon possible actions, or against my project, because I am mistaken regarding it or the world (606)—which being in error, needless to say, does not represent freedom. More seriously, this means that having conceived of the project of changing my initial choice, I have no means of evaluating alternative choices. Nothing survives the dissolution of the meaningful world, no value in terms of which I could rank possible choices, for the choice is itself the source of all values. Thus all choices are of equal value; that is, before the choice, they are valueless, and after the choice the new project is posited as a plenitude of value. As Sartre puts it, all choices are equally "*unjustifiable*" (598).

But this amounts to saying that there is no choice. Indeed, in his *War Diaries*, Sartre seems to recognize this. Choices are not merely "unjustifiable", they are *impossible.* For the choosing subject finds itself in the position Sartre occupies when he contemplates the possibility of rejecting his project to write:

I only ever *dream* of questioning my desire to write, because if I really tried even for an hour to hold it in abeyance, place it in paranethesis, all reason for questioning anything whatsoever would collapse. (WD: 29-30)

If choice is a matter of all or nothing, as Sartre clearly thinks, then we do not choose at all.

This has far-reaching consequences for Sartre's entire system. If voluntary deliberation is always a deception, then so is the choice of project. For what is it that can motivate such a choice? I must choose to reject my project in the name of the values of my *new* project, for my old, offering as it does a *total* interpretation of being, can never present me with any reasons for rejecting it. But if I believe that I am choosing to reject an old project in the name of a new, I necessarily deceive myself, for the values of the new project only exist after the choice. When I believe that I am choosing, I have in fact always-already *chosen.*

One can thus apply to the project of the for-itself exactly the description Sartre gives of the so-called "impermeability to experience of the primitive" (NE: 355; translation modified):

Within the primitive's *Weltanschauung* everything that happens gets interpreted in terms of the cardinal categories of this *Weltanschauung*, (thus) a *lack* internal to this *Weltanschauung* will never lead to its abandonment. (NE: 355)

It is not only the 'primitive' who cannot learn from experience, for the structure of the for-itself's choice is such that anything which occurs within its world is necessarily interpreted in terms of the categories of that world. Nothing can come from *outside* to motivate a choice, for there is no outside. But neither can anything from *inside* my project provide me with reasons for rejecting it, for the choice offers only a plenitude of reasons for persevering in it.[3] As Sartre himself acknowledges:

> our actual choice is such that it furnishes us with no *motive* for making it past by means of a further choice. In fact, it is this original choice which originally creates all causes and all motives which can guide us to partial actions; it is this which arranges the world with its meaning, its instrumental-complexes, and its coefficient of adversity. The absolute change which threatens us from our birth until our death remains perpetually unpredictable and incomprehensible. Even if we envisage other fundamental attitudes as *possible*, we shall never consider them except from outside, as the behavior of Others. And if we attempt to refer our conduct to them, they shall not for all that lose their character as external and as transcended-transcendences. To 'understand' them in fact would be already to have chosen them. (BN: 598-9)

In fact, we are forced to a surprising conclusion: freedom exists *nowhere* in *Being and Nothingness*, neither before the founding choice of the original project, nor within the boundaries of that project, nor in the movement of rejection of an original project. And Sartre has eliminated freedom from the world of the for-itself, paradoxically, by granting it too much freedom. So absolute is the choice of the for-itself that nothing pre-exists that choice, which could influence it, nor does anything survive its dissolution. The choice is absolute, but this amounts to saying that it is arbitrary, which means that it is not a choice at all. As Sartre should have realized— writing, as he was, a book which engages in an almost continual dialogue with Hegel— absolute freedom is as abstract as total determination, and ultimately indistinguishable from it.[4]

Inside the Magic Lantern

And it is here that we rejoin Foucault. For his work, too, is largely concerned with change. As he wrote in the preface to *The Order of Things*:

> my main concern has been with changes (...) the suddenness and thoroughness with which certain sciences were sometimes recognized, and the fact that at the same time similar changes occurred in apparently very different disciplines. (OT: xii)

This passage, which occurs only in the English translation of *Les mots et les choses*, is written in response to the criticism that the latter work denies the possibility of change. As Foucault points out, he does no such thing. Far from denying change, he constantly highlights the discontinuity between one episteme and another. His problems arise, however, not from the denial of change, but, as in Sartre's case, from too absolute a conception thereof.

Of course, Foucault's work at this period is far from being concerned with the question of the freedom of the subject. On the contrary, he wants to show that the category 'subject' is itself determined by a particular configuration of epistemological space. Individuals are defined as a function of the way being presents itself to be thought:

> at any given instant, the structure proper to individual experience finds a certain number of possible choices (and of excluded possibilities) in the systems of the society; inversely, at each of their points of choice the social structures encounter a certain number of possible individuals (and others who are not). (AK: 380)

We find ourselves immersed in a mode of thought as far removed from Sartre's as possible. Individuals do not give meaning to the world; on the contrary, there are individuals only if being is structured in such a way that, as Heidegger would say, 'it gives' (*es gibt*) man. Thus the decisions these individuals make are merely actualizations of some of the limited number of possibilities the *episteme* makes available:

> When we investigate the knowledge that made all those various options simultaneously possible, we perceive that the opposition between them is superficial; and that, though it is logically necessary, it is so on the basis of a single arrangement that simply creates, at a given point, the alternatives of an indispensable choice. (OT: 181)

There is, therefore, no more freedom in the episteme than in the world of *Being and Nothingness*: being gives itself to be thought prior to our existence, it gives our existence to us. Within the epistemological arrangement thus defined, we can do no more than actualize the options made possible by that arrangement. And if the arrangement is to be changed, it will be, as it were, of its own accord. No action of ours, no reflection, no critique can influence it to change. On the contrary, critique is always interior to the episteme; it thinks as it is directed to think. Criticism, in the Kantian sense, cannot produce change in the *episteme*, for it is part of the functioning of that *episteme*: "the Kantian critique (...) marks the threshold of our modernity" (OT: 242). Criticism:

> opens up (...) the possibility of another metaphysics; one whose purpose will be to question, apart from representation, all that is the source and origin of representation; it makes possible those philosophies of Life, of the Will, and of the Word, that the nineteenth century is to deploy in the wake of criticism (...) our thought today still belongs to the same dynasty. (OT: 243)

And it is precisely in this dynasty that Foucault would place Sartre, to judge by his remarks on phenomenology:

> that with which phenomenology was to oppose (positivism) so tenaciously was already present in its underlying structures (...) Involved, but forgotten to its advantage. So much so that contemporary thought, believing that it has escaped it since the end of the nineteenth century, has merely rediscovered, little by little, that which made it possible. (BC: 199)

It seems, then, that we have discovered an important continuity between the earlier and the later Foucault. In both, the thought which claims to criticize a certain arrangement of knowledge, or a certain political practice, is intimately involved with the functioning of that very arrangement. Reflection, it seems, can accomplish nothing in the way of change, for it cannot think its own limits, although it continually addresses itself to them. Thus:

> Discontinuity— the fact that within the space of a few years a culture sometimes ceases to think as it had been thinking up till then and begins to think other things in a new way— probably begins with an erosion from outside, from that space which is, for thought, on the other side, but in which it has never ceased to think from the very beginning. (OT: 50)

But that which is on the outside is nothing less than Being itself. And if it is possible to think Being as it really is, not as it gives itself to be thought, as Heidegger and Foucault sometimes appear to suggest, neither are able to show how, on their own terms, such thought is possible. It is true that Foucault assigns a "somewhat enigmatic place" in *The Order of Things* to Nietzsche, who:

> sent all these stable forms up in flames (...) then used their charred remains to draw strange and impossible faces; and by a light that may be either— we do not know yet which— the reviving flame of the last great fire or an indication of the dawn, we see the emergence of what may perhaps be the space of contemporary thought. It was Nietzsche, in any case, who burned for us, even before we were born, the intermingled promise of the dialectic and anthropology. (OT: 263)

But we are not to see in this body of work the signs of courageous individual decision, or of thought which will not recognize boundaries for itself. If Nietzsche inaugurates a new mode of reflection, which will burst the boundaries of the modern *episteme*, this is not due to his individual brilliance or daring. It is due, simply, to the fact that Being gave itself to be thought differently. The questions raised by Mallarmé and Nietzsche are the questions of a new *episteme*. They are therefore the questions which arise subsequent to a change in *episteme*, just as the motives which cause a change of original project can only arise after such a change. Consequently, if the answers to these questions are not clear, we can nevertheless say with Foucault: "I now know why I am able, like everyone else, to ask them— and I am unable not to ask them today" (307).

For the Foucault of this period, then, *Gelassenheit* is indeed the appropriate attitude to adopt. We cannot hurry the change of *episteme*, we can only await it. The suspicion arises, however, that if we even want such change, this can only be because it has already occurred. Change:

> cannot be 'explained' or even summed up in a single word. It is a radical event that is distributed across the entire visible surface of knowledge (...) Only thought reapprehending itself at the root of its own history could provide a foundation, entirely free of doubt, for what the solitary truth of this event was in itself. (217-8)

Discontinuity is as mysterious, ineffable, and as impermeable to our acts as Being itself. And this is so because it is neither more nor less than a sending of Being.

Foucault's refusal to explain change is superfluous, then, for he cannot attempt to explain it within the bounds of his thought. Change cannot come from outside the *episteme*, for the *episteme* has no outside (apart, as we have seen, from Being itself). As Foucault writes:

> In any given culture and at any given moment, there is always only one *episteme* that defines the conditions of possibility of all knowledge, whether expressed in a theory or silently invested in a practice. (OT: 168)

And change cannot come from within the *episteme*, since all thought can do within the boundaries within which it operates is to actualize the prefabriacted possibilities of that *episteme*. Change cannot be explained, therefore, it can only be pointed to. It is true that Foucault embraces this consequence with enthusiasm; far from constituting an aporia in his thought, it is precisely the conclusion towards which, under the manifest influence of Heidegger, he had been working. But for a style of thought which aspires to political engagement, it is a paralyzing conclusion. And it is one which, as he became increasingly critical of Heidegger, Foucault was soon to reject.

Already in the preface to the English translation of *Les Mots et les choses*, Foucault is backing away from the overly totalizing presentation of the *episteme* in that work. Not that the preface contains any self-criticism, merely the assertion that the notion of *episteme* had been misread as total, whereas what he was writing was "a strictly 'regional' study" (x). This is patently untrue: *The Order of Things* abounds in assertions such as the one quoted above, to the effect that there is only one *episteme* at any one time in any one culture.[5] But the very fact that Foucault felt the need to reassess his work in this way is revealing of the new direction he was to take in the coming years.[6]

EIGHT

Accepting The World

It is right that a person, no matter who, be they at the other end of the world, should rise up because they cannot bear that someone else should be tortured or condemned. This is not to interfere in the internal affairs of a state. Those who protest for the sake of a single Iranian tortured in the depths of a Savak prison concern themselves with matters as universal as can be.

— Foucault, "Lettre ouverte à Mehdi Bazargan."

In the book on ethics which he had promised at the end of *Being and Nothingness*, but which was not, in fact, published until after his death, Sartre returned to the question of freedom. He had realized that the possibility of free choice is intimately tied up with that of ethics: how can we reasonably blame a person for acting in a manner that is strictly determined? It is in this sense that the question of freedom is bound up with that of intersubjectivity. It is no accident that, in *Notebooks for an Ethics*, Sartre attempts to elaborate a more coherent doctrine of absolute freedom at the same time as his most positive ever reading of the intersubjective relation.

Unfortunately, Sartre's solution to the problem of intersubjectivity in this work is vitiated by a still too dualist ontology. Once again we are presented with the model of a for-itself which gives meaning to the world through its choice of itself, and once again a change in project is predicated on the ability of the for-itself to suspend that meaning:

At every instant of the world, there is always the possibility of *waking up*. This awakening (...) is reflection. For non-complicitous reflection, my choice becomes the adoption of a possible and the significations of the world appear as correlative to this adoption (...) It is the setting within parentheses, not of the world (for doubt is impossible given sensory intuition), but of the world's significations. (NE: 359; translation modified)

Thus the for-itself will effect the ultimate in phenomenological *epochés*, or a new form of Cartesian doubt (both of which are invoked in the above passage) and erase all significations from the world. All that will remain is, not the *cogito*, but the *cogito* faced with the in-itself. It need hardly be added that this is precisely the sort of ahistorical ontology to which Foucault objects:

> If there is one approach I do reject (…) it is that (one might call it, broadly speaking, the phenomenological approach) which gives absolute priority to the observing subject, which attributes a constituent role to an act, which places its own point of view at the origin of all historicity— which, in short, leads to a transcendental consciousness. (OT: xiv)[1]

If the significations can be stripped from the world, this can only be because they have been placed there by a constituent act, and the suspension of these significations reveals, very precisely, transcendental consciousness. That Foucault's criticism is here appropriate is further indicated by Sartre's application of this *epoché* to intersubjective relations. The gift, Sartre writes, "is freedom and liberation" (369):

> In giving, my freedom springs forth over the collapse of the world. At the same time, I recognize the other's freedom, for I consider the other as essential and the world as inessential. (NE: 369)

The gift, too, functions as an *epoché*; it too brackets the world. The difference between the two *epochés* lies in the fact that in this second bracketing, not one but two *cogitos* survive, encountering each other against the background of meaningless being. It goes without saying, of course, that one cannot suspend the meaning of the world, that the *epoché* is a cultural instrument which carries with it a world of significations, and that no instrument is free of these meanings. The gift, claims Sartre, will place me "above every type of universe in a kind of absolute beyond the ages, an *ahistorical* absolute" (369). But there is no ahistorical absolute, nor are there any "ahistorical human relations" (370). The act of giving only has a meaning because it occurs in a particular cultural context in which such actions play a role. And if there were any means of exiting from history, there would still not be any freedom, as I have already shown.[2]

But in fact Sartre had already begun to sketch the less rigidly dualist ontology which would be the condition of developing a more adequate account of intersubjectivity, and in the very same book which contains his analysis of the gift. For his criticism of the ethics of Right is predicated on the assumption that it is *not* possible to suspend the meaning of the world. The reality of a right "is a demand":

> it is addressed to freedom, since it posits that it is possible for man to disengage himself entirely and at any moment whatsoever from the concrete process. (NE: 138)

The demand assumes it always possible for the individual at any instant to suspend the meaning of the world, for it demands that one should act in a certain manner *regardless of the situation*. Thus,

> the demand 'treat me like a freedom' is purely negative since all concrete contents are destroyed along with the world and since I am a purely formal end. (139; translation modified)

Sartre makes two criticisms of this negative conception of liberty (ignoring for the moment his ironic charge that it destroys the world): that it locates liberty in the subject, as a given property, thus missing the fact that liberty only exists as a concrete operation; and that the political implications of the demand that one destroy the world are, paradoxically, conservative. Sartre insists that "precisely because it is negative and a nihilation of the world as such, it favors the status quo" (147).[3] And here Sartre sketches for the first time a theme to which he will often return; that if one wishes to change the world, it is necessary first to accept it, if only in order to use it as an instrument of change. The project of change is always the project of changing something in the world, not of rejecting the world altogether. What is more, my project of changing my world is itself an expression of that world: "I can *express* my epoch only in surpassing it" (490). There is, then, no outside to the epoch because there is no outside to meaning.

If meaning is brought to the world by the free and gratuitous act of the for-itself, then there is no freedom. But if, on the other hand, meaning is immanent in the world and we are unable to take our distance from it, if, that is, we find ourselves back in the *episteme* of *The Order of Things*, then freedom is equally expelled from the world. To put it another way, critique can only occur on condition both that there is meaning inherent in the world— whether this meaning be historical or somehow 'natural'— and that we are able to reflect on this meaning, that is, withdraw in relation to it while remaining entirely within it. And indeed this is the position toward which Sartre was already moving by the time of the *Notebooks for an Ethics*.[4]

For at least on some of the pages of the *Notebooks*, the for-itself arises in an already meaningful world. That is, the subject is *interpolated*, received into a world which pre-exists it:

> the situation (...) is already experienced (*vécue*) and thought about by other For-itselves for whom I exist before being born and who make claims on my freedom. In other words, I am an already pledged freedom. In surpassing their situation, these For-itselves have assigned me a future: they have already defined me as French, bourgeois, Jewish, etc.; they have already determined my earnings, my obligations, my chances; they have *already made the world meaningful*. (NE: 57-8; italics mine, Sartre's italics deleted)

Thus, we can accept Sartre's assertion that the world is made meaningful by the for-itself, but only on the condition we recognize that each for-itself does not undertake this act on its own account, *ex nihilo* and freely. Meaning comes from the for-itself, but the for-itself is always born into a world that is already a plenitude of meaning. It is indeed we who decide, but we decide "as intersubjectivity" (NE: 102).[5] And we make our decision taking as our unavoidable point of departure the meaningful world into which we are born. Thus we create the world and ourselves, but we do so by surpassing it. And this surpassing is of one particular aspect of that world only. It is in this sense that we can say that that which is surpassed is conserved in the surpassing:

> In truth, human freedom is such that the one who does not revolt accepts, and revolt can be engendered only by a disavowed acceptance and a semi-complicity (...)
>
> revolutionaries (...) have a bad conscience in the beginning because they are fighting in and against themselves. Because man is facticity and freedom, and because his freedom takes up his facticity. (NE: 264, 269)

Authentic action, then, is the project to change a part of the world while accepting, at least provisionally, the remainder. And the values in the name of which this change is accomplished are values of this same world.[6] This necessary acceptance of the values of the world means that person who aims to change the world may find herself, like Foucault's prison reformers, merely realizing or even reinforcing precisely that aspect of the world she wished to reject, actualizing one of the possibilities of the configuration with which she is faced:

> Thus, at this level, an individual may avoid being a class individual, and may sometimes transcend his class-being (...) However, *in fact* (...) all he has done is to realize, in his person, one of the possibilities in the structured field of his class possibilities. (CDR: 330-1)

But it is also possible for individuals to realize a small, but real, margin of liberty, to make of themselves something other than the world has made of them, to become, in the marxist vocabulary of the *Critique*, in some small way their own product, and not *just* the product of their world. Once Sartre had realized that freedom is not the *ex nihilo* creation of the self and the world out of the in-itself plus nothingness, his conception becomes markedly less grandiose, less celebratory: "Freedom is not a triumph. For Genet, it simply marked out certain routes which were not initially given" (Sartre, 1974e: 35). But freedom becomes no less valuable for that. More sober, but also more effective, it is more able to justify its demands, for they are made *in the name of the values of the same world to which it stands opposed.*

The position Sartre begins to outline in *Notebooks for an Ethics*, and which underlies the *Critique*, is one in which the for-itself arises in an already meaningful world, in terms of which it forms projects. But the meaning of that world is in turn illuminated, and potentially altered, by those projects.[7] Between the for-itself and the world, there exists a reciprocal interaction:

> everything happens as if by springing forth into the world, I uncover a future of this world that awaits me. But this future in which I am engaged and that I contribute to constituting in the time it unveils, is like a face of objects not yet turned toward me (...) They designate themselves as potentialities and usable tools by their future, but reciprocally it is their potentialities that uncover their future. These two moments are one. (NE: 240)

This is precisely the condition of critique. Meaning must be inherent in the world, and it must come to the world by the for-itself. It must have its own coefficient of adversity, but it must be to some degree, no matter how small, changeable by intentional action. One can no longer pretend it is possible to change the world globally, or by fiat. To act on the world is to act really and materially, using the instruments at hand (ideological as well as physical), accepting and transforming the significations they bring with them.

Foucault and the Possibility of Critique

Have we solved the problem with which we began? Can we critique states of domination in the name of the values they produce? Will that not return us to the situation outlined by Foucault in *Discipline and Punish*, wherein prison reform merely repeats "(w)ord for word, from one century to the other, the same fundamental propositions" (DP: 270)? Foucault himself must have felt it possible. For his solution to the problem concerning prisons was to participate in their critique; not only by writing *Discipline and Punish*, but also by helping to form the *Groupe d'Information sur les Prisons*. The difference between GIP and all previous attempts to critique the prison was certainly not, as might be suspected, that it allowed the prisoners to speak for themselves: *Pauvre Jacques* and the *Gazette de Sainte-Pélagie* had given a voice at least to former prisoners in the first half of the nineteenth century.

Foucault's criticisms of the prison, of the disciplinary society, of the deployment of sexuality are made, I believe, largely in the name of the values these institutions secrete. And it could not be any other way. Foucault was a man born at a certain time into a certain society and inculcated with its values. If he found some aspects of that society objectionable, this could only be for one or both of two reasons: because there are competing value systems in that society, that is, theoretical options contained within a single epistemo-ethical configuration; or because the society behaves, in certain matters and to a certain extent, contrary to its own dominant values.

That there are competing value systems in the name of which Foucault condemns some of the practices of his society, and which he believes might be activated to change some of those practices, is shown by Foucault's interest in and advocacy of minor knowledges:

> it is through the re-emergence of these low ranking knowledges, these unqualified, even directly disqualified knowledges (such as that of the psychiatric patient, of the ill person, of the nurse, of the doctor (...) of the delinquent, etc) and which involve (...) a particular, local, regional knowledge, a differential knowledge incapable of unanimity (...) that criticism performs its work. (Foucault, 1980c: 82)

But at least as important are those other knowledges produced by a deformation or inversion of the dominant knowledges, such as those produced by Marcuse or Reich. Or those produced by precisely the humanism Foucault had expended so much energy in combating. Resistance to disciplinary power in the name of "life and man as a living being" (HSI: 144) had instituted:

> a very real process of struggle; life as a political object was in a sense taken at face value and turned back against the system that was bent on controlling it (...) The 'right' to life, to one's body, to health, to happiness, to the satisfaction of needs, and beyond all the oppressions or 'alienations,' the 'right' to rediscover what one is and all that one can be, this 'right'—which the classical juridical system was utterly incapable of comprehending—was the political response (*réplique*) to all these new procedures of power which did not derive, either, from the traditional right of sovereignty. (HSI: 145)

Foucault is not advocating a return to such methods of combat; he has convincingly shown how easily any discourse which critiques in the name of "what one is" can be colonized by power. But neither is he claiming that nineteenth century humanism was simply a ruse of discipline: the struggle was "very real." Like Reich's critique, then, this humanism presented a form of resistance that was effective, yet remained within the boundaries of that which it criticized:

> The importance of this critique and its impact on reality were substantial. But the very possibility of its success was tied to the fact that it always unfolded within the deployment of sexuality, and not outside or against it. (131)

The eventual aim is not to turn this deployment against itself, but to overturn it, for it produces effects contrary to those it claims. It does not free, it tightens constraint. But the only means of producing this overturning is to work within it. By "réplique", then, Foucault means neither "reply", nor "replica",[8] but both at once. The "réplique" made by the humanists to the extension of disciplinary power was effective resistance to that power made in the name of values which it had itself made possible. This resistance, it is now clear, was able to be inverted in turn; far from leading to the overthrow of discipline, it reinforced it. But this does not imply that *all* attempts at resistance will be similarly doomed to failure. Power, in its functioning, inevitably produces possibilities of resistance:

> there are no relations of power without resistances; the latter are all the more real and effective because they are formed right at the point where relations of power are exercised. (Foucault, 1980f: 142)

And these possibilities of resistance enable real, effective, and potentially far-reaching and enduring effects to be produced upon that power. The reply made by homosexuals to the deployment of sexuality is an example of a "réplique" which, although susceptible to re-colonization to the extent it is made in the name of their *being*, has so far proved an effective form of resistance (Sawicki, 1991: 56):

> There is no question that the appearance in nineteenth-century psychiatry, jurisprudence, and literature of a whole series of discourses on the species and subspecies of homosexuality (...) made possible a strong advance of social controls into this area of 'perversity'; but it also made possible the formation of a 'reverse' discourse: homosexuality began to speak in its own behalf, to demand that its legitimacy or 'naturality' be acknowledged, often in the same vocabulary, using the same categories by which it was medically disqualified. (HSI: 101)[9]

It is in part due to what one might call the *undecidability* of the concepts through which power operates that Foucault has recourse so often to the notion of *strategy*:

> power (...) should not be conceived of as a property, but as a strategy (...) its effects of domination should not be attributed to an 'appropriation', but to dispositions, manoeuvres, tactics, techniques, functionings. (DP: 26; translation modified)

Power operates strategically, through the concatenation of "a multiplicity of often minor processes (...) Discipline is a political anatomy of detail" (DP: 138-9). The resistance to power must similarly resort to strategy.[10] Hence resistance is most effective when focused on specific struggles, rather than on the project of rejecting the whole:

> The overthrow of these 'micro-powers' does not, then, obey the law of all or nothing; it is not acquired once and for all by a new control of the apparatuses nor by a new functioning or a destruction of the institutions; on the other hand, none of its localized episodes may be inscribed in history except by the effects that it induces on the entire network in which it is caught up. (DP: 27)

What, then, do we oppose to the regime of truth? The answer is by now clear. Truth can only be resisted in the name, precisely, of truth itself:

> It is indeed in this field of obligation to truth that we sometimes can avoid in one way or another the effects of a domination, linked to structures of truth or to institutions charged with truth (...) We escaped then a domination of truth, not by playing a game that was a complete stranger to the game of truth, but in playing it otherwise. (ECS: 15)

That one opposes power in the name of a truth which it itself makes possible, that one criticizes truth by demonstrating that there are "other rational possibilities, (by) teaching people what they ignore about their own situation" (ECS: 15), that, in short, it is in the name of current values that one critiques, explains Foucault's somewhat ambiguous attitude to the Enlightenment, especially apparent in *Discipline and Punish*.[11] I have already pointed to the connection Foucault establishes between the gaze and the Enlightenment, between an eye which sees all and an intellectual movement which has as its aim the illumination of everything. *Discipline and Punish* seems to continue to insist on this connection between Enlightenment and discipline:

> although, in a formal way, the representative régime makes it possible, directly or indirectly, with or without relays, for the will of all to form the fundamental authority of sovereignty, the disciplines provide, at the base, a guarantee of the submission of forces and bodies (...) The 'Enlightenement', which discovered the liberties, also invented the disciplines. (DP: 222)

In this and other similar passages, many have seen Foucault as denouncing the Enlightenment, which stands revealed as nothing more than a cynical mask for the real operations of power.

But matters are more complex than these commentators appreciate. Foucault also notes that disciplinary power functioned "in opposition to the formal framework that it had acquired" (222), that the models of the prison eventually adopted, "although they correspond on a number of points with the general principles of penal reform (...) fail to do so on an even greater number; sometimes they are even quite incompatible" (120).[12] The ambivalence Foucault demonstrates toward the Enlightenment is explained, then, by the fact that he opposes the uses to which its doctrines have been put, but opposes these uses *in the name of values which stem from these same doctrines*.[13] It is thus that he placed himself in "the *critical* tradition of Kant" (Foucault, 1994a: 314). The values on which Foucault bases his critique are our values, and one of the charges he makes against our societies is simply that they are *hypocritical*. That this is the case is evident from many of Foucault's own political pronouncements. I cite two from among many:

We demand that the fundamental rules of justice should be respected (...) People have always, in Europe, fought for this justice. Today once again we must struggle for it, every times it is threatened. (Cited in Mauriac, 1976: 546-7)

There exists an international citizenry that has its rights, that has its duties, and that is committed to rise up against every abuse of power, no matter who the author, no matter who the victims (...) Men's misfortunes must never be the silent remnant of politics. It is the basis of an absolute right to rise up and address those who hold the power. (Cited in Eribon, 1991: 279)[14]

It should be apparent by now how we ought to reply to those who see in Foucault's work a Nietzschean denial of all rationality and morality. One of the most persistent objections to Foucault's overall project is that he cannot justify the norms implicit in his critique of contemporary society. Thus, essay after essay on Foucault point out that his work has a normative content (Habermas, 1987: 275-6; Fraser, 1989: 27), that it is reliant upon the very notions of rationality and freedom it criticizes (Rochlitz, 1992: 255), and that by relativizing all truth claims it undercuts the very ground upon which critical discourse could stand (Taylor, C., 1986: 94; McNay, 1992: 153). Perhaps it comes as a surprise to such critics that Foucault should criticize his society in the name of values secreted by that society. But it should not do so: very simply, we cannot perceive an injustice *as* an injustice without reference to the norms which constitute our ethical subjectivity. Foucault did not somehow identify certain practices as inequitable and then search around for norms in the name of which to reject them.[15] The perception of an injustice and the application of norms is always, and necessarily, simultaneous.[16]

Thus there was thus nothing "crypto" about Foucault's normativism. Thus, too, it is clear how we ought to reply to one of the most common criticisms addressed to Foucault's work: that he cannot justify his political interventions. Thus Wolin: "why should the specific intellectual employ his or her knowledge in political struggle and why should he side with the dominated?" (Wolin, S.S., 1988: 196). It ought to be apparent that it is the question, not Foucault's lack of a reply to it, that is incoherent. Why should we side with the dominated? Simply because they are the dominated. The perception of domination supplies its own justification, the only possible such justification. Ethics does not exist outside of our concrete ethical judgments, which inform and shape our perceptions. Thus Fraser (who her stands representative for an entire body of critical opinion) makes a fundamental error in her influential essay on Foucault's "normative confusions", by making the assumption that if Foucault criticizes his own society, he requires an alternative normative system. It is not a fault of Foucault's that he, as

Fraser correctly points out (1989: 30), presupposes the normative framework of the very society he criticizes, for in fact that society is vulnerable to criticism in the name of just these norms.

I suspect, however, that few of Foucault's critics would be satisfied with this defense of his work. They would insist that it ignores the fact that Foucault appears simultaneously to call into question the very standards to which he appeals when engaged in political activity. Richard Rorty concludes that Foucault's political project ends up in incoherency if its ultimate aim "is not to extend the visiting rights of prisoners to thirty minutes or to procure flush toilets for the cells, but to question the social and moral distinctions between the innocent and the guilty." Rorty comments:

> Prisoners need flush toilets for their cells a lot more than anybody needs to question (...) the distinction between the guilty male rapist and his innocent female victim. (Rorty, 1993: 64)

Thus Rorty proposes that we follow Vincent Descombes, in distinguishing between two Foucaults: an American Foucault, who can be read as "an up-to-date version of John Dewey"; and a French Foucault, the "*fully* Nietzschean one", who calls into question distinctions such as that between the guilty and the innocent (Rorty, 1991: 193).

Rorty is right to make such a distinction, but wrong in the consequences he draws from it. As a private individual, Rorty believes, Foucault can indulge in fantasies of a revaluation of all values, but, as a public intellectual, he must renounce such fantasies in favor of "the standard liberal's attempt to alleviate unnecessary suffering" (1991: 194). Rorty fails to see that the two levels are connected in Foucault's work. Foucault does not simply attempt to make his society run a little more efficiently, and a little less harshly: that is his project only when an activity provokes in him the visceral reaction of "*intolerable!*".[17] But the point of his genealogical analyses is to examine what, in practices which do *not* provoke such a reaction, might help to contribute to practices which do. As he told Dreyfus and Rabinow, "people know what they do, they frequently know why they do what they do, but what they don't know is what what they do does."[18] Foucault analyses these practices at the level of what they do, unbeknownst to their authors. It is this level which is missing from Rorty's good "American" Foucault.[19] And there is no incoherency in such analysis. To conduct a piece of theoretical research with the ultimate effect of calling into question the distinction between the guilty and the innocent does not necessarily imply any abandoning of the moral standards from which we all begin (although it might imply a work which modifies them). This is precisely the effect of

Discipline and Punish. We close Foucault's book with an understanding of prisoners as in some sense victims, though guilty ones, victims of a system which turns the petty offender into a minor cog in the prison-machine.[20]

The Truth of the Subject/The Subject of Truth

But this leaves one problem unresolved. If one is to oppose truth in the name of truth, what about the truth of the subject? The dilemma can be expressed in the following manner: in what way is it possible to formulate a discourse concerning the truth of the subject which will not inevitably become a means of subjection?[21] Can one produce a truth which will not be a *deep*— essential— truth, to which the subject must dedicate itself, and yet which must be accepted *as truth* (and which will therefore have truth effects, that is, real, material effects upon people and, ultimately, institutions)?

Let us return to Sartre. I have already mentioned that *Notebooks for an Ethics* contains Sartre's most positive ever reading of the intersubjective relation. And I have pointed out some of the flaws inherent in this attempt to found "ahistorical human relations" (NE: 370). But Sartre also sketches another possibility for the 'conversion'; the name Sartre gives to the movement by which a subject goes from acceptance to revolt. I have demonstrated the fundamental condition upon which the conversion can take place; that the for-itself must be thought of, not as being, but as existence. In the conversion, the for-itself

> is asked to refuse the I and the Me as forms of the Other's ontological priority, to that extent he can and must in authenticity assume the objective transformation of himself. (NE: 418)

To refuse the priority of the Other over the for-itself, or to recognize that the only values which can motivate the actions of the for-itself are its own (albeit largely shared) values, but still to assume its being-for-others, its objectivity, as the only aspect of its being which is, now, in being: these are the conditions of the conversion. This is not a form of ethical voluntarism. Sartre does not ask the for-itself arbitrarily to take up an attitude because such an attitude would lead to moral action. The conversion consists in recognizing the structure of being which all for-themselves share.

To recognize that one's values cannot arbitrarily be changed is not, however, to reinscribe them in Being, as somehow natural or true. It remains the case that the for-itself ("as intersubjectivity") is the source of all value. The conversion cannot bracket all the values of the individual, nor can it justify them. It is limited, in fact, to placing an additional mediation between the for-itself and itself:

> it realizes a type of unity peculiar to the existent, which is an *ethical* unity brought about by calling things into question and a contractual agreement (*accord*) with oneself. In other words, unity is never given, it is never in *being*. Unity is willed. (NE: 479; translation modified)

The for-itself needs to recognize that the unity of the subject, insofar as it is the basis of totalization of others and of itself,[22] must be realized, not as unity of being, but as the unity of an accord with itself. Thus the for-itself is the mediation between itself (on the plane of the immediate) and itself (as reflection):

> Pure, authentic reflection is a willing (*vouloir*) of what I will (*veux*) (...) that takes a reflective distance on itself as a quasi object in order *also* to be able to will itself in terms of quasi objectivity. (NE: 479-80)

The for-itself wants what it wants; Sarte has abandoned the nonsensical demand that ethical action requires it to want what it does not want, and not to want what it wants. The latter formula defines, not ethics, but the condemnation to be free, insofar as it demands that the for-itself assumes its facticity. But here facticity is not at issue. We consider there to be a *decision* to want what one does not want, when the possibility exists of not so deciding.

It may indeed seem that nothing has changed, apart from an additional mediation. But where formerly Sartre had denied that the for-itself was trapped within its project, he now recognizes this inevitability:

> But (pure reflection) does not will it as accessory reflection does, which *does not* call into question the reflected-upon project. It calls the project into question before willing it (...) (it is) not just a *choice* of some maxim but a choice of itself inasmuch as it is a choice of A. (NE: 480)

In one sense, then, nothing has changed. The for-itself is still unable to evaluate its own project in terms of anything other than this project— except that, now that the project is defined in terms of a reciprocal interaction between world and subjectivity, the for-itself is able to have *experiences* which might lead it to modify or even radically transform its fundamental project. And there is a sense in which the dice remain loaded: "the mediation of the project by itself leaves its autonomy to the project and its essentialness to the sought-for goal" (481). In other words, the project remains that in terms of which I must necessarily evaluate the project. But this additional mediation between the for-itself and its project, this putting in question of the for-itself by itself (itself merely an elaboration of the fundamental structure of the for-itself, the being whose being is perpetually in question for-itself), is the only possible way for the individual to criticize itself without resorting to the categories of Being. It is the *project* of the for-itself that is in question, not its nature: "the authentic For-itself, refusing being and the Psyche, unveils itself to itself (...) in the immediacy of its perpetual calling into question" (478). The renunciation of the attempt globally to modify the project, in favour of a critique likely to result only in gradual and partial change, in the slow coming into being of an accord between the for-itself and itself, is not the renunciation of important and effective modifications of the self. It is precisely the slow work of a liberty upon itself which Sartre illustrates in *Saint Genet*. This "daily labour, long and disappointing", in which the self acts upon itself by the mediation of the world, revolutionizes neither the world nor the self— not, at least, in any period of time reasonably described as short term. But it is the indispensable condition for the realization of a real margin of liberty in the world.[23]

Ascesis: the Self as Aesthetic Object

The word "authenticity" will long have aroused the suspicions of any self-respecting Foucauldian— of all those, in fact, who regard Sartre as long since *dépassé* (to use a Sartrean term). And, it is true, we will find no authentic/inauthentic duality in Foucault.[24] However, the model Sartre proposes in *Notebooks for an Ethics* (and which underlies much of his later work) can be used to shed light on those most obscure of Foucault's works, the second and third volumes of the *History of Sexuality*, with their problematical 'return of the subject.' How can Foucault propose such a return, and that in the books immediately following his most powerful demonstration of the *subjection* of the individual through, precisely, the production of a truth concerning the subject? He can do so, I believe (and he cannot *not* do so if he is to provide any sort of ground— but neither 'ground', nor 'foundation', nor any other metaphor which suggests a stable, fixed base is adequate— for his critique),[25] because he is proposing a new type of relation between the self and itself; a relation where the self no longer *questions* itself in order to reveal its hidden truth, but rather places itself *in question*, not as to its being, but as to its acts.

It is thus that Foucault advocates a (wary, suspicious) return to the Greeks.[26] For in the Greeks we find a notion of concern with the self which does not proceed through the categories of Being, or, perhaps more accurately, can be reactivated today in such a way as to make the path through these categories unnecessary. When we examine the concrete formulations of this concern with oneself, it is striking how close they come to Sartre: in Epictetus, for example, "Man is defined (...) as the being who was destined to care for himself" (CS: 47). The whole Greek thematic of the "relation to self" could, in fact, be described as profoundly Sartrean. For it is not here a matter of judging one's guilt, that is, of applying categories of *being* to oneself, but of evaluating one's actions:

> The purpose of the examination is not therefore to discover one's own guilt (...) it is (...) to commit to memory (...) legitimate ends, but also rules of conduct that enable one to achieve these ends through the choice of appropriate means. The fault is not reactivated by the examination in order to determine a culpability or stimulate a feeling of remorse, but in order to strengthen (...) the rational equipment that ensures a wise behavior. (CS: 62)

One questions oneself, not in order "to try and decipher a meaning hidden beneath the visible representation", as in Christian spirituality (or psychoanalysis), but in order to decide whether what one represents to oneself "can depend on the subject's free and rational choice" (CS: 64), or, to the contrary, lies beyond our control and therefore should not be of concern for us.

It is true that the Greek subject was by no means unique in being defined by a relation to itself; this is precisely the (self-) definition of the subject for Foucault. At least, so we may deduce from the fact that, "in order to analyze what is termed 'the subject'":

> It seemed appropriate to look for the forms and modalities of the relation to self (*rapport à soi*) by which the individual constitutes and recognizes himself *qua* subject. (UP: 6)

It is true, moreover, that all ethics aim at what Foucault calls a mode of being of the subject:

> A moral action tends toward its own accomplishment; but it also aims beyond the latter, to the establishing of a moral conduct that commits an individual, not only to other actions always in conformity with values and rules, but to a certain *mode of being*, a mode of being characteristic of the ethical subject. (UP: 28; italics added)

It must immediately be added that the 'being' Foucault has in mind here is not the fixed being of a nature or an essence, but precisely a being which the subject gives to itself. It is, to use Sartrean terminology, the being which is returned to the subject by the world and by others.[27] Ethics aims at:

> self-formation as an 'ethical subject,' a process in which the individual (...) decides on a certain mode of being that will serve as his moral goal. (UP: 28)

This being does not *precede* the subject; it is created. This explains the attraction for Foucault of Greek, as opposed to Christian, ethics. In Christian ethics, "the main emphasis is placed on the code" (UP: 29), and, in consequence, "subjectivation occurs basically in a quasi-juridical form, where the ethical subject refers his conduct to a law" (29). In the ethical space defined by Christianity, the rules of the game leave very little margin for invention. The establishment of the relation of self to self takes place to as great an extent as in any other ethics, but remains, as it were, in the background: the subject is aware, not of the process of self-constitution, but only of the system of what is prohibited, permitted and prescribed. In Greek ethics, by contrast, the accent is placed on the forms of subjectivation and the practices of the self. Here:

> the emphasis is on the forms of relations with the self, on the methods and techniques by which he works them out, on the exercises by which he makes of himself an object to be known, and on the practices that enable him to transform his own mode of being. (UP: 30)

In this ethics, the process of self-constitution is thus foregrounded: the self is aware of itself as forming and being formed. Whereas the Christian form of subjectivity can give rise to the illusion that the subject *is*, Greek self-subjectivation keeps the space of the game open, to the extent that the subjects are always aware that they are the source of their own being.

Foucault recognizes that the forms of being available to the subject are always rigorously structured. The subject cannot invent its own mode of subjectivation *ex nihilo*:

> the subject constitutes himself in an active fashion, by the practices of self (but) these practices are nevertheless not something that the individual invents by himself. They are patterns that he finds in his culture and which are proposed, suggested and imposed on him by his culture, his society and his social group. (ECS: 11)

Nevertheless, throughout *The Use of Pleasure* and *The Care of the Self*, he persists in speaking as though the subject invents itself, of the "*ethical work* that one performs on oneself (...) to attempt to transform oneself into the ethical subject of one's behavior" (UP: 27). It is here that the notion of the mediation of self by self comes into play. It is, of course, true that subjects are constituted according to models proposed and imposed by their society. But this inevitable occurrence is not to be lamented: freedom lies neither in an initial arbitrary self-creation without such models, nor in their later rejection. Freedom is the margin of liberty realized by the subject when it reflects upon itself using those very models as its starting point, when the self, in its relation to self, is the mediation between self and itself. As Sartre puts it, "what is important is not what people make of us but what we ourselves make of what they have made of us" (SG: 49).[28] That one has to take a certain, determined, starting point for the "exercise of self upon self" (ECS: 2) is not a limit on freedom, but its indispensable condition.[29] In the preceding chapter I pointed out, somewhat unfairly no doubt, the extent to which a nominalist definition of existentialism could be applied to Foucault. It only remains to highlight the existentialist genealogy of the notion of the relation of the self to itself:

> Kierkegaard was perhaps the first to point out (...) the incommensurability of the real and knowledge, (...) ideas do not change men. Knowing the cause of a passion is not enough to overcome it; one must live, one must oppose other passions to it, one must combat it tenaciously, in short one must 'work oneself over' (*se travailler*). (SFM: 12-13)

The irony of Foucault's return to the Greeks might just be that it makes available to us once more the texts of a tradition much less removed from us in time.

NINE

Excursus: Intersubjectivity

one's point of reference should not be to the great model of langauge (*langue*) and signs, but to that of war and battle. The history which bears and determines us has the form of a war rather than that of a language: relations of power, not relations of meaning.

— Foucault, "Truth and Power."

One of the aspects of modern philosophy most often exposed to postmodern critique is the attempt to think reality in terms of subjects and objects, for-themselves and in-themselves. We have already seen Derrida differentiate ours from the preceding period in terms of the "ends of man", the death of the subject. Sartre's project, for Derrida, falls into the modern pattern, established by Descartes, of subject/object dualisms. Moreover, his work is often seen as containing an intensifying twist on this theme: not only is the relation between the individual and the world conceived in terms of a subject opposed to objects, the relation between individuals themselves is also thought in precisely the same terms. The for-itself is subject only for-itself; its being for-others is its being as an object. Thus the encounter of two subjects is presented by Sartre as a battle in which each individual struggles to impose objectivity upon the other; such an imposition represents victory and the temporary death of the other's subjectivity.

Merleau-Ponty's *The Visible and the Invisible* develops its critique of Sartre along precisely these lines. It is by transcending the subject/object dualism that Merleau-Ponty hopes to achieve true intersubjectivity, what he calls a *chiasm*. The first obstacle to the achievement of such intersubjectivity, Merleau-Ponty argues, lies in Sartre's idealistic attribution of meaning-giving powers to the individual for-itself: in Sartre's work, "strictly speaking there is no intermundane space (*intermonde*); each one inhabits only his own, sees only according to his own point of view" (Merleau-Ponty, 1968: 62). Sartre's subject can never encounter another subject, simply because it does not inhabit the same world as other subjects. Subjects are each the center of their world, in which nothing else appears except objects. For Merleau-Ponty, this "high-altitude thought (*pensée en survol*)" (69) is the inevitable result of Sartre's privileging of the gaze as the primary mode of contact between the individual and the world:

> For a philosophy that is installed in pure vision, in the aerial view (*survol*) of the panorama, there can be no encounter with another: for the look dominates; it can dominate only things. (77)

Thus only if Sartre is right in believing that the gaze is the primary mode in which we come into contact with the world is he also right to believe that everything I encounter in the world is first and foremost an object for me. Merleau-Ponty does not accept that this is the case. For him, our contact with things is much more direct than Sartre would have it:

> we do not wait until we have observed it to say that the thing is there; on the contrary it is the appearance it has of being a thing that convinces us immediately that it would be possible to observe it. (77)

Given Sartre's dualist ontology and his privileging of the gaze, Merleau-Ponty concludes that in Sartre's work, "(p)hilosophically speaking, there is no experience of the other" (71).

We have already examined the object of Merleau-Ponty's first accusation, although from a different angle. We too have concluded that Sartre errs on the side of idealism in making the for-itself a constituting subject. But we have also seen Sartre respond to this objection, by asserting a dialectical interplay between subject and meaning. Merleau-Ponty's first objection, then, cannot be sustained against Sartre's later works, those published after Merleau-Ponty's death. One the other hand, we have seen no evidence that Sartre overcomes the antagonistic relation between for-themselves. In the *Critique*, individuals inhabit the same world, but this only intensifies the conflict between them, for this world is fundamentally a place of scarcity. Though "(w)e are united by the fact that we all live in a world that is determined by scarcity" (CDR: 136), that union is nevertheless negative; we are united insofar as we struggle against each other. Each individual now seeks the death of the other because that other is in direct competition for scarce resources. Thus 'man' has been:

> watched from time immemorial by the cruel enemy who had sworn to destroy him, that hairless, evil, flesh-eating beast— man himself. (Sartre, 1961: 177)

Thus despite his affirmation of a common world, Sartre's outlook appears bleaker than ever. The possibility of realized intersubjectivity must wait for the moment of the fused group when, briefly, each will perceive the other as the same in a common action, before the subsequent inevitable lapse back into seriality and alterity.

Given that the gaze occupies a place of prime importance in Foucault's work too, we need to reply to Merleau-Ponty's criticisms, in order to determine the value as social theory of the work of both Sartre and Foucault. Not a few features of Foucault's work make it a likely target for Merleau-Ponty's critique. We have pointed to the importance of the gaze. We can now add what Merleau-Ponty seems to regard as its inevitable corollary, an antagonistic view of intersubjective relations. When asked who in the social world fights against whom, Foucault replied:

> This is just a hypothesis, but I would say it is all against all (...) Who fights against whom? We all fight each other. (1980g: 208)

It appears, then, that Foucault remained trapped in much the same dualist and antagonistic mode of thought as Sartre. He was never able to get beyond thinking the relation between individuals, and between individuals and the world, as a relation between subjects and objects.[1] And this despite his critique of modern power as the power that subjects and objectifies, that produces "the subjection of those who are perceived as objects and the objectification of those who are subjected" (DP: 184-5). It may be that Foucault was led away from the notion of the chiasm precisely by this analysis. Given the interrelatedness of subjection and objectification in producing docile bodies, Foucault may have felt that a conception of individuals as simultaneously subject and object for each other would merely play into the hands of a power that worked through a correlative increase in both dimensions. The point, Merleau-Ponty could have replied, is not to think subjectivity and objectivity simultaneously, but to reject these terms altogether.

It is in this light that we should examine Sartre's alleged solipsism, and the similar pattern of thought in Foucault. Given their dualism, both thinkers come to the conclusion that the relations between individuals are always relations of power:

> The essence of the relations between consciousnesses is not the *Mitsein*; it is conflict. (BN: 555)

> in human relations, whatever they are— whether it be a question of communicating verbally, as we are doing right now, or a question of a love relationship, an institutional or economic relationship— power is always present. (ECS: 11)

Now, it should be immediately apparent that, given the inevitability of power, the individual is not isolated. The social atom in both Foucault's and in Sartre's world can never be *l'homme seul*. Society is built upon power relationships which imply a gazing subject and a gazed-at (temporary) object: in the *Critique*, thirds unifying with their gaze the initial binary relation, in Foucault's work, the competing strategies of individuals and groups.² Relations of power imply relations of reciprocity between those who enter into them, even if this reciprocity is negative. Power unites those it divides, and to the extent that it divides them.³

It is precisely this level of power which is missing from *The Visible and the Invisible*. Merleau-Ponty thus ends up falling into much the same kind of errors he finds in *Being and Nothingness*. By positing a contact with being which precedes vision, Merleau-Ponty wishes to establish our connection with "brute or wild being", that is, the being of the world

> before it is a thing one speaks of and which is taken for granted, before it has been reduced to a set of manageable, disposable significations. (102)

In other words, he wishes to establish our connection with being as it is, before it is endowed with 'merely human' significations. But it is precisely Sartre's belief, in *Being and Nothingness*, in the possibility of some sort of contact with the in-itself prior to meaning which led him to posit the for-itself as constitutive subject, and thus to think of each for-itself as inhabiting its own world, which owes its existence to it alone. Certainly, Merleau-Ponty does not go so far as this; for him, the significations with which the world is endowed are irreducibly social. But the pre-social is nevertheless both real and active in the social. It represents "the wild region", where all cultures are born and through which different cultures communicate with each other (115); it is the region of experiences which have not yet been "'worked over'" (130), of the ahistoric foundation of history. By founding culture upon an unchanging body, Merleau-Ponty seeks a still point in the flux of history. No matter how irreducibly new a culture may be, "it slips through ways it has not traced, transfigures horizons it did not open" (152). Conversely, if power penetrates even this still point that is the body, if it circulates "through progressively finer channels, gaining access to individuals themselves, to their bodies, their gestures and all their daily actions" (1980e: 151-2), if the body is "directly involved in a political field; power relations have an immediate hold upon it" (DP: 25), then this one still point is submerged beneath the tide of history. The body in its direct contact with being-in-itself cannot found history, for neither pole, neither *the* body nor being-in-itself, exists.⁴ They cannot found history for they only appear in history. Finally, then, Foucault's and Sartre's work is more radical than Merleau-Ponty's. Nothing remains in their worlds which has not been already "worked over", and which will not be reworked again and again. To say that power is everywhere is also to say that history is everywhere.⁵

Thus, the notion of the chiasm, as elaborated by Merleau-Ponty, cannot be sustained by a radically historicized mode of thought, and Merleau-Ponty's criticisms of Sartre (and, implicitly, of Foucault) fail. On the other hand, few if any commentators have seen that Sartre does indeed provide the intersubjective relation his work is so often criticized for lacking, a relation in which two individuals or groups exist as simultaneously object and subject for each other. This 'chiasm' occurs precisely where power plays in its most naked form. That is, the chiasm occurs, not in relations of positive reciprocity, mutual aid or love, but in those of mortal conflict.

Sartre had already established the basis for the chiasm in the fundamental structure of comprehension, the "knowing" (*connaissance*) that is "simply the dialectical movement which explains the act by its terminal significations in terms of its starting conditions" (SFM: 153). All human actions are comprehensible to the individual, indeed, comprehension is so integral an element of human understanding that its lack is the symptom of a pathological state (CDR: 101). Given sufficient information, I will always comprehend the actions of the other. It is this comprehension which warrants Sartre's speaking of our "complicity in principle with any undertaking, even if one then goes on to combat or condemn it" (CDR: 101).[6]

Of course, this is not yet what we, following Merleau-Ponty, will call the chiasm. There is no reason why such comprehension could not be apply equally where it is a question of the activities of machines, for example. But let us examine what occurs in the case where the individual does decide "to combat or condemn" the action so comprehended.

In the case of antagonistic action, or direct struggle, comprehension does not cease to exist. Rather, it becomes intensified. Comprehension becomes a matter of urgency for the individual or group, since the object of the actions of the other is the defeat, subjugation or destruction of that individual or group. In warfare, to take the example of struggle at its most intense, each side attempts simultaneously to predict the actions of the other, in order to defend against it and to calculate its most vulnerable points. If it successful in so predicitng, it can attempt to turn the enemy's action against itself, by laying traps for it. Thus:

> the action of the enemy is known; it is known that he is going to move to a particular place in order to attain a specific objective But for us this objective is simply the spring of the trap which will make him go through a particular mountain pass, for example (...) of course the enemy has his own cards: he will foresee the trap and we will foresee his foresight. (CDR: 807n.)

Comprehension here becomes a matter of life and death. Thus, "struggle is (...) a deepening of the comprehension of others" (CDR: 815); "the enemy is even more directly comprehended than the ally" (807).

Now, in this comprehension, a relation is constructed very different from that established between two for-themselves encountering each other under normal circumstances. In the 'normal' encounter, as we have seen, one for-itself assumes subject status, the other object. In the new relation, each individual or group is *simultaneously subject and object, for themselves and for the other*.[7] In order to foresee the enemy's attacks and defend against them, it is necessary for the antagonists to assume their being as objects:

> This means that *our* activity as a *praxis-subject* (...) must always include knowledge of itself as a *praxis-object* (that is to say, as an objective movement of groups or troops, seen, for example, from an exclusively quantitative point of view). (CDR: 807)

While it is true that the for-itself must always assume its being-for-others, the relation realized here between the subject and its objectivity is given an intensity born of necessity: "Struggle is the only human practice which realizes everyone's relation to his object-being in urgency (and sometimes in mortal danger)" (CDR: 808-9). Whereas before it was necessary to assume one's exteriority in shame or in pride, now it is necessary because it is through this very objectivity that one is at risk. The for-itself does not feel ashamed before this objectivity; it desperately seeks to understand it and to transform it in order to defend itself.

At the same time as the for-itself assumes its objectivity in urgency, it comprehends the enemy-object as subject of praxis, the very determination of the Other fated always to escape its comprehension in *Being and Nothingness*. Once again this comprehension of the Other as acting subject is a matter of urgency. Each antagonist needs to understand the other in order to predict his or her action, in order to defend themselves against it and turn it to their advantage:

> in other words, the free practical dialectic of the one involves the grasp of the free dialectic of the other both as *freedom* and as a *double means* (a means of predicting the enemy action and thus outwitting it, and a means of making *the Other* an accomplice in an action aimed at subjecting him, by proposing a false goal for his freedom). (CDR: 808)

Thus it is only in the relation of struggle that the chiasm occurs, that two acting subjects appear to themselves and to their opponents as simultaneously subject and object, interiority and exteriority:

> In its basic principle, struggle is, for everyone, an occasion upon which to develop the multiplicity of human dimensions in a synthetic tension, since one has to be an object-

subject for a subject-object who is the Other, and since one interiorizes an other comprehended freedom within one's own freedom. (CDR: 808; translation modified)

Does this represent an alleviation of Sartre's pessimistic view of human relations, or an aggravation thereof? On the one hand, we now see subjects encountering each other as subjects; on the other, this encounter takes place only in situations of conflict. It is tempting to dismiss this experience of the chiasm as a peculiarly Sartrean twist to the dialectic of intersubjective relations: only someone combining a Cartesian starting point with a deep-rooted pessimism would proceed to a thought which located intersubjectivity only in struggle. But before we so dismiss Sartean intersubjectivity, recall that Sartre had previously given conflict a very wide definition: it was, in fact, "the essence of the relations between consciousnesses" (BN: 555). Or, as Foucault put it, "in human relations (...) power is always present" (ECS: 11). It does not follow from this, of course, that there is no difference between, say, a student-teacher relation and a struggle to the death between two opposing armies. To say that power is always-already present does not imply that it is always present in the same form or to the same degree. But it does follow that any relationship is always to some degree, however minimal, a contest. Thus it is, for example, that Sartre can speak of "*Dialogue* (in the sense of rational antagonism)" (CDR: 516). In a history which derives its coherence from "a logic of opposing strategies" (Foucault, 1980b: 61),[8] the chiasm of the struggle offers not only a chance to comprehend one's adversary and oneself, but perhaps also a basis for positive reciprocity.[9] For the concern that seeks to entrap the Other, like the concern Genet shows his readers, must "prefer the reader to himself, if only so as the better to destroy him, and that earnest hatred has the same concern as love" (SG: 444). It remains only to point out that this comprehension, this basis for the chiasm, is in the future perfect: one understands the Other in the light of the future toward which their actions aim; if one is able to realize one's being as subject (or one's own being as object) it is, now, only a probable being. It will assume its full being only from the perspective of the future: a future that will have been. Perhaps, then, in this comprehension of the future perfect there appears the faint outline of a sketch for the perfect future.

TEN

On Not Being Up To Date: Les Temps (Post)Modernes

While revolts take place in history, they also escape it in a certain manner (...) In the end, there us no explanation for the man who revolts. His action is necessarily a tearing that breaks the thread of history and its long chains of reasons, so that a man can genuinely give preference to the risk of death over the certitude of having to obey

— Foucault, "Is it useless to revolt?"

The future perfect is the mode of thought appropriate to a time of great and constant change, whether that change is a change in epoch or merely within an epoch. Only a thought in the future perfect can take responsibility in the face of a future which is uncertain, only such a thought can continually transform the rules to meet new challenges, and illuminate the present in the light of a time that will have been. The 'not yet' of the future perfect expects the future as that which cannot be expected, at the same time taking responsibility for the actions which have brought it about. Heidegger counsels that we should be toward our own death, regard ourselves as already having been. But if the end is thus given, thus known and taken into account, time becomes the mechanical unfolding of the already given. Instead, the future perfect must conserve the incalculability of the future, even the incalculability of that future which we know to be certain:

> We ought (...) to compare ourselves to a man condemned to death who is bravely preparing himself for the ultimate penalty, who is doing everything possible to make a good showing on the scaffold, and who meanwhile is carried off by a flu epidemic. (BN: 683)

Or, to quote a less controversially postmodern source, if we await death in the 'not yet' of the future perfect:

> the expecting and waiting is absolutely incalculable; it is without measure and out of proportion with the time of what is left for us to live. One no longer reckons with this 'not yet,' and the sigh that it calls forth does not bespeak the measurable but instead the nonmeasurable: whether it lasts a second or a century, how short will life have been. (Derrida, 1993: 69)

The future perfect teaches us to expect the future as the new, as that which cannot be expected. Thus— to return one last time to the explicit confrontation between Sartre and Foucault— when Sartre accuses Foucault of having written a book (*The Order of Things*) which merely filled a preexisting demand, the criticism is worth taking seriously:

> The success of his book is proof enough that it was anticipated. But true original thought is never expected. Foucault gives the people what they needed: an eclectic synthesis in which Robbe-Grillet, structuralism, linguistics, Lacan, and *Tel Quel* are systematically utilized to demonstrate the impossibility of historical reflection. (Sartre, 1971: 110)

Despite the enigmatic presence of Nietzsche, then, in *The Order of Things*, despite Foucault's attempt to break away from a modern thought "doomed to Time, to its flux and its returns, because it is trapped in the mode of being of History" (OT: 220), Foucault's work is *timely*.

But *The Order of Things* is not the only thing which Sartre was thus to describe as timely. There was, for instance, the "providential" influence upon him of Heidegger. He had read "What is Metaphysics?" (in what Derrida was to call Corbin's "monstrous translation") "without understanding it", when it was published in the journal *Bifur* (WD: 182-3). Sartre gives the date of this initial encounter as 1930. It was in fact 1931, and the encounter was not entirely fortuitous: the journal also contained a portion of one of Sartre's earliest works, "La légende de la vérité."[1] This 1931 essay was, then, doubly untimely, untimely because Sartre was not yet ready for Heidegger (nor was he to be in 1934, when he attempted for a second time to read his work), and untimely because misplaced in time: Sartre has the date wrong.

Then, at a time when history "surrounded and gripped" Sartre, in 1938, a French translation of selections from Heidegger appeared, also under the title *Qu'est-ce-que la métaphysique?*, and including the 1931 translation of that essay. This translation appeared "(j)ust when it was needed", when Sartre "was ready to understand Heidegger" (WD: 185). Moreover, its intervention was, once again, not entirely fortuitous: the translation was *expected*. Corbin's translation was in response to a growth in "curiosity" concerning Heidegger (which curiosity, presumably, was much chastened by a reading of *Sein und Zeit*, since the latter purports to show that curiosity is one of the structures of *das Man*— despite which Sartre feels able to cite "an article on 'das Man' in Heidegger" precisely as a manifestation of French curiosity about the German philosopher (WD: 185)). Thus *Qu'est-ce-que la métaphysique?* (the book, not the article, whose appearance was untimely) arrived just at the *right moment*. I have explained how I was vaguely waiting for it— longing for somebody to provide me with tools to understand History and my destiny. But precisely, there were many of us who had those longings— and who had them at *that particular moment*. It was we who dictated that choice (i.e., of a translation of Heidegger rather than of Husserl). (WD: 186)

Heidegger, it seems, no less than Foucault, was "anticipated." He gave the people "what they needed." Like a good entrepreneur, he— or his translator— had seen a niche in the market and moved to fill it. The intervention of "the prophet of the postmodern" (Hoy, 1988: 18) was a timely one. But, as we know, "true original thought is never expected."

It is tempting to conclude from this minor episode of intellectual history that Derrida is right, that Sartre had never understood Heidegger, for he had never read him on his own terms. Perhaps, then, we should follow Derrida, and consign Sartre to the scrap-heap of history, ranking him among those who once performed a useful and necessary function, but now no longer speak to us. On this reading, Sartre would serve as a transition point between anthropological French thought and Heidegger *an sich*. Thus, Sartre's adoption of Corbin's "monstrous translation", while "philosophically very *risky*", had its own necessity:

we doubt neither the historic necessity of this *risk*, nor the function of awakening whose price it was, within a conjuncture that is no longer ours. All this merits recognition. Awakening and time have been necessary. (Derrida, 1978b: 338n42)

Sartre's translation, while objectively 'wrong', was nevertheless appropriate for the time. It served to awaken French thought from its anthropological slumber, to ready it for the encounter with Heidegger and the entry into a post-humanist postmodernism. Sartre's work served as a timely bridge, but now it is *passé*, or even *dépassé*. It is now high time that we encountered the untimely *as such*. And by this criterion, Sartre, by his own admission, is a "has-been."[2]

Foucault's first encounter with Nietzsche, like Sartre's with Heidegger, was also *untimely*. He had, he tells us, "tried to reach Nietzsche in the fifties but Nietzsche alone did not appeal to me" (1988e: 250). Just as Sartre needed his way to Heidegger prepared by reading Husserl (and French thought had needed the way beyond humanism cleared by Sartre), so Foucault had needed Heidegger to reach Nietzsche. Here, though, the process follows a different path. Instead of the first named philosopher serving as a ladder to the second, which ladder is then largely (in the case of Husserl) or completely (in the case of Sartre) expendable, it is the combination of Nietzsche and Heidegger which for Foucault provided access to both: "Nietzsche and Heidegger: that was a philosophical shock!"

(1988e: 250). A shock, by definition, cannot be expected, at least not in the shocking form it takes. A paradox, then: Nietzsche alone came along at the wrong time for Foucault, or at least in the wrong order or combination; he had tried to read Nietzsche at an inopportune, unseasonal, untimely time. Yet Nietzsche and Heidegger together were exactly the shock Foucault had been waiting for:

> I was surprised when two of my friends in Berkeley wrote something about me and said that Heidegger was influential. Of course it was quite true, but no one in France has ever perceived it. When I was a student in the 1950s, I read Husserl, Sartre, Merleau-Ponty. When you feel an overwhelming influence, you try to open a window. (Foucault, 1988b: 12-3)

Heidegger (and Nietzsche, who here goes unmentioned) thus came along at exactly the right moment for Foucault; they represented a window for him, a way out, an *Ausgang* from immaturity, perhaps. If it was not exactly they who were expected, then at least Foucault (and with him, perhaps, Derrida and his entire generation) was looking for something to free themselves from Husserl, Sartre, and Merleau-Ponty. When it came, it was a shock, but a not entirely unexpected shock.

What Foucault found in Nietzsche, what was missing from Sartre and allowed Foucault to escape from his overwhelming influence, was a notion of history, more precisely a history of truth:

> My relation to Nietzsche, or what I owe Nietzsche, derives mostly from the texts of around 1880, where the question of truth, the history of truth and the will to truth were central to his work. (1988c: 32)

These texts, presumably, do not include "The Uses and Disadvantages of History for Life" (1874), or any of the other *Untimely Meditations*. Nevertheless, it is to that text which Heidegger— the thinker who provided Foucault with access to Nietzsche, at the same time as Nietzsche provided access to him— is referring when he attempts to show us the essential use of history for "a critique of the 'Present'", which critique "becomes a way of painfully detaching oneself from the falling publicness of the 'today'" (BT: 449). Nietzsche and Heidegger had long ago, at a time when the world was not yet ready to hear them, already shown us how the "authentic" attitude to adopt before history is the future perfect, that which detaches itself from the 'today.' In this future perfect, the "today" is "interpreted in terms of understanding a possibility of existence (...) an understanding which is repetitive in a futural manner" (BT: 449), in order to see, in the light of this future, what it will have been.

It is, presumably, this history that is missing from Sartre. We have already heard Derrida complain that what is lacking in Sartre "is a history of concepts", particularly of that concept known as 'man' (Derrida, 1982b: 116). Without such a history, the reflection on 'today' is not possible, if what was true for Nietzsche is true for everyone:

> it is only to the extent that I am a pupil of earlier times (...) that though a child of the present time I was able to acquire such untimely experiences. (Nietzsche, 1983: 60)

Sartre, thus lacking an "authentic" history, or suffering from its abuse, was unable to have such untimely experiences, was unable to act counter to his time and thus "for the benefit of a time to come." As much as his work and his actions "mark an epoch" (Foucault, 1968a: 21), it is an epoch that is past. At best, Sartre might himself have participated in the movement which led to his own surpassing, for the rupture took place:

> around 1950-55, at a time, moreover, when Sartre himself renounced, I believe, what one could call philosophical speculation properly speaking, and when finally he invested his own philosophical activity in behavior that was political. (1996d: 51)[3]

If Sartre was present at the time when he himself became untimely, was an all too timely factor in making himself a has-been (at a time (1953) when Foucault, fortuitously, was reading the *Untimely Meditations* (Macey, 1993: 34),[4] then he served as a bridge to the post-Sartrean world, that which asks the question of today:

> philosophy from Hegel to Sartre has essentially been a totalizing enterprise, if not of the world or of knowledge, at least of human experience. I would say that perhaps if there is now an autonomous philosophical activity (...) then one could define it as a diagnostic activity. To diagnose the present is to say what the present is, and how our present is absolutely different from all that is not it, that is to say, from our past. (Foucault, 1996d: 53)

Yet perhaps the division between "philosophy from Hegel to Sartre" and diagnostic philosophy is harder to mark than it first appears. As we have seen, in the interview entitled "Replies to Structuralism", Sartre accuses Foucault's all too timely work of being "the latest barrier (...) against Marx" (Sartre, 1971: 110). Foucault reacted with "amused astonishment" to this comment:

> I was in the Communist Party some time ago for a few months, or a little more than a few months, and at that time Sartre was defined for us as the last rampart of bourgeois imperialism, the last stone of the edifice, etc. So it is with amused astonishment that I find this phrase coming from Sartre's pen now, fifteen years later. Let's say that he and I have turned around the same axis. (1996d: 54)[5]

In their revolutions around the same axis, in their exchanging of positions in which each keeps the same relative position, had Foucault moved from being timely to being untimely, and Sartre conversely? Or had it been the other way around? At which point in their revolution had each adopted a more critical, a more revolutionary position? And at which point, which timely or untimely time, was each at their most unmodern?

This was not to be the only point upon which Foucault and Sartre "turned around the same axis." In the interview quoted above Foucault replied to a question about Nietzsche with a question of his own:

> Did you know that Sartre's first text— written when he was a young student— was Nietzschean? "The History of Truth," a little paper first published in a *Lycée* review around 1925. He began with the same problem. And it is very odd that his approach should have shifted from the history of truth to phenomenology, while for the next generation— ours— the reverse was true. (1988c: 32)

This time, it is not just Foucault and Sartre who have revolved around the same axis, but Sartre and Foucault's entire generation. Foucault's work, perhaps, was not so untimely, for it was caught up in a generational shift. In thus shifting perspective, he was simply a child of his time. And now it is Sartre who appears untimely: because it was not his generation who travelled from Nietzsche to phenomenology, but he alone; because his starting point, which, as a good dialectician, he must have to some degree conserved, was Nietzschean; and finally because "The History of Truth" is a mythical work. Mythical in two senses. Firstly because it does not exist, at least not in the form in which Foucault suggests. In fact, the work he has in mind can be none other than "La légende de la vérité", published, not in 1925, but in 1931, in the same issue of *Bifur* in which Corbin's "Qu'est-ce-que la métaphysique?" appeared. Foucault was wrong. History was not Sartre's starting point: it was myth.[6]

If nothing else, this series of slightly comical *contretemps* illustrates the difficulty of applying the concept of the untimely, of that which must be awaited as the unexpected. If Sartre's philosophy is no longer appropriate to our time— if it is anachronistic— does this make it more or less fitting for a postmodernity which must be thought of as the untimely?[7] If Sartre is indeed wholly and irretrievably in the past— a has-been— does this not make the confrontation with his thought all the more pressing? For such studies of the past are "untimely":

> that is to say, acting counter to our time, and thereby acting on our time and, let us hope, for the benefit of a time to come. (Nietzsche, 1983: 60)[8]

The thought of the untimely, then, has the effect of making us less sure of our certainties. It becomes much more difficult to think, when the necessity of the untimely is made apparent. Thinking becomes a labor of thought upon itself, a long, slow process of reshaping the rules by which we think, in order to think anew, to think differently. The future perfect makes us more suspicious of concepts, it teaches us to regard everything, not as bad, but as dangerous:

> which is not exactly the same as bad. If everything is dangerous, then we always have something to do. So my position leads not to apathy but to a hyper- and pessimistic activism. (Foucault, 1983b: 231)[9]

The future perfect makes it much more difficult to pronounce, once and for all, that any thought is simply *passé*, that it has moved entirely into the past, any more than to acclaim the arrival of a thought which is entirely new. If we are still to be able to think, to practise philosophy in this most untimely of ages, when philosophy has "if not vanished (...) at least been dispersed"— a philosophy, that is, after philosophy— it can only be such a thought of and in the future perfect.

Foucault himself, despite moderating his initial vituperative assessment of Sartre's work, would never countenance the suggestion that they might, philosophically, have something in common: "My view is much closer to Nietzsche's than to Sartre's" (1983b: 237). Moreover, there is no evidence that Foucault, however much admiration for Sartre's work he might occasionally express, ever changed his opinion that it belonged to another, past, era.[10] I have already quoted from one of Foucault's last texts, the pseudonymous article on himself for the *Dictionnaire des philosophes*, where he speaks of Sartre's work in precisely such a past tense: of "the break introduced by Michel Foucault" in a philosophy dominated by Sartre and by Marxism (Foucault, 1994a: 314). Foucault always endorsed the rhetoric of ruptures and of generational shifts, which would situate Sartre in the untimely era we have left behind— while Foucault's own work, presumably, would represent the new "unsurpassable philosophy of our time." But, given the blurring of temporal boundaries necessitated by the future perfect, Foucault ought to have exercised more restraint in his assessment of what is contemporary with us— the more so since he himself, by his own admission, is if not obsolete than at least out of date:

> What are we calling post-modernity? I'm not up to date. (1988c: 33)

Being up to date is, precisely, the question. Even if neither Sartre nor Foucault were up to date, abreast of their time, writing for their age— and they have now been dead twenty and fifteen years respectively— their significance to us, today, might be all the greater. Perhaps Sartre was wrong; perhaps it is after a writer is buried a *second* time that his or her work, entering into new conjunctions and combinations unforeseeable by its author, takes on its greatest relevance.[11]

ELEVEN

The Ethical Problem

any Ethic which does not explicitly profess that it is *impossible today* contributes to the bamboozling and alienation of men. The ethical 'problem' arises from the fact that Ethics is *for us* inevitable and at the same time impossible.

— Sartre, *Saint Genet.*

If there is one thing which Sartre and Foucault have always had in common, at least in the eyes of many commentators, it is their failure to advance a viable ethics.[1] Foucault's work in the theoretical and political fields presents us with the image of a relativist unable to justify the normative stances he so regularly took. Sartre's parallel refusal to accept any values as simply given— an attitude he stigmatizes as the "spirit of seriousness"— similarly prevents him from articulating any justifiable moral judgments. Both thinkers seek to elaborate a form of political critique, but by over-generalizing their critique they cut the ground out from under their own feet. They therefore find themselves able neither to condemn existing injustices nor to present alternative practices or institutions.

In fact, it is possible to read both Sartre and Foucault as presenting forms of thought which are simple reversals of Hegel's dictum that everything which is rational is real. For there is in both men a marked tendency to equate the real, the actually existing, if not with the irrational, then at least with a suffocating limit on freedom. Foucault puts it most strongly in his review of André Glücksmann's *Les maîtres penseurs*:

> The morality of knowledge, today, is perhaps to render the real acute, harsh, angular, unacceptable. And thus irrational? Of course, if to render it rational is to pacify it, to fill it with a tranquil certitude, to make it pass into some grand theoretical machine designed to produce dominant rationalities. Of course once again, if to render it irrational is to make it cease to be necessary, so that it becomes accessible to captures, to struggles, to being grasped. Intelligible and vulnerable to attack to the extent that it is 'derationalized.' (Foucault, 1977e: 84)

This suspicion of the actual finds expression in Sartre's attempt to formulate a notion of freedom so radical it would be untainted by the meanings inscribed in the world, and in Foucault's restless need to move on, to begin again, to think anew. Hence his famous declaration in *The Archaeology of Knowledge*:

> I am no doubt not the only one who writes in order to have no face. Do not ask who I am and do not ask me to remain the same: leave it to our bureaucrats and our police to see that our papers are in order. At least spare us their morality when we write. (AK: 17)

Thus both thinkers are inclined to view any constituted moral system with suspicion. Sartre sees in the moral obligations which pervade any society no more than a mystification and a justification for oppression. Rights, he tells us in the *Notebooks for an Ethics*, are instituted by the dominant class in order to justify their pre-eminence. The conqueror "recognizes the situation of the conquered as a situation of rights so that the conquered will recognize the situation of the conqueror" (NE: 142). And Sartre does not hesitate to generalize his negative concept of right: "the Evil in violence does not come from the fact that it destroys Right but from the fact that it creates it", for "every state of affairs creates a state of right" (NE: 264).

The "conquered", then— that is, the oppressed— always find themselves in a situation in which their oppression is *justified*. It is right that things should be this way. To refuse this state of affairs is thus necessarily to refuse the right which appears to vindicate it. The dominant class, therefore, is always in the right: it is the Other who appears to strike first. "Objectively revolt is a crime: it is defined as such by the master's order" (NE: 402). What is more, and what is worse, this system of values is interiorized by the very people it is designed to oppress. Because the state of affairs is transformed into a state of right and lived as such,

> revolutionaries never fight *just* against a state of affairs, they fight first of all and above all against a Right, and they have a bad conscience in the beginning because they are fighting in and against themselves. Because man is facticity and freedom, and because his freedom takes up his facticity. (NE: 269)

An analogous current of thought can be glimpsed in Foucault's work. Here, too, there is sometimes a tendency to see the real as consecrating a state of domination. Foucault is, as he says, "a little bit Nietzschean about this":

> it seems to me that the idea of justice in itself is an idea which in effect has been invented and put to work in different types of societies as an instrument of a certain political and economic power or as a weapon against that power. (Foucault, 1974: 84-5)

Indeed, Foucault goes even further than Sartre, insofar as he appears to identify this system of constraints with historically variable systems of truth.[2] Hence his construal, in "The Discourse on Language", of "the opposition between true and false" as a "system of exclusion" (1972c: 217).

Everything that is real is rational— but it is precisely the rational which represents fundamental oppression.

Given this inability on the part of both thinkers to formulate moral principles which could ground their own critical projects, we should not be surprised at the eventual foundering of their ethical enterprises. Small wonder that Sartre never felt sufficiently satisfied with his *Ethics* to publish it. Small wonder that Foucault finally retreated into an aestheticized understanding of *ethos*, conceived as a concern with the self which is turned away from the world. Small wonder both men's flirtation with anarchism. For anarchism seems the only consistent stance one can adopt if one regards all existing values and practices as fundamentally masking states of domination. Domination vanishes only in the moment of what Sartre will call, both in the *Critique* and the *Notebooks for an Ethics*, the Apocalypse:

> the ethical moment is that of the Apocalypse (...) Festival, apocalypse, permanent Revolution, generosity, creation— the *moment of man*. The Everyday, Order, Repetition, Alienation— the moment of the Other than man. (NE: 414)

The Rules of the Game

But we have already seen the failure of Sartre's project to elaborate an unconditioned freedom, and of Foucault's paradoxically parallel attempt to sketch a complete system of constraint within the episteme. Ultimately, both men come to accept and consistently apply the reciprocal implication of freedom and constraint, or, if you like, to recognize the necessity of maintaining the tension between the transcendental and the empirical poles, without allowing either to collapse into the other. The foregoing analysis of Foucault's and Sartre's ethical failure may thus be seen as a caricature of their work, which insists on reading the later work in the light of the earlier, and, where differences are apparent, always taking the earlier position as that to which the thinker would ultimately adhere. Such readings are all too common.

Yet the ethical labyrinth into which we have seen them led is not merely a result of the incoherencies of their early work, nor does it just represent an aporia into which an unnuanced mode of thought ineluctably led them, and which can be abandoned, now that we have seen the necessity of maintaining both the empirical and the transcendental poles in an irreducible tension. Rather, the impasse in which Foucault and Sartre found themselves points to a genuine dilemma inherent in all ethical systems, especially insofar as any such system would be an ethics of freedom. For an ethics cannot consist simply of a body of rules which must always be followed, regardless of the situation. And this for two reasons. Firstly, because no ethical system can ever hope exhaustively to list the concrete situations with which the subject of ethics may be confronted. Quite simply, reality can always be counted upon to present unforeseen circumstances, circumstances which, moreover, might often be ambiguous in their ethically relevant aspects. Thus, an ethics must present us with a few general rules, following which action in the world can be carried out— a Ten Commandments, say, or a categorical imperative. But such rules risk being elaborated at such a level of generality that they do not allow themselves to be used to differentiate ethically between two opposed courses of action. "Thou shalt not kill" appears clear enough. But it is easy to imagine situations in which its application becomes far from simple— war and self-defence are classic examples. Similarly, Sartre has shown how the categorical imperative may be too abstract to allow us to distinguish which is the right course of action when we are confronted with two alternatives. In "Existentialism is a Humanism", he presents us with the example of a man torn between caring for his mother and leaving her to fight for his country:

> The Kantian ethic says, Never regard another as a means, but always as an end. Very well; if I remain with my mother, I shall be regarding her as the end and not as a means: but by the same token I am in danger of treating as means those who are fighting on my behalf; and the converse is also true. (EH: 355)

Thus, it appears, our involvement in the world and our necessary interiorization of its values notwithstanding, there will always necessarily be an element of invention, of creation, perhaps even of gratuity in our ethical choices. Though we might make decisions in an ethical framework, our concrete actions can never be deduced from, or reduced to, that framework. Or as Sartre puts it in another context, "action is irreducible: one cannot comprehend it unless one knows the rules of the game (...) but it can never be reduced to these rules" (CDR: 457).

There is a second dilemma to which ethics seems necessarily to lead. It concerns the is/ought distinction we saw Foucault and Sartre collapse in their early work: to what extent can the ethical demands we formulate be said to transcend their rootedness in an existing state of affairs? That is, can we uphold values which are not simply apologies for the domination of one group of people over another? In a society based on oppression, it would seem, our values are expressions of that oppression; or, if we manage somehow to formulate alternatives, they will be unjustifiable (in fact, will appear to most people quite simply as evil). In Sartre's work, this aporia is explicitly presented only in a more radical form, in which the existing values are rejected, not as masks of the will-to-power, but simply due to the fact that they are in being:

> Ethics' dilemma: if the goal is *already* given, it becomes a fact and being, not a value. If the goal *is not* given, then it is gratuitous, it is the object of a whim. (NE: 449)

Nevertheless, the dilemma to which this points remains, even after we recognize the futility of attempting to reject all such given values, even after we recognize that our actually existing system of values provides us with our only basis for critique (as well as with the moral motivation which makes us feel that critique is necessary).

The two elements of the ethical dilemma come together in the problems surrounding the application of rules. And, although this may be a more general dilemma, the problems which arise from the attempt to formulate and follow rules of ethical behavior are exacerbated to a hitherto unparalleled degree in the modern and postmodern worlds. If reality could always be counted upon to present unforeseen circumstances, how much more is this true of the era in which "all that is solid melts into air", when "everything that is received must be suspected, even if it is only a day old" (Lyotard, 1992b: 21). This, then, is the ethical *aporia* of today, of an impeccably postmodern today:

> In order to be responsible and truly decisive, a decision should not limit itself to putting into operation a determinate or determining knowledge, the consequence of some preestablished order. But, conversely, who would call a decision that is without rule, without norm, without determinate or determined law a decision? (Derrida, 1993: 17)

But Derrida is as insistent as Sartre that, even if this aporia exists in a heightened form 'today', the "other *today* which should be anticipated *as* the unforeseeable" (Derrida, 1992: 18), it is not exclusively a modern dilemma, but the necessary condition of all ethics:

> ethics, politics, and responsibility, *if there are any*, will only ever have begun with the experience and experiment of the aporia. When the path is clear and given, when a certain knowledge opens the way in advance, the decision is already made, it might as well be said that there is none to make: irresponsibly, and in good conscience, one simply applies or implements a program. (1992b: 41)

Ignorance is the necessary condition of ethics. If one knows, or believes that one knows, the situation in all its ethically relevant features, if one is able to anticipate all the possible effects of one's action, of all the other actions that may be able to impact upon it, of its necessary inscription into the whole complex field of the practico-inert, then one would not be making a decision but simply applying the appropriate rule: "we have to conceive of ethics as occurring in principle in ignorance" (NE: 12).

Thus ethics can never simply be reduced to a set of rules. Such rules can neither prescribe all instances of concrete behavior, nor, to the extent that they do guide behavior, can such rule-following be considered as a sufficient condition for ethical action. Yet neither can we have an ethics which would dispense with rules— given both the practical necessity of interiorizing the values of our society, and the theoretical difficulty with calling any arbitrary values 'ethical.' Ethics can neither simply apply rules, nor dispense with them. That is, the very condition of ethics is the aporia Foucault identified in *The Order of Things* as an insurmountable obstacle to a modern ethics:

> for modern thought, no morality is possible. Thought had already 'left' itself in its own being as early as the nineteenth century; it is no longer theoretical. As soon as it functions it offends or reconciles, attracts or repels, breaks, dissociates, unites or reunites; it cannot help but liberate or enslave. Even before prescribing (...) thought (...) is in itself an action— a perilous act. (OT: 328)

No ethics is possible in the modern world, it appears, simply because the situation in which the attempt is made to apply ethical rules is always necessarily different from that in which they were formulated— necessarily, because the very act of formulating the rules has altered the situation. Thus "*any* ethic is both impossible and necessary" (SG: 224). A postmodern ethics, then, would be one which managed to accomplish this necessary impossibility: to give us the rules for acting in a reality whose parameters we cannot foresee.

Towards an Ethics of the Future Perfect

If, as Sartre says, truth is circular (CDR: 454n), it is perhaps time to return to our beginning. We began with postmodernity, which we defined— if we have a right utilize so strong a word— as the thought and the epoch which is 'after now.' I said then, and I repeat now, that it is not my intention to prove the postmodernity of either Foucault or Sartre, nor to defend the future perfect as the necessary and sufficient constituting ingredient of a postmodern attitude, theoretical or practical production. But I do wish to show that ethical— as well as creative— action *is* necessarily in the future perfect. And it is so because of the ambiguous status of rules in any ethics.

If an ethics can neither be reduced to a set of rules, nor dispense with such rules, its relation to those rules can only be in the future perfect. Acting subjects are thus in a position analogous to that of Lyotard's artist: whereas the artist works "without rules and in order to establish the rules for what *will have been made*" (1992b: 24), the ethical subject acts with reference to a pre-existing set of rules, even attempts to apply them, but in the process of acting in a complex concrete world must necessarily creatively distort these rules. Thus the rules which *will have been followed* will not be identical to those given as the point of departure.

It is exactly this metaphor of the artist to which Sartre resorts when describing moral action, in "Existentialism is a Humanism":

> does anyone reproach an artist, when he paints a picture, for not following rules established *a priori*? Does one ever ask what is the picture he ought to paint? As everyone knows, there is no pre-defined picture for him to make: the artist applies himself to the composition of a picture, and the picture that ought to be made is precisely that which he will have made. As everyone knows, there are no aesthetic values *a priori*, but there are values which will appear in due course in the coherence of the picture (...). It is the same upon the plane of morality. There is this in common between art and morality, that in both we have to do with creation and invention. (EH: 364)

Sartre overstates his case in insisting that no values exist *a priori*, at least if we interpret him as meaning that values need to be invented on each particular occasion. Nevertheless, the fact remains that even if all ethical action can be described as an attempt to realize such values, we still necessarily have to do with creation and invention, and therefore with the future perfect.

And such was, I believe, Sartre's mature position, outlined in "Determinism and Freedom" (Sartre, 1974b) and, so far as I have been able to ascertain, in the rest of the Rome lecture on ethics from which "Determinism and Freedom" is drawn, as well as in the as yet unpublished Cornell lecture on the same topic.[3] In "Determinism and Freedom", Sartre distinguishes between two types of future: the pure future and the future of repetition. The first is the future of creation; the future which is "in no way determined by the past" (245). As such, it is "*neither knowable nor predictable*" (245). It is "*a future to be created*" (245). At the same time, however, Sartre has also moved towards recognizing the relevance of existing values for action in the pure future, admitting that I create this future "out of what is presently given to me" (246). Nonetheless, this future will be irreducibly new. If I am able to see in the means at hand a sketch of a future which is different from the present, nevertheless the line of causality does not run from the present to the future, but in the opposite direction: I "*explain the present through the mediation of the future*" (246). This is the future which will be created by action in the future perfect, action which cannot be reduced to any set of rules, nor deduced from an existing state of affairs.

To this pure future, Sartre opposes the future of repetition, which he also refers to as— the future perfect![4] This is the future defined with reference to the past, the future which can be predicted in advance. This future assigns me a "destiny", my future as preordained. Thus:

> This future of mine is really a *prior future* (*futur antérieur*): it presents itself to the moral agent I am today as *my future* and a repetitive fact. (248)

I believe, however, that we can reject Sartre's terminology while retaining his analysis. For his *futur antérieur* can be substituted, precisely, McCleary's "prior future", or *a priori* future, while in the place of his "pure future" we can set our future perfect. Sartre uses *futur antérieur* to refer to a future constructed upon the model of an already existing past, a future which will repeat this past: precisely a "prior future." I shall continue to use future perfect to refer to both an irreducibly new *present* (the present in which one cannot say of the for-itself, *it is*, but only, *it will have been*) and a future which will be constructed, taking the past as its inevitable starting point, but which will in no way be able to be reduced to that past.[5] Here it is not only the future which will have been— once it has become a past future— but also the rules which will appear to have been followed in bringing it about. For the fact that the future will always have been irreducibly new does not detract from its intelligibility. It remains perfectly comprehensible and, once constructed, its connection with the past can be seen to be strong, even to involve links of causality.[6] But full comprehensibility cannot exist before the future comes to be— one cannot take a given situation and exhaustively predict how the individuals in that situation will transcend it. Often— too often— such predictions will be accurate enough. But two factors intervene to prevent full *prior* comprehensibility. One is the necessary ensnarement of the action in the field of the practico-inert, in which sheer complexity makes its result difficult, if not impossible, to predict. Its transformations can, in retrospect, be seen to be necessary; at this level, necessity is "a strictly predictable but completely unforeseen alteration of the ends pursued" (CDR: 340). The resulting passivized praxis is counter-finality, which, as we have seen, is as much a characteristic of Foucault's social world as of Sartre's.

The more important, at least for our purposes, reason for the sheer unpredictability (which unpredictability, as I hope is clear by now, has nothing to do with either randomness or arbitrariness) of what will have been done is the incalculable dimension of freedom. The for-itself not only follows rules in its actions, it also invents them. The rules it will have followed do not precede the action in which they are implemented. This is the case, not only for action in the realm of ethics, but for all *praxis*, no matter how banal:

> *praxis* is directly revealed *by its end*: the future determination of the field of possibilities is posited at the outset by a projective transcendence (*dépassement*) of material circumstances, that is to say, by a project; at each moment of the action, the agent *produces himself* in a particular posture, accompanied by a specific effort in accordance with present givens in the light of the future objective. I have called this *praxis free* for the simple reason that, in a given set of circumstances, on the basis of a given need or danger, it creates its own law. (CDR: 549)

Praxis is free—in the sense that it is able to realize a small but genuine margin of liberty—because, although the past remains the essence of the for-itself, it is not a determining essence. Thus I always have open to me the "possibility of producing myself in opposition to or independently of my past" (DF: 245). This independence from my past is a relative independence. I can neither change my past actions, nor can I wish their social significations away. Nevertheless, the determining force of my past on my present and future can never be exhaustive. To translate this into Marxist terms—as Sartre himself does, in "Determination and Freedom"—Marx's assertion that "man makes history, but he does so on the basis of circumstances which are not of his choosing" is correct, so long as both sides of the equation—the acting subjects on the one hand, the circumstances into which (to use a term from another Marxist tradition) they are *interpolated* on the other—are given equal emphasis. This is another way of saying that the tension between the empirical and the transcendental poles must be maintained. On this basis, then, the future will be both an application of past laws, practices, instruments and rationalities *and* the appearance of the irreducibly new:

> Thus the historical future is partially predictable—it is alienated by the system which has been produced by praxis—and partially unpredictable—it develops within and outside the system as a *future to be created*, both by means of and in opposition to determining structural factors. (DF: 250)

Or, as Derrida puts it: "We must thus be suspicious of *both* repetitive memory *and* the completely other of the absolutely new" (Derrida, 1992: 19).

As well as an outline of Sartre's position on human action, "Determinism and Freedom" contains a brief critique of structuralism. For the structuralists, Sartre tells us, "*history is an internal product of the system.*" Thus:

> This historical pluralism succeeds in subordinating history as a movement to the structural order. The future is still *predictable*, but with well-defined limits—and defined in a positivistic sense. In this sense, the future is already in the past. It *will be* as a *prior*

future (*futur antérieur*); it will realize, for the social agent it produces and conditions, the future being which is present implicitly in his past. In other words, the future is something to be predicted rather than *created*. (DF: 250)

This passage can be read as an *untimely* criticism of *The Order of Things*, untimely because written two years before its publication. In Foucault's structuralism, history is indeed to be predicted rather than created, at least within the *episteme*. The movement from one *episteme* to another, on the other hand, cannot be predicted— but neither can it be comprehended. If history is only the development of the immanent order of the *episteme*, the change of *episteme* can only be a *radical* discontinuity:

for an archaeology of knowledge, this profound break in the expanse of continuities, though it must be analyzed and minutely so, cannot be 'explained' or even summed up in a single word. It is a radical event that is distributed across the entire visible surface of knowledge. (OT: 217)

Thus we may note that, despite Sartre's emphasis on the necessary unpredictability of human creation, his own foresight, was, on this occasion, impeccable.

But we have already seen Foucault reject much of the theoretical apparatus of *The Order of Things*, in favor of a perspective which allows for the dimension of human transcendence. Does his work then implement a thought of, or in, the future perfect? If the argument I have been presenting to this point is valid, then insofar as Foucault recognizes the importance both of the historical conditioning of the subject and of its ability to transcend such conditioning, his thought must be in the future perfect. We will not find any explicit thematizing of this thesis in Foucault's later work. But bearing it in mind will help to clarify many issues which have seemed obscure to commentators.

First among these issues is the place of aesthetics in his late work. In the elaboration of an "aesthetics of existence", several commentators have seen a recognition on Foucault's part of his inability to formulate a basis for political critique, and a concomitant withdrawal into an abstract, aestheticized, realm of the solitary subject (During, 1992: 181; Said, 1988: 10). Certainly Foucault's two last works propose no ethical principles, no rules which we could seek to apply. Instead, *The Use of Pleasure* and *The Care of the Self* can more profitably be read as meditations on the status of such rules. Rather than seeking to diagnose an inadequate existing set of rules and codes, to which he might oppose a better, Foucault examines the application of rules in ethical action.

Foucault's originality in the analysis of ethics lies in his distinction between what are for him its two principal components: the "codes of behaviour" and "forms of subjectivation" (UP: 29). Although no ethical system can ever completely dispense with either component— indeed, the two are always necessarily interrelated— some moralities emphasize one aspect, some others:

> in certain moralities the main emphasis is placed on the code, on its systematicity, its richness, its capacity to adjust to every possible case and to embrace every area of behavior (...)

> On the other hand, it is easy to conceive of moralities in which the strong and dynamic element is to be sought in the forms of subjectivation and the practices of the self. In this case, the system of codes may be rather rudimentary. Their exact observance may be relatively unimportant, at least compared with what is required of the individual in the relationship which he has with himself. (UP: 29, 30)[7]

These two elements, while not isomorphic with Sartre's "prior future" and "pure future", are importantly related to them. The prior future is, precisely, the future prescribed by codes, especially by the mythical code which could "adjust to every possible case." Given such a code, one would be able to predict exactly how a subject acting ethically will react to any situation known by that subject in its ethically relevant aspects. Conversely, if the morality with which a subject evaluates a situation places the emphasis upon "practices of the self", it may be clear neither how the subject will act, nor how they ought to act. In other words, the degree of creativity, of invention, will be much greater. The future created by such a subject will be irreducibly new to a greater extent than that created by the subject's attempt to apply a rigorous code.

Hence the attraction of the notion of aesthetics for Foucault. As we have seen, for both Lyotard and Sartre, aesthetics provides the model of an activity which is strongly codified, yet in which production is a failure if it can simply be reduced to the codes which govern the field of activity. And Foucault too gives an example from the realm of aesthetics, from the field of music.[8] In the work of Pierre Boulez he finds just such a creative transformation of rules:

> He expected from thought precisely that it would permit him ceaselessly to do something other than he had done. He asked it to open, within the so regulated, so well thought-out, game that he played, a new free space (...) What, therefore, is the role of thought in action, if it is to be neither simple savoir-faire nor pure theory? Boulez demonstrates this role: to give the strength to break the rules in the very act which puts them into play. (Foucault, 1982: 52)

Most often Foucault describes the space of ethical activity he wishes to open, not as an aesthetic field, but as a game. By so doing, he again draws attention to the rule-governed nature of such activity, as he points out with reference to the production of 'true' discourses:

> when I say 'game' I mean an ensemble of rules for the production of the truth. It is not a game in the sense of imitating or entertaining (...) it is an ensemble of procedures which lead to a certain result, which can be considered in function of its principles and its rules of procedures, as valid or not, as winner or loser. (ECS: 16)

'Game' may seem an infelicitous metaphor, insofar as calling an activity a game appears to draw attention more to the fixity of the rules than to the ability of the players to transform them (despite the fact, as Sartre point out— with reference to soccer— that the players' concrete activity can never simply be reduced to the rules (CDR: 457)). But it is just such possibilities of transformation that Foucault wishes to highlight:[9]

> what has always characterized our society, since the time of the Greeks, is the fact that we do not have a complete and peremptory definition of the games of truth which would be allowed, to the exclusion of all others. There is always a possibility, in a given game of truth, to discover something else and to more or less change such and such a rule and sometimes even the totality of the game of truth. (ECS: 17)

The space of the game is thus the space of the future perfect, the space in which rules exist, but cannot be exhaustively codified until after they have been applied.[10]

Far from simply being an aestheticization of ethics, or irresponsibly reducing morality to a game, in the sense of a mere entertainment, Foucault's aesthetics of existence thus has a hidden moral charge.[11] It stands opposed to domination:

> we can imagine that there are societies in which the way one determines the behavior of others is so well determined in advance, that there is nothing left to do. On the other hand, in a society such as ours (...) the games can be extremely numerous and thus the temptation to determine the conduct of others is that much greater. However, the more that people are free in respect to each other, the greater the temptation on both sides to determine the conduct of others. The more open the game, the more attractive and fascinating it is. (ECS: 20)

That is, the harder it is to determine the behavior of others, the more they are free, the more fascinating the game. Freedom is thus an indispensable precondition of the game: "Liberty is the ontological condition of ethics" (ECS: 4). And freedom only exists where the codes allow the subject room for manoeuvre. Foucault advocates an aesthetics of existence over a more strongly codified morality simply because in such an ethics the possibilities for freedom are greater.[12]

Thus Foucault's ethics, while advocating a minimal codification, does not have as its ultimate horizon the elimination of codes altogether:

the important question (...) is not whether a culture without restraints is possible or even desirable but whether the system of constraints in which a society functions leaves individuals the liberty to transform the system. (1988a: 294)

Neither of the two poles of morality can be abandoned, neither *ethos* nor codes. The problem of the abuse of power must therefore necessarily be "posed in the terms of the rules of law", as well as those of "*ethos*, of practices of self and of freedom" (ECS: 18-19).

This still does not, however, directly address the issue as to whether Foucault is aestheticizing ethics— that is, as During puts it, "championing a world in which modes of self-fashioning have priority over political activity" (1992: 181). And it must be admitted that it is impossible to read the most trenchant critique of the discourse of aesthetics, Bourdieu's *Distinction*, without a frisson of recognition. In fact, it would be hard to avoid the conclusion that many of its assertions are implicitly directed at Foucault, were it not for the fact that Bourdieu's explicit comments on the latter are so positive (Bourdieu, 1984b; 1985). For example, there would appear to be ample warrant, from Bourdieu's perspective, to regard Foucault's aesthetic of existence as a "denial of the social world"; that is, the world of political action:

The pure aesthetic is rooted in an ethic, or rather, an ethos of elective distance from the necessities of the natural and social world, which may take the form of moral agnosticism (...) or of an aestheticism which presents the aesthetic disposition as a universally valid principle and takes the bourgeois denial of the social world to its limit. (Bourdieu, 1984a: 5)

It is not difficult to read Foucault's last works as endorsing just such a withdrawal from the world into a concern with the self. It is here, I believe, that Sartre's work can serve as a necessary corrective. For Sartre, work on the self can only be accomplished through the necessary mediation of the world: I do not have a self at all, in the sense of an internal principle of self-identity, but only the image of myself returned to me by my actions and encounters in the world. Thus "one creates oneself in creating the thing and in the same way as one creates it" (NE: 131). We cannot hope to work on ourselves, to transform ourselves into works of art, except by working on the world. Moreover, as we have seen, Foucault's self is equally a being-in-the-world. Thus, the call for an aesthetics of existence is designed to highlight the impossibility of fixing once-and-for-all either our identities or the ethical maxims to which we subscribe. It is not designed to deny the possibility of action in the world, nor to advocate a refraining from such action. Foucault, as much as Sartre, would have recognized that such a withdrawal was itself a mode of action, and a conservative one. Equally, he would have seen Rorty's call for us to separate our political activity from our attempts at self-fashioning (Rorty, 1991: 196-7) as hopelessly abstract. As Bernauer puts it, "(r)ather than promoting a self-absorption, Foucault deprives the self of any illusion that it can become a sanctuary separated from the world (...) Foucault's notion of self-formation is always presented in the context of a struggle for freedom within an historical situation" (Bernauer, 1990: 181).

The Ethics of Thought

Foucault's late work proceeds on two fronts. On the one hand, he presents us with an analysis of ethics, which both advocates and shows the possibility of a morality which would emphasize practices of the self at the expense of codes. On the other hand, his writings present us with a model for that ethics, a work-in-progress which attempts to create new rules for thought on the basis of the existing ones. With the publication of *Discipline and Punish*, the former archivist whose work could not be used for speaking of our own historical *a priori* "since it is from within these rules that we speak", (AK: 130) becomes an unabashed historian "of the present" (DP: 31). Now, to be a historian of the present involves taking a peculiar attitude towards one's own time.[13] And it is here that we come back to Heidegger. For it was Heidegger who first adumbrated the question of a "history of the present" (BT: 445), and detailed the attitude necessary for the historian to adopt toward this present:

> in so far as this 'today' has been interpreted in terms of understanding a possibility of existence which has been seized upon (...) authentic historiology becomes a way in which the 'today' gets deprived of its character as present; in other words, it becomes a way of painfully detaching oneself from the falling publicness of the 'today.' As authentic, the historiology which is both monumental and antiquarian is necessarily a critique of the 'Present.' (BT: 449)

Thus the historian, in disclosing the 'today' as the bearer of possibilities, that is, in thematizing it, withdraws from that present, since it remains impossible to speak of the ground from which one speaks. It is only possible to take the present as one's object to the extent that one transcends that present. But, as Sartre's work shows, such transcendence is not as impossible as it sounds— the impossibility lies rather in *not* so transcending. Whenever we act or speak in a manner not strictly determined by what is in being— that is, all the time— we transcend that being. Which is not to say that we free ourselves from it, but only that we realize a small margin of liberty within it. When one thus withdraws from the present, one enters into a relationship where it is regarded as a present *past*; that is, one tries to see with the eyes of the future. That present is regarded as having *already* been. At the same time, to thematize the present is to thematize the future. For the future is not nothing, it has its own being. The possibilities that traverse the social field should not be thought of "as a zone of indetermination, but rather as a strongly structured region" (SFM: 93). By this Sartre refers both to the pure future, that which is not yet, but in the light of which I transcend my present, and to the future of repetition "which the collectivity forever maintains and transforms" (SFM: 94); most obviously, by way of the reproduction of the relations of production. Since these futures are not nothing, but at work on the present, as the goal towards which I transcend my present, as the past which I recreate by my transcendence, Sartre can rightly conclude that:

> So long as one has not studied the structures of the future in a defined society, one necessarily runs the risk of not understanding anything whatsoever about the social. (SFM: 97)

But to say that that which is *not yet* somehow *is*, that it *has being*, even if only in the mode of "what *has not yet* been" (SFM: 92), is to say that it *will have been*. Since "nothing is *settled* except *past being*" (CDR: 671), only that which was, that which has an essence, can be taken as an object for study. The historian of the present thus adopts a future perfect relation to the (absent) present.[14]

For Foucault, such a relation to one's own time is a distinguishing characteristic of modern thought. Modern philosophy, for Foucault, is that kind of thought which takes the present as a horizon of reflection, not in order to contemplate it, but to critique it:

> For the attitude of modernity, the high value of the present is indissociable from a desperate eagerness to imagine it, to imagine it otherwise than it is, and to transform it not by destroying it but by grasping it in what it is (...) extreme attention to what is real is confronted with the practice of a liberty that simultaneously respects that reality and violates it. (1984: 41)

That is, modern thought, in taking as its object the present which will have been, illuminates it in the light of the pure future, the future which has being only as the future to be created. Foucault thus establishes a continuity between his work and the form of thought, inaugurated by Kant, which takes its own present as its object. In this sense, Foucault is happy to place himself within the Enlightenment tradition. But this is the most critical of traditions, so much so that Foucault sees a permanent critique of ourselves, and thus of the tradtion itself to the extent that it is formative of us, as the only way in which one can remain faithful to it:

> Let us leave in their piety those who want to keep the *Aufklärung* living and intact. Such piety is of course the most touching of treasons. What we need to preserve is not what is left of the *Aufklärung*, in terms of fragments; it is the very question of that event and its meaning (the question of the historicity of thinking about the universal) that must now be kept present in our minds as what must be thought. (Foucault, 1988d: 94-5)

The Enlightenment is thus the name for *any* period which takes itself as its own object, as symbolized by the fact that it is "the first period that names itself" (1988d: 89). It is also the *only* period which so names itself, if we accept Foucault's characterization of Baudelaire's modernity as in essential continuity with the Enlightenment— unless, that is, postmodernity represents a break in this continuity. But the name 'postmodernity' suggests that it does not represent such a break: any period which is 'after now' occupies precisely the position in relationship to itself first adumbrated by the Enlightenment; that is, it takes itself as its object. Postmodernism is thus the latest in a succession of names the Enlightenment has given itself; an anachronistic Enlightenment.[15] At most, it is modernity for the first time conscious of itself as needing to be understood "according to the paradox of the future (*post*) anterior (*modo*)" (Lyotard, 1992b: 24).[16]

TWELVE

Postmodern, Posthumanist, Post-Sartre

All those who adopt a universalist perspective *here and now* are *reassuring* to the established order (...) the human universal is *yet to come*

— Sartre, "A Plea for Intellectuals."

In the course of this study I have run several risks. The risk of presenting a 'normalized' Foucault, stripped of what Rorty describes as "self-indulgent radical chic" (1986: 47), but equally without the power of radical contestation celebrated by many commentators. The risk of eliding the differences between a thought which remains totalizing and subject-centered, and a thought of, precisely, difference. The danger of closing the gap in which new thought, new practices, can arise, by reducing the apparently new to the already said. I recognize both that these are real dangers, and the possibility that I have not always managed to avoid them.

It is equally true, however, that writing always runs a number of risks, the writing that would celebrate difference no less than that which points to similarities and continuities. As Foucault said, the call for radical rupture, as much as the call for seamless continuity, can be abused:

> The pressure of identity and the injunction to break things up are both similarly abusive.

> The periods dominated by great pasts— wars, resistance movements, revolutions— rather demand fidelity. Today, we rather go for ruptures. (Foucault, 1997: 137)

The risks I have run, the risk of betraying what could be called, for want of a better word, the spirit of Foucault's work, is equally the precondition of remaining faithful to it. Only by accepting this, or another, risk, is it possible to live up to the Foucauldian spirit by producing something new.

Nevertheless, it is not sufficient simply to accept the risk and confidently expect the new. Vigilance is called for if the conjunction of the old with the new is not to result merely in a repetition of one or the other. Before we find that Foucault was merely an updated Sartre, an untimely thinker for these times, before we reduce postmodernism to a synonym of the Enlightenment, we had better bear in mind the fact that the same late works

which have led us to re-emphasize the degree of Foucault's— and our—
continuity, not only with the Enlightenment, but even with Classical
thought ("A way of thinking in which we recognize the origin of our own"
(UP: 7n)), are placed under the sign of what appears to be an overall
discontinuity. Quoted on the back cover of the original French editions of
both *The Use of Pleasure* and *The Care of the Self* are the following lines of René
Char:

> L'histoire des hommes est la longue succession des synonymes d'un même vocable. Y
> contredire est un devoir.
>
> (The history of humanity is a long succession of synonyms of one and the same term.
> To contradict this is a duty).

These lines point to what appears to be the largest single obstacle to any
attempt to find in modernity and postmodernity simply "synonyms of the
same term": the issue of humanism. Modernity is resolutely subject,
consciousness, humanity centered, while postmodernity refuses the notion
of any center at all, and defines the subject as an effect of discourse. Sartre
is thus a paradigmatically modern thinker, for, while he recognises the
exclusionary nature of "bourgeois humanism", he responds to it by
attempting to produce "a true and positive humanism" (CDR: 800).

In fact things are not so simple. For the humanism, in the name of which
Sartre develops his critique of bourgeois humanism and of the modern
world, is a humanism without a center: the place to be occupied by
humanity stands empty. This is so simply because that humanity does not
yet exist: *"man does not yet exist"* (Sartre, 1974c: 250). For Sartre:

> man has to be made: it is what is lacking in man, what is in question for each of us at
> every moment, what, without having ever been, is continually in danger of being lost.
> (CP: 179-80)

Thus bourgeois humanism is opposed by a humanism which would be truly
inclusive, which Sartre believes to be the "humanism of need", "the only
humanism which has as its object the whole of humanity" (CP: 179).

For us, of course, it is evident that Sartre's humanism of need does not
take the whole of humanity as its object— this is indicated by his free use of
'man' as interchangeable with 'humanity.' The humanism of need, it seems,
is a masculinism. Need this imply, however, that we should reject the notion
of humanism as necessarily exclusionary? Or merely that this exclusion
should provide us with the impetus toward a new, truly inclusive,
humanism? Should we see the exclusion of half the human population as
the final dialectical contradiction before the final synthesis, humanity as a
totality?

Between the two exclusive options, that of seeking to define, once and for all, an acceptable definition of humanity to occupy the center of a new humanism, and that of rejecting the idea of humanism *tout court*, there lies a third: that of a humanism in the future perfect. Such a humanism would retain the idea of humanity as a totality, but as a purely regulative notion, one towards which we should strive. Humanity is not contingently missing from the center of Sartre's humanism; it is not an alienated humanity, that of the modern world, perhaps, which cannot play the role of subject and object of history at the present moment. That is, humanity is not *in being* by definition, not due to some accident:

> Man is all the time outside of himself: it is in projecting and losing himself beyond himself that he makes man exist (...) This relation of transcendence is constitutive of man. (EH: 368)

If humanity is essentially self-transcending, the "(i)mpossibility of a *totalizing* definition" (NE: 67) is a necessary impossibility. Thus, for Sartre, the species humanity does not exist except as "what *he has been*" (NE: 69). The humanism in the future perfect must necessarily reject all definitions of humanity in the name of that humanity which is not yet. Except that this 'not yet' is a permanent state, a 'to come' which always remains in the future (*a-venir*).[1]

In an interview originally published as the afterword to the second edition of their book on Foucault, Dreyfus and Rabinow questioned him as to the similarities between his view of the subject and Sartre's. His response is worth quoting in full:

> I think that from the theoretical point of view, Sartre avoids the idea of the self as something which is given to us, but through the moral notion of authenticity, he turns back to the idea that we have to be ourselves— to be truly our true self. I think that the only acceptable practical consequence of what Sartre has said is to link his theoretical insight to the practice of creativity— and not to authenticity. From the idea that the self is not given to us, I think that there is only one practical consequence: we have to create ourselves as a work of art. In his analyses of Baudelaire, Flaubert, etc., it is interesting to see that Sartre refers the work of creation to a certain relation to oneself— the author to himself— which has the form of authenticity or inauthenticity. I would like to say exactly the contrary: we should not have to refer the creative activity of somebody to the kind of relation he has to himself, but should relate the kind of relation one has to oneself to a creative activity. (1983: 237)[2]

Yet I believe I have shown that Sartre's subject meets exactly the criteria Foucault demands of it. It is precisely the creative, and self-creating, subject Foucault advocates.[3] And the notion of authenticity, concerning which Foucault is so critical, is intimately bound to this activity of self-creation, not to the uncovering of any true self. Authenticity for Sartre lies precisely in the rejection of the notion of the self as given, in the acceptance of our necessarily creative but situated existence, not in being our true self.[4]

Just as the notion of humanity lies always and unavoidably in the perpetual future, so the thinking which would be adequate to this notion remains to come. And here it is Foucault who shows us the way, who takes future perfect thought as his object. Throughout his last writings and interviews there runs a recurrent theme, that of a thought which would be perpetually remaking itself, without sacrificing any of the rigour necessary to a mode of thinking which wishes to say something new. The best known example of Foucault's new ethics of thought occurs in *The Use of Pleasure*, where Foucault seeks to explain the kind of curiosity that led him to abandon the project he began with *The History of Sexuality, Vol. I*, in favor of thinking anew, the kind of curiosity "which enables one to get free of oneself":

> what is philosophy today (...) if it is not the critical work that thought brings to bear on itself? In what does it consist, if not in the endeavour to know how and to what extent it might be possible to think differently. (UP: 8-9)

Such is the style of thought Foucault and Sartre each sought to adumbrate, a thought constantly ahead of itself, creating concepts to which no entity can ever correspond, illuminating the present in the light of a future which will never exist, playing a game with rules which have not yet been formulated, exploring the limits of our thought and of our being. Such a thought "does not 'liberate man in his own being'; it compels him to face the task of producing himself" (Foucault, 1984: 42). For such a thought, "mankind is a *mankind to be created*" (DF: 251). Such a thought:

> will not deduce from the form of what we are what it is impossible for us to do and to know, but it will separate out, from the contingency that has made us what we are, the possibility of no longer being, doing, or thinking what we are, do, or think. It is not seeking to make possible a metaphysics that has finally become a science; it is seeking to give new impetus, as far and wide as possible, to the undefined work of freedom. (Foucault, 1984: 46)

What Will Postmodernism Have Been?

Are we living in a postmodern epoch? Ultimately, only an analysis of the concrete conditions of social, economic and historic life, of which thought is only one aspect, however important, can decide. However, insofar as a reading of the paradoxical formulations of the thinkers who are taken, or take themselves, to be the representatives or heralds of the postmodern world can determine, postmodernity represents not so much a break with modernism as modernity in a heightened state— conscious of itself as after now. I will go no further with attempting to answer this question: a minefield of paradoxes lies that way (the first, and only the first, of which, centered around the notion of discontinuity, can be sketched in the form of two inconsistent syllogisms: modernism represents a continual break with the past; postmodernism is a break with modernity; therefore postmodernism is modernism. Or postmodernism is a continuation of modernism; therefore postmodernism is not a continuation of modernism).

The fact that I do not feel that the question can be answered does not mean I believe it unimportant. What modernity and postmodernity have in common, the urgent message they have for us, lies precisely in the necessity of reflecting upon the present. What the work of Sartre and Foucault presents us with is precisely such a reflection, a reflection which would take seriously the difference of today from yesterday, without assuming that this difference freed them from the responsibility of thinking this 'today', using concepts borrowed from all our yesterdays. Theirs is a thought which is oriented towards the future, towards bringing about a difference which would not be just any difference, but a determinate difference worth striving for, and in full knowledge that the tomorrow they contribute to bring about, when it will have been, will be quite unlike any that have gone before it, and any that we had imagined as our goal. It is true that such a thought is always "in the position of beginning again" (1984: 47), that we cannot ever move beyond our historical limits, into a realm of freedom which would not be, at the same time, a realm of necessity. Equally, we can never hope truly to begin anew. All attempts to start from scratch find they are preceded, overhung, by the whole weight of history:

> We have no language— no syntax and no lexicon— which is alien to this history (of metaphysics); we cannot utter a single destructive proposition which has not already slipped into the form, the logic, and the implicit postulations of precisely what it seeks to contest. (Derrida, 1978c: 280-1)

Or, to put it another way, "in the beginning, there will have been, ghost of the future perfect" (Derrida, 1989a: 127n8).

Perhaps the rewards justify the risks of which I have spoken. But I have not yet addressed the greatest risk of all. Perhaps my entire project, from beginning to end, risks irrelevancy. For what could be more irrelevant than a work which relies so heavily on the writings of Sartre: no matter how dressed up by references to thought more contemporaneous with us, this body of work remains no more than a part of our prehistory. This is confirmed each time he is discussed:

Smiles are quick to surface whenever anyone is still interested in Sartre or still writes about him, as though the person were all but suspect of still being 'with' Sartre, of being stuck with him. (Hollier, 1986: 92)

The risk my work runs, then, and I with it, is that of being out of date, of being irredeemably untimely. But perhaps this risk, too, is worth taking. There may, after all, be certain advantages to be had in looking at our times with foreign eyes. As Sartre put it, "in our societies in motion delays (*retard*) sometimes give a head start" (Sartre, 1964: 40; translation slightly modified). More than that, perhaps such a *retard* is the very condition of this work, of all work on postmodernism.

Indeed, Foucault finds such a *retard* even in Sartre's last works:

The first pages of Sartre's *Flaubert* are unreadable due to the five or six first pages on language which are 75 years behind the times (*de retard*), ignorant of all that linguistics had discovered. (Foucault, 1994b: 262)

Yet while Sartre was behind the times theoretically, Lacan, who was setting the pace for the theoreticians of the younger generation, found himself politically anachronistic, while Sartre was "converging" with the young Lacanians in the street and at the barricades. Thus, Foucault goes on, "Sartre died contemporary with those who were educated in the image of a thought formed in rupture with him" (263). If the postmodern is constitutionally at variance with its own time, as its name would seem to suggest, then the only route by which to approach it is via the untimely. Perhaps, then, the detour through this most untimely of thinkers will, in the end, have been necessary.

NOTES

Chapter One

1. This is much more the case in the European than in the Anglo-American tradition. Analytic philosophy is much more problem-oriented than is Continental, and accordingly rather less interested in history.

2. 'Post-contemporary', proposed by some people as an alternative to the term postmodern, would thus be an exact synonym.

3. Hoy's date receives— equivocal— implicit support from Richard Rorty's statement that "it seems best to think of Heidegger and Derrida simply as post-Nietzschean" rather than "postmodern", for "it seem safer and more useful to periodize and dramatize each discipline or genre separately, rather than trying to think of them as all swept up together in massive sea changes" (Rorty, 1991: 1-2). It remains only to add that such resistance to totalizing periodization is itself characteristic of postmodernists in all disciplines and genres.

4. Jay refers, of course, not to postmodernists but to post-structuralists. However, although postmodernism and post-structuralism cannot simply be equated— not all so-called 'post-structuralists' would be happy to be referred to as 'postmodern', and, certainly, not all postmodernists are post-structuralist— there is a very real sense in which post-structuralism represents the theoretical or philosophical underpinnings of postmodernity. Jameson, for example, is far from being alone when he asserts that "what was variously called 'poststructuralism' or even simply 'theory' was also a subvariety of the postmodern, or at least proves to be that in hindsight" (1991: xvi). Mark Taylor puts the case even more strongly: "To think after the end of philosophy is to think poststructurally" (Taylor, 1987: XXV).

5. I use the term 'Man' here to designate the subject of modern philosophy, in full awareness of the fact that, although it is not equivalent to any empirical human being of either sex, this subject nevertheless specifically excludes women. It is, in part, precisely because of the exclusions to which this notion commits us that Derrida wishes to call humanism into question.

6. *Futur antérieur* is, of course, the normal French term for the tense we call the future perfect.

7. It is fitting, therefore, that Lyotard's definition of modernity is exactly the same as his definition of postmodernity: "Modernity consists in working at the limits of what we thought to be generally accepted, in thought as in the arts, in the sciences, in matters of technology, and in politics. A modern painter is a painter for whom the nature of painting is at stake in the picture he or she is making" (Lyotard, 1993: 24).

8. For Jürgen Habermas, one of the most influential and implacable foes of postmodernist "young conservatives" (among whom Habermas numbers Foucault), it is precisely the future perfect which distinguishes the authentically modern from the

merely ephemeral. The modern shares with the "merely stylish" the state of being "'the new' which will be overcome and made obsolete through the novelty of the next style". But the modern alone "preserves a secret tie to the classical": the modern work, unlike the ephemeral, "becomes a classic because it has once been authentically modern" (Habermas, 1983: 4). That is, the classic *will* once *have been* modern: Habermas follows Baudelaire's understanding of a modernity which finds "confirmation as the authentic past of a future present" (Habermas, 1987: 9). The 'will have been' marks the difference between the modern and the faddish, the authentic and the inauthentic. For Habermas as much as Lyotard, then, the modern is a retrospective category, not the distinctive mark of our present.

9.   The major reason that Jameson presents for the change in cultural sensibility from the modern to the postmodern—that modernism arose from the experience of uneven development, and that postmodernism is the result of the completion of the modernization process itself—also tends in the direction of Lyotard's paradoxical definition of postmodernity. For Jameson, postmodernity is the result of a modernity so complete that it no longer has anything with which to compare itself: "Ours is a more homogeneously modernised condition; we no longer are encumbered with the embarrassment of non-simultaneities and non-synchronicities". It is in this sense that Jameson believes that it is possible to affirm "either that modernism is characterized by a situation of incomplete *modernization*, or that postmodernism is *more* modern than modernism itself" (1991: 310). We have only changed, Jameson asserts, in the sense that we no longer feel it is necessary to be modern; it is merely "something that happens to us". But even the pinpointing of this single element as the difference between the modern and the postmodern experience is questionable: in Lyotard's call for a "war on totality" we detect more than a hint of a project whereby we *become* postmodern.

10. Both quoted in Bradbury and McFarlane, 1983: 33.

11. We can well agree with Derrida that "*la réalité humaine*" is a "monstrous translation" of Heidegger's *Dasein*, but it should be pointed out that the word is strictly untranslatable. Sartre sometimes settled for the literal *être-là*, but this has the disadvantage of substituting a neologism in French for a common German word. Derrida's solution, to leave it as *Dasein*, similarly replaces the familiar with the foreign. Foucault himself was faced with the same problem, when he collaborated on a translation of Ludwig Binswanger's Heideggerian *Traum und Existenz*. After much discussion, he and his co-translator settled upon *présence* as the translation for *Dasein* (Eribon, 1991: 45). It goes without saying that such a translation, too, has its problems, in the light of the postmodern problematization of presence.

12. The quote from Heidegger is from the "Letter on Humanism" (Heidegger, 1977a: 202. The *Letter*, of course, was itself written in response to Sartre's "L'existentialisme est un humanisme" lecture (Sartre: 1946). Derrida is thus not applying Heidegger to Sartre, but wholeheartedly endorsing the German's own already elaborated assessment of Sartre's work.

13. Derrida adds in a footnote that this applies not only to Sartre's early work, but to the *Critique of Dialectical Reason* as well.

14. For example, Hoy, 1988: p.18.

15. As Lebrun notes, after Foucault we cannot "use 'philosophical' words without mentioning or researching their date of birth or the date when they came into use" (Lebrun, 1992: 35).

16. The assertion that, for most commentators, Sartre represents a high modernist philosophy, Foucault a postmodern thought hardly needs justification. I will cite only two of the more highly regarded critics. Jameson regards Sartre as a paradigmatic modernist, in that "existentialism in philosophy" forms one of the movements which represent "the final, extraordinary flowering of a high-modernist impulse which is spent and exhausted with them" (1991: 1). Unlike Derrida, however, Jameson regards Heidegger too as modern: it is to the latter's reading of Van Gogh's "A Pair of Boots" that Jameson opposes the post-modernist painting he takes as exemplary (1991: 7-8). Turning to Foucault, for Deleuze the latter's work "celebrates the dawn of a new age" (1988: 1).

17. Interestingly, McKenna, whose definition of postmodernism I have adopted, has recourse to certain works of Sartre's to illustrate aspects of the postmodern: "'Mais il faut choisir: vivre ou raconter,' as Sartre's Roquentin observes in an archly postmodern moment of *La Nausée*, contesting false beginnings, false endings, and the 'total partiel' we make of them" (232). Similarly, he notes Sartre's use of the future perfect in *The Condemned of Altona*, where, at the end of the play, Franz's "voice comes to us on a tape recorder, so that he addresses us as one who will have been killed" (233). LaCapra too argues that *Nausea* "goes further" that any of Sartre's philosophical works (LaCapra, 1978: 95), and Derrida himself, in "The Ends of Man", finds in it a deconstruction of humanism (Derrida, 1982b: 115n.)— all of which appears to illustrate that as far as the distinction between literary and philosophical genres is concerned, deconstruction has got no further than the stage of overturning hierarchies, rather than undoing them. I will not follow Derrida in attempting to demonstrate that Sartre's literary works, despite him, undo the distinctions carefully drawn up in the philosophical production. Instead I will be concerned with illustrating how Sartre's *explicit* philosophical theses foreshadow those of Foucault, and of Derrida himself (Actually, I do not believe that *The Condemned of Altona* illustrates the postmodern future perfect. The future perfect, as McKenna notes, is "the temporal modality, or at least the grammatical translation, of historical becoming" (232). When we hear Franz's message, becoming, for him at least, is at end, and his voice comes to us from one who simply has been killed. Only when he actually taped his message and his death was an unrealized possibility did he speak as one who will have been killed).

18. For Ozouf, the essential difference marked by the passage "from Sartre to Foucault" concerns not just totalization or humanism, but also a new problematization, if not rejection, of the "word-nugget which for so longed served us as talisman: revolution" (Ozouf, M. [1984]).

19. Thomas R. Flynn promises us just such a substantive comparison, in the second volume of his *Sartre, Foucault and Historical Reason*. Volume One (Flynn, 1997) concentrates upon Sartre's philosophy of history and historiography. Flynn proposes to compare Sartre with Foucault on just this ground of historiography; I therefore expect his concerns to be tangential to mine.

20. For Bernauer, the difference between Sartre and Foucault is so great it even extends to the absences they appear to share: "However Foucault's faith or absence of it is

described, it seems singularly inappropriate to claim, as Jean-Maries Auzias has in his recent book, that 'radical atheism' is the point of convergence between Sartre and Foucault. On this topic too, the two thinkers would be quite far from one another" (Bernauer, 1990: 229n86).

21. After writing this, I came across an article in which the same paragraph from the same text of Heidegger's is used to justify the comparison, not of Foucault and Sartre, but Foucault and Heidegger. (Ijsseling, 1986: 418). Ijseeling notes the problematic nature of examining the relation between Foucault, who took the notion of 'influence' as an explicit object of criticism, and any other thinker. Ijessling wishes to locate the *traces* of a reading of Heidegger in Foucault's writings; such traces of Sartre, often explicit and indicated by the proper name, are far from rare in Foucault's work. I, however, do not intend to take these traces as my theme— at least not primarily— but to examine certain *consonances* between their thoughts, regardless of the question of influence.

Chapter Two

1. James Miller's recent biography of Foucault interprets almost the entirety of his philosophical development as a reaction against Sartre. As early as his student days at the école normale, Foucault found "Sartre's challenge (...) irresistible" (45), the success of *Madness and Civilization* left him unsatisfied because he had "failed to reach the larger audience that *Being and Nothingness* had tapped" (118), even his political activities took as their primary goal, not their ostensible aim, but the image of the engaged intellectual promoted by Sartre (188). Unfortunately, Miller's reading of the Sartre/Foucault confrontation has the effect of reducing the latter's work to a mere psychological, and not philosophical, reaction to the older man's. That Foucault might have criticized Sartre for reasons akin to what Harold Bloom has termed "the anxiety of influence" is possible, but uninteresting from our point of view. Where Miller does suggest more properly philsophical reasons for Foucault's opposition to Sartre he, like most commentators, constructs a straw Sartre for Foucault to knock down, including the strange suggestion that Sartre promotes the idea of the self as object for itself (54), which ignores his sustained attack on the notion of self as object.

2. *The Order of Things* itself is reported by Raymond Bellour to have originally contained some "pages on Sartre" which were removed from the published version (Mentioned by Bellour in the discussion following Lebrun, 1992: 37).

3. "L'Homme est-il mort?", in *Arts et loisirs*, June 15, 1966. Cited in Eribon, 1991: 161.

4. Another reference to Sartre, and to his magic lantern, in the original French version of AK has been detected by several commentators (Eribon, 1994: 176; O'Farrell, 1989: 132-3n.44).

    To the last *flâneurs*, is it necessary to point out that a tableau (...) is formally a series of series? In any case, there is no question of a small fixed image which one places in front of a lantern in order to fool children who, at their age, of course prefer the vivacity of the cinema.

Perhaps because the translator felt that the reference was too obscure, the note goes untranslated.

5. I believe the following, listed in the order in which they were written, constitutes a full list of all Foucault's writings which contain references to Sartre of any importance, excluding *The Archaeology of Knowledge* and other texts in which references to him are implicit:

————"Dream, Imagination and Existence", trans. F. Williams, in Binswanger, L., and Foucault., M., *Dream and Existence*, Seattle: Review of Existential Psychology and Psychiatry, 1986 (Originally published 1954);

————"The Order of Things", in *Foucault Live* (Originally published in *Les Lettres Françaises* 1125, March 31, 1966);

————"Entretien", *La Quinzaine Littéraire* 5 (May 16, 1966);

————"Une histoire restée muette", *La Quinzaine Littéraire* 8 (July 1, 1966);

————"Foucault Responds to Sartre", in *Foucault Live* (Originally published in *La Quinzaine Littéraire*, March 1, 1968);

————"Une mise au point de Michel Foucault", *La Quinzaine Littéraire*, March 15, 1968;

————"The Archaeology of Knowledge", in *Foucault Live* (Originally published in *Magazine Littéraire* 28, April-May 1969);

————"Theatrum Philosophicum", in LCMP (Originally published in *Critique* 282, November 1970);

————"An Historian of Culture", in *Foucault Live* (Originally published in Italian, in *Bimestre* 22-3, September-December, 1972);

————*Remarks on Marx*, Semiotext(e), 1991 (Originally published in Italian, as *Colloqui con Foucault*, 1981, this series of interviews was conducted in 1978);

————"Introduction" to Canguilhem, G., *The Normal and the Pathological*, trans. C. Fawcett. New York: Zone Books, 1989 (Originally published in the first edition of the English translation, in 1978);

————"Appendice", in Eribon (1994). This reproduces part of a hitherto unpublished interview Eribon conducted upon the occaison of Lacan's death, in September 1981;

————"Truth, Power, Self: An Interview with Michel Foucault", in Martin, L.H., Gutman, H., and Hutton, P.H. (eds), *Technologies of the self: A Seminar with Michel Foucault*, London: Tavistock Publications, 1988 (interview conducted on October 25, 1982);

————"Critical Theory/Intellectual History", in *Politics, Philosophy, Culture* (Originally published in German, in *Spuren* 1-2, 1983);

————"On the Genealogy of Ethics: An Overview of Work in Progress", in Dreyfus, H.L., and Rabinow, P., *Michel Foucault: Beyond Structuralism and Hermeneutics*, The University of Chicago Press, 1983;

————"Foucault, Michel. 1926"-, trans. Catherine Porter, in Gutting, G. (ed.), *The Cambridge Companion to Foucault*, Cambridge University Press, 1994 (Originally published in Huisman, D. (ed.), *Dictionnaire des philosophes*, Presses Universitaires de France, 1984).

In addition, the Bibliothèque du Saulchoir holds a typescript entitled "Sartre" which consists of extracts from discussions held at Berkeley. Most of this typescript, however, is printed in "On the Genealogy of Ethics", cited above.

6. The phrase, or a close permutation of it, occurs fairly frequently in journalistic literature on Foucault. Merquior quotes one example in his *Foucault* (London: Fontana, 1985), p.155.

7. Sartre, J.-P., "A propos de la justice populaire", in *Pro justicia*, no. 2 (1973), pp. 22-3. Cited by Eribon, 1991: 247.

8. Eribon reports a rather different response by Foucault to Sartre's funeral: "On the morning of Saturday, April 19, 1980, Catherine Von Bülow telephoned Foucault to ask if he was going to Sartre's funeral. 'That goes without saying,' answered Foucault" (Eribon, 1991: 279). Claude Mauriac's description of Sartre's funeral would appear to support Von Bülow's, rather than Defert's, account. Mauraic reports meeting Foucault at the funeral and asking him: "Who, in this crowd, has read Sartre; I mean, really read? But they are here, they know they are required, like us, to be here". He adds that Foucault "agreed", but quotes no response. (Mauriac, 1981: 517). On the other hand, Mauriac agrees with Defert that it was necessary to attend, not as readers of Sartre's texts, "but of his life" (518).

9. I find it harder to justify the exclusion of Sartre's late magnum opus, *The Idiot of the Family*, which was after all felt by him to be one of his most important works. But if it is true, as has been claimed by some, that this work is "poststructuralist" (Wood, P. R., 1989: 878), then this might in itself constitute a ground for leaving it out of account: it might be more interesting to see how compatible Sartre's work is with certain strands of poststructuralist thought taking as our point of comparison those works which predate poststructuralism. The length of *The Idiot of the Family* is also not wholly incidental to my decision to exclude it; so massive is it that it really requires an entire volume to itself.

10. Thus, for example, there can be no doubt that Sartre is a deeply sexist writer, yet I have chosen to ignore his sexism. I believe I am justified in so doing because his sexism is not internally related to or entailed by those aspects of his thought which I believe to be valuable. Thus Michelle Le Doeuff, for example, is quite right to stress Sartre's sexism— that it is not internally related to major currents of his thought does not imply that it is incidental— but it is equally necessary to point out that Sartre is sexist "[a]gainst all the general assumptions of his own doctrine" (Le Doeuff, 1991: 68). That is, Sartre's sexism exists as a contradiction in his thought, not an integral element (Simone de Beauvoir had already pointed out this contradiction in an interview she conducted with Sartre: to Sartre's claim that he took his *machismo* "to be a characteristic trait of mine", de Beauvoir replies: "That's odd, since you were the first to say that psychology, interiority, is never anything but the interiorizing of a situation" (Sartre, 1977c: 96).

11. On the other hand, since the flaws I will be pointing to in Sartre's work are more frequently present in the early work than the later, I will be the more concerned to offer an interpretation which would account for the entire oeuvre the later the chronological point we reach. It is this, at the horizon total, interpretation which justifies my use of the proper name 'Sartre' as an anchoring point for my arguments.

12. Foucault's introduction to the Binswanger, "Dream, Imagination and Existence", includes a brief critique of Sartre's theory of imagination, as presented in *The Psychology of Imagination*. For Foucault, Sartre's definition of imagination as a kind of positing of its object as *irréel* is too negative: "we must ask whether the image does indeed, as Sartre would have it, designate— even negatively and in the mode of unreality— the real itself" (Foucault, 1986a: 67).

Chapter Three

1. To cite two examples among many: Hoy (1998: 18) describes Heidegger as "the prophet of the postmodern". For Mark Taylor, the "space of postmodernism is opened by Heidegger's effort to think what philosophy leaves unthought" (Taylor, M., 1987: XXX).

2. The 'always already', which ensures that the question of the origin cannot be raised, is perhaps the decisive difference between modern and postmodern thinking— in that sense, Foucault is correct in locating the retreat and the return of the origin at the center of modern thought. For the 'always already' is also the 'after now', that which ensures that we are never contemporary with ourselves. It is for this reason, too, that the widely proclaimed linguistic turn of postmodern thought *is* distinctively postmodern. Language, like all 'always already' systems into which we are interpolated without recourse, justification, or appeal, cannot be traced back to its origin because any attempt to analyze it must be conducted from within it. As Frank puts it, "the signs, through whose application we theoretically survey (articulate) reality, are put at our disposal by structure. As soon as we use them, our assertion that *we* are the ones who established them comes too late" (Frank, 1989: 93). In an important sense, however, we, who cannot claim to found such structures, *are* these structures. They shape us, form and determine our patterns of thought, the organization of societies, even the content of our dreams. Thus, when we twist back on ourselves to thematize these structures, we assume a position at right angles to ourselves. We place ourselves temporally *after* our own present.

3. As Lyotard notes elsewhere, "Heidegger's 'politics' constitute an affair because they mean that the task of rewriting and deconstruction that they have undertaken along with Heidegger is not innocent of the worst kind of erring" (Lyotard, 1993: 140).

4. Quoted in the summary of discussions following his paper (Lebrun, 1988).

5. Dreyfus (1992): 95. The quote is from the summary of discussion following the paper.

6. In a later essay of Foucault, however, Derrida does note the "invasion" of *The Birth of the Clinic* by a "vocabulary and thematics (...) that always seemed to be difficult to dissociate from Heidegger, who as you know is practically never evoked, or even named, by Foucault" (1998: 104; translation modified). The distinction Derrida here draws between the adoption of trademark terminology and evocation is a fine one, to say the least: one would have thought that just such a technique of using terminology to evoke a philosopher is familiar to all readers of Derrida.

7. In his comparison of Foucault and Heidegger, Spanos comes to a diametrically opposite conclusion, claiming that Foucault "fails adequately to perceive the possibility of an *ontological* critique of the disciplinary society"; that he fails to see the extent to which the aspects of modernity to which he objects have their roots in "the circular/specular discourse of metaphysics" (Spanos, 1993: 158, 180). Spanos limits his exploration of Foucault's texts to the post-archaeological period: an examination of the 1960s works would, as I will show, soon reveal the extent to which his writing, during that period at least, was informed by precisely the destruction of the ontotheological tradition which Spanos contends is needed to complete his work.

8. Spanos asserts that, due to their excessive concentration on the notion of discontinuity, most Foucault specialists have overlooked the source of the Enlightenment gaze in the

Roman (mis)appropriation of Greek thought. Thus "they have missed or denied the affinities between his genealogy of the disciplinary society and Heidegger's destruction of the ontotheological tradition" (1993: 155). Spanos himself appears to overlook the extent to which the notion of the episteme (and therefore of discontinuity) itself finds its source in Heidegger, but he does point to an important difference between the thinkers: whereas, at least prior to *The Archaeology of Knowledge* Foucault thinks of the episteme as essentially discontinuous, Heidegger sees the epistemes as introducing, as Spanos aptly puts it, "difference-in-continuity" (170). Heidegger's epistemes overlay an essential continuity which stretches from Roman times to modernity as concerns the thinking of Being, and an even longer *durée* in the continuity between the Greek and German languages (During, 1992: 102).

9.   In the earlier "Age of the World Picture" (1977b), a then more subjectivist Heidegger credited (or blamed) Descartes with the creation of "the metaphysical presupposition for future anthropology" and the founding of "modern, and that means at the same time Western, metaphysics" (140).

10. Lebrun, who asserted that "*Les Mots et les Choses* owes nothing to Heidegger" attempts to demonstrate Foucault's rejection of phenomenology precisely through his interpretation of the *mathesis* "By this means, Foucault (...) begins to reject the analysis of *mathesis* made by Husserl in *Krisis*" (Lebrun, 1992: 22). Although it is clear that Foucault's analysis of the *mathesis* differs from Heidegger, he follows Heidegger's clue in rejecting the equation of eighteenth century knowledge with mechanization and mathematicization. Foucault does mean to distance himself from phenomenology; he does not, as Lebrun believes, include Heidegger under that heading.

11. Ferry and Renaut note that Foucault's depiction of the classical age as the age of representation but not of man "has an anti-Heideggerian flavour" (1990: 101).

12. With regard to Foucault's later work, however, Dreyfus's statement is perfectly correct. Foucault himself notes in a late lecture that whereas for Heidegger "it was through an increasing obsession with *techné* as the only way to arrive at an understanding of objects, that the West lost touch with Beings", he turns the question around and asks "which techniques and practices form the Western concept of the subject, giving it its characteristic split of truth and error, freedom and constraint" (This statement, quoted by the editor in a footnote to Foucault, 1993: 223-4, is drawn from a transcript of a lecture given by Foucault at Berkeley in 1980).

13. In a late interview, Foucault uses precisely the word "influential" to describe Heidegger's impact upon him. (Foucault, 1988b: 12).

14. Megill expresses the relation between the two philosophers well in speaking of "a kind of anti-Heideggerian Heideggerianism" (Megill, 1985: 220).

15. Paul Rabinow has pointed out the disparity between the analysis of modernity in late Foucault and the "countermodern" attitude evinced by Heidegger throughout his work, and the importance of this difference for any attempt to reconcile their work (Rabinow, 1994). As I will show, this difference is apparent long before the texts which Rabinow analyses are written.

16. Bourdieu devotes his analysis almost exclusively to *Being and Time*, leaving him open to the accusation that he condemns Heidegger for precisely the positions that he implicitly rejects or at least substantially modifies after his period of active involvement with Nazism; I have already pointed out Heidegger's decreasing subjectivism. Despite this, however, I believe that it can be shown that for Heidegger authenticity (translators of the later works usually use the word "proper", but the German word remains the same as that translated by Macquarrie and Robinson as "authentic" [*Eigentlich*]) remains linked with being set apart—appropriated into the proper, Heidegger might have said. For example, in the 1953 essay translated as "Language in the Poem": "The stranger (...) has been set apart because he is one of the select", and "the nature of apartness (...) gathers to itself also those who follow him who died early, by listening after him and carrying the music of his path over into the sounds of spoken language so that they become men apart. Their song is poetry" (Heidegger, 1982a: 186, 188).

17. It is for this reason that Scott is incorrect in finding a parallel between Heidegger and Foucault in a distrust of "universalization and totalization" (Scott, 1990: 110). It is at this point that Foucault departs from Heidegger, not the one respect in which they are "similar".

18. R. Kevin Hill notes that Foucault "claims to show that Heidegger's interpretation of death as the hidden truth of our nature is itself a historically conditioned event", which claim would, if true, undermine Division Two of *Being and Time* (Hill, 1989: 335).

19. Again, it might be necessary to establish that a valorization of being-toward-death, Dasein's "ownmost potentiality-for-Being", which undoes "all its relations to any other Dasein" (BT: 294), remains a theme in post-*Kehre* Heidegger. In fact, death for the later Heidegger continues to be that which "presences, even as the mystery of Being itself (...) death harbors within itself the presencing of Being" (1971c: 178-9). In death, for Heidegger, "the supreme concealedness of Being crystallizes" (1971e: 200). As Derrida notes, "the distinction between (properly) dying and *perishing*" extends, for Heidegger, "well beyond *Being and Time*" (1993: 35).

20. In *Aporias*, Derrida points to the same reversibility present in the notion of death, with all the consequences this reversibility will have for Heidegger's attempt to situate authenticity in being-towards-death: "Everyone's death, the death of all those who can say 'my death', is irreplaceable. So is 'my life'. Every other is completely other. [*Tout autre est tout autre.*] (...) nothing is more substitutable and yet nothing is less so than the syntagm 'my death'" (Derrida, 1993: 22).

21. It is here that I part ways with Dreyfus's interpretation of Heidegger. For Dreyfus, post-*Kehre* Heidegger makes "no attempt to find an ahistorical, hidden, deep truth" (1984: 76). If Heidegger makes no such attempt, it is because he believes he is already in possession of such a truth. On this point, see Palmer, 1984: 93; Wolin, R., 1992: 140.

22. It could be argued that Derrida is being unfair to Foucault, in as much as his own work, while never attempting to represent the unrepresentable, is often concerned to gesture towards it. Foucault's discourse could be read as a similar gesture. In a later essay, which resumes Derrida's meditation upon Foucault's history of madness, Derrida concedes that though Foucault's discourse may indeed find itself in "a maddening situation", nevertheless "a certain mad panic is not necessarily the worst thing that can happen to a

discourse on madness as soon as it does not go all out to confine or exclude its object, that is, in the sense that Foucault gives to this word, to *objectify* it" (Derrida, 1998: 100-101).

23. This is not the only reason that Foucault has for assigning literature a privileged place in his thought. Language is, of course, one of the primary markers of the finitude of humanity: as that which always precedes us, that to which we are always already committed when we begin to think, its investigation might mark a fundamental change in our space of knowledge, from a position in which 'man' is central to one in which language takes his place:

> From within language experienced and traversed as language, in the play of its possibilities extended to their furthest point, what emerges is that man has 'come to an end' (...) he arrives not at the very heart of himself but at the brink of that which limits him. (OT: 383)

And, Foucault believes, it is literature which most unflinchingly extends this play of possibilities: in contemporary writing, "every work is an attempt to exhaust language; eschatology has become of late a structure of literary experience, and literary experience, by right of birth, is now of paramount importance" (1977a: 86).

24. John Rajchman devotes chapter two of his book *Michel Foucault: The Freedom of Philosophy* to an analysis of Foucault's nominalism (Rajchman, 1985).

25. The contradiction is not, as might be incorrectly guessed, between the original version of *Maladie mentale et personnalité* (1954), and Foucault's later revision of it, published as *Maladie mentale et psychologie* (1962). Both quotes are drawn from part two of the later work, which part is almost wholly different from the earlier version. That is, the contradiction is not between an earlier and a later Foucault, but internal to Foucault's thought at this time.

26. Dreyfus, in his preface to *Mental Illness and Psychology*, notes the "tension in *Madness and Civilisation*", arising, he claims, from Foucault's employment of "an unstable synthesis of early Heidegger's existential account of Dasein as motivated by the attempt to cover up its nothingness and later Heidegger's historical interpretation of our culture as constituted by its lack of understanding of the role of clearing". Thus, he argues, to understand the tension, "one must return to Heidegger". (Dreyfus, 1987: xxvii). Dreyfus's argument is predicated on his reading of Heidegger's turn as a rejection of the "hermeneutics of suspicion"; later Heidegger, according to him, "rejects his earlier claim that there is any underlying ahistorical truth about human beings" (xxix). In fact, as we have seen, Heidegger retains a concept of the essence of Being, and of the essence of humanity (for him, the turn away from the danger would come when "mortals (...) find the way to their own nature"; the interpretation of being which produces this danger "threatens man (...) with the death of his own nature" (Heidegger, 1971b: 93, 116)). Just as Dreyfus fails to see the essentialism inherent in later Heidegger, so he misses that present in Foucault's work throughout the 1960s: "When in his next books, *The Birth of the Clinic* and *The Order of Things*, Foucault rejects hermeneutics, he is rejecting, with Freud, Marx, and the early Heidegger, his own brand of the hermeneutics of suspicion, the claim that madness has been silenced and must be allowed to speak its truth" (xxxiii). Foucault's "turn" thus appears to have paralleled Heidegger's and to have been led by it— which is true enough, as far as it goes, but this turn does not (yet) take Foucault beyond a position which could appropriately be described as a negative theology.

27. Mahon notes that there is a clash between a positive and a negative conception of power within *Histoire de la folie* (Mahon, 1992: 5).

28. The "reply" that Foucault attributes to Mallarmé, that it is the word that speaks "in its enigmatic and precarious being" recalls Heidegger's contention that "[i]n its essence, language is neither an expression nor an activity of man. Language speaks" (Heidegger, 1971e: 197).

29. There is, of course, no logical barrier to holding a positive conception of power as it operates *inside* the episteme, while retaining a belief in an absolute outside; Foucault's distinction between "*folie*" and "*maladie mentale*" in *Histoire de la folie* points in this direction. Perhaps he thought he had resolved the contradiction between the ontic and the ontological in just this way. But already his formulation of the notion of power as positive is too strong to allow for such a reconciliation; it will not allow him a space which would not have been created by the workings of power. And even the distinction between *la folie*, the outside of the episteme, and *maladie mentale*, unreason captured, classified and tamed, is not consistently drawn by Foucault; as he told *Le Monde*,

> Madness cannot be found in its raw state. Madness only exists in society, it does not exist outside of the forms of sensibility that isolate it and the forms of repulsion that exclude or capture it. (Foucault, 1996a: 8)

Chapter Four

1. "What saves the Fourfold-play from being merely a fantasied future or a regression to past history is that it is the simple Event that 'lasts', what 'eternally' rules human thought and events". (Fell, 1979: 257-8).

2. In "What Calls For Thinking?", Heidegger suggests that while the pre-Socratics may have not have been able to think Being as it is, perhaps Socrates himself came closer: "All through his life and right into his death, Socrates did nothing else than place himself into this draft, this current [i.e. of Being withdrawing], and maintain himself in it. This is why he is the purest thinker in the West. This why he wrote nothing" (1977f: 358). Just how Heidegger *knows* this is unclear, since Plato's thought is "already" metaphysical. Either, it seems, Plato was able to hint— at some moments in his work, despite his metaphysics and perhaps even despite himself— at Being as it is in its presencing, which is no lesser achievement than that which Heidegger claims for himself, in which case it appears that metaphysics is in no way inferior to what Heidegger calls, portentously, "thinking", or Heidegger must look elsewhere for the origin of metaphysics.

3. Thus "the thinking of this *Frühe* to come (...) opens onto what remains *origin-heterogeneous*..The entirely other announces itself in the most rigorous repetition" (Derrida, 1989a: 112-113).

4. In fact, language and the fourfold play in which mortals and earth are together authentically belong together. It is in naming that mortals make their contribution to the play of the fourfold: naming, as we have seen in chapter two, is what gives being to the thing. But once again, to be authentic, the naming cannot be done in just any manner, and it is this that provides Heidegger with a mechanism to explain how it happens that there is a natural way for earth and mortal to be. To be authentic, the naming, as we might guess

by now, must be done in German. The affinity between German and Being is guaranteed by the origin; it is due to "the special inner relationship between the German language and the language and thinking of the Greeks. This has been confirmed to me again and again by the French. When they begin to think they speak German" (Heidegger, 1990: 63). Furthermore, as Derrida notes that while "the joint privilege of German and Greek (...) with regard to thought, the question of Being, and thus to spirit, is implied by Heidegger everywhere", Heidegger also contends that "the Greek language has no word to say (...) *Geist*". Thus German is "the only language, at the end of the day, at the end of the race, to be able to name this maximal or superlative [*geistigste*] excellence which in short it shares, finally, *only up to a certain point* with Greek" (Derrida, 1989a: 69-71). Just as the origin has retreated beyond even the pre-Socratics, and thus must be located in the future, so the language of the pre-Socratics is unable to capture that origin, which task is left to the inheritor of Greek proximity to the origin, which can add to its inheritance spiritual riches of its own, and which points toward the future return of the origin.

5.   Fell takes Heidegger's rootedness in the commonplace as his decisive advantage over Sartre, who ultimately topples over into idealism, in that he "exhibits a metaphysical horror of the commonplace" (Fell, 1979: 179) and so traces the origin back to the for-itself. In so doing, Fell argues, Sartre misses the real locus of being in "The regular recurrence of day and night, of the season (...) of warmth and cold, of water and desert, of mountain and valley (...) It is they that form the grounding ethos" (382). It is hard to understand how the myth that this describes the commonplace can persist, when the world which surrounds most of us in the West is not this world. "Sartre's disaffection with nature and rural settings, and his preference for the artifactual and for cities" does not imply a "horror of the commonplace". The commonplace, in fact, is the very world that Sartre affirms: quite simply, most of the world's populations live in cities.

6.   In seeking to retrieve the lost origin, Heidegger places his faith in the distant past and its possible repetition in the future. Fundamentally, then, Heidegger is not a postmodernist if by postmodernism one means the thinking that is 'after now'. As Hoy says, "The ability to act without nostalgia is what carries the French postmoderns beyond Heidegger, whose tone remains one of regret over the historical withdrawal of Being" (Hoy, 1988: 30).

Chapter Five

1.   However, it must be noted that AK is not just a formulation of the methodology Foucault had previously applied, but also a revision of that methodology. In particular, as Gutting has pointed out (and despite the interpretation of the earlier work that Foucault offers in AK), between OT and AK Foucault abandons the notion of the *episteme* as the all-inclusive system of knowledge for an entire epoch. Such a conception had made criticism of OT a simple matter of finding counter-examples: one had merely to locate a text that did not fit into the schema that Foucault provided. In response to this criticism, Foucault proposes a new conception of the system of knowledge as consisting of both geographically and temporally local formations, and reads this conception back into OT (Gutting, 1989: 177-8). The later conception is infinitely more defensible; unfortunately, it also has less value as an explanatory or heuristic device.

2. In "Guetter le jour qui vient" (1963a), Foucault clearly identifies dialectics—in both its Socratic and Hegelian forms—with thought which has fallen from an original purity: the effort "to shake up dialectical language which forcibly assimilates thought to philosophy, and to leave to this thought the game without reconciliation, the absolutely transgressive game, of the the Same and of Difference" would be the restoration "of a *thought* which cannot be reduced to philosophy because it is more orignary and sovereign (*archaic*) than philosophy" (716).

3. With the rejection of an unrepresentable—but evocable—referent underlying reasonable discourse, Foucault also gradually abandons literature as an important element in his thought. For the early Foucault, literature was able to hint at the unrepresentable, and to symbolize, by manifesting nothing less than the being of language, Being itself. In AK, however, the literary text is simply a text inserted into a network of other, similar and dissimilar, texts. For the Foucault of the 1970s, literature is a nexus of power/knowledge relations. As Hollier puts it, "From one book to the next, Foucault turns his back on terror, on the association of literature and the thematic of death" (Hollier, 1992: 138).

4. The original quote is from OT: 318.

5. Once again, there is a significant difference between OT and AK on this question. In an interview published in March 1966, that is, shortly after the publication of OT, Foucault affirms that that work is indeed "the analysis of our own sub-soil" (1996b: 14). By investigating our own unthought, by attempting to elucidate our own a priori conditions of knowledge and experience, Foucault thus necessarily falls into the doubles of the analytic of finitude in the earlier work—although in the very same interview, Foucault also suggests that perhaps we need to undertake a different and less aporetic kind of analysis of our own subsoil:

> as soon as it's a matter of determining the system of discourse within which we are still living, at the moment we are obliged to put into question the words that still resonate in our ears and which are indistinguishable from those we are trying to speak, the archaeologist, like the Nietzschean philosopher, is forced to resort to the blows of the hammer. (1996c: 30)

In the "Reponse au Cercle d'épistémologie" (1968b), which is clearly a sketch for AK, Foucault recognises that any attempt to study his own episteme inevitably raises the question of the legitimacy of the apparently transcendental viewpoint he assumes:

> I analyze the space from which I speak [...] At each instant, with regard to each of my statements, therefore, I risk provoking the question of where it can come from [...] to the question, 'From where do you claim to speak?' [...] I will respond only: I believed that I was speaking from the same place as these discourses, and that in defining their space I was situating my propositions. But now I must recognize that from where I have shown that they speak without saying it, I can no longer myself speak, but only from this difference, from this infinitesimal discontinuity which has already left my discourse behind it. (21)

The attempt to outline the modern episteme is either conducted from a *post*modern space, or it must launch itself beyond modernity in its very performance. Foucault's thought, then, must either itself be postmodern, keeping the transcendental and the empirical poles separate, and thus unable to tell us about our present, or it is itself modern, and, like all modern thought, "both a knowledge and a modification of what it knows" (OT: 327): the condition it analyzes is no longer the condition in which it finds itself. It is the present, not the past or future origin which recedes for this mode of thought:

> In order to think the system, I was already constrained by a system behind the system, which I do not know and which will recede to the extent that I discover it, that it discovers itself. (1966a: 15)

6. It is for this reason that Dreyfus and Rabinow are wrong to assert that Foucault escapes the retreat and return of the origin double because "Archaeology simply is an ahistorical discipline with an ahistorical technical language which is able to survey and order history precisely because it is not in history"; thus, it "need not even raise the question of origin" (1983: 97). If Foucault feels that he need not raise the question of origin, it is not because he regards himself as temporarily stepping outside history when he speaks as an archaeologist. On the contrary, he recognises that it is a particular historical "archive system that makes it possible today to speak of the archive in general" (AK: 130). He does not raise the question of the origin simply because at this stage he believes that the origin is outside the realm of possible knowledge for us: such a question leads inevitably, for reasons to do with the structure of knowledge, to an endless movement from one pole of a binary opposition to the other and back again.

7. This, I take it, is what Foucault means when he notes that his discourse, "far from determining the locus in which it speaks"

> is avoiding the ground on which it could find support. It is a discourse about discourses: but it is not trying to find in them a hidden law, a concealed origin that it only remains to free; nor is it trying to establish by itself, taking itself as a starting point, the general theory of which they would be the concrete models. (AK: 205)

By not formulating a general theory of discourses, Foucault is able to avoid having to determine the locus from which *he* speaks; he is able to leave unasked the question concerning the validity and status of his discourse, thus keeping the transcendental and the empirical poles rigorously separate.

8. In an interview translated as "The Discourse of History", Foucault speaks of "this modern age which begins around 1790-1800 and goes to around 1950" (1996c: 30). All the evidence within OT, however, points to an uncertainty concerning the possible dating of a 'new age'. Foucault would *like* to be speaking from the vantage point of a different episteme, but feels unable to affirm that he does so. Hence the hesitation evident in the text over whether he can rightfully claim a transcendental viewpoint upon the modern age, or continues to speak from within the very space he condemns.

9. Moreover, Foucault suggests that his attack on humanism, and that of his contemporaries, should also be understood as essentially political:

> our work is a political undertaking, to the extent that all government, East or West, smuggle their bad merchandise under the banner of humanism. (1966a: 15)

I do not wish to underestimate the possible political importance of anti-humanism— although I believe Derrida is right in maintaining that humanism "has remained *up till now* (...) the price to be paid in the ethico-political denunciation of biologism, racism, naturalism, etc" (1989a: 56). Moreover, it is clear from Heidegger's example that antihumanism does not necessarily imply an escape from the analytic of finitude. The important question remains whether it is possible to develop a form of thought which will not separate the transcendental from the empirical, that is, a form of thought which will be really "valid for our diagnosis", but which will not be a humanism. This question I wish to leave open for the time being.

10. "Sartre is (...) very much a modern", Jameson, 1991: 363.

11. Michel Haar has attempted a fuller demonstration of the extent to which Sartre's thought is metaphysical, in his "Sartre and Heidegger" (Haar: 1980). According to Haar, Sartre "tries in general to preserve the fundamental structures of metaphysics" (168), especially by committing the ultimate sin from a Heideggerian point-of-view: attempting to think being as presence. For, despite Sartre's assertion that the future "constitutes the meaning of my present for-itself" (BN: 128), Haar argues, "this constitution turns out to be an illusion; I shall never be in the present that filled gap that I have the project to be (...) Thus the future, linked to the in-itself, is an inauthentic dimension: it represents 'the ontological mirage' of the Self (BN: 137). It is not the source but simply a frame, a pre-outline 'within which the for-itself will make itself be as a flight making itself present to Being in the direction of another future' (BN: 128)" (183). In fact, it is Haar who would privilege the present, in his demand that the for-itself at some future present *be* "that filled in gap" that it has the project to be. Sartre does not render the future inauthentic by refusing to the for-itself the ability to ever complete its project of becoming God; he holds it perpetually open *as* future. In fact, Sartre's present is in the mode of the 'after now': I am not my present (or I am my present in the mode of not being it), but this present that I am not *will have been* as the past of my future project: "Essence is what has been" (BN: 72).

12. According to Aronson, Sartre was unable "to transcend his original commitment to interiority, to the *cogito*" (Aronson, 1980: 352).

13. Admittedly, phenomenology is a broad school and not every attack upon it by Foucault should be seen as directed at Sartre; usually, however, it is clear that Foucault intends Sartre *as well* as Husserl and Merleau-Ponty when he says 'phenomenology'.

14. Knee adds, "From this angle, can we not see Sartre's efforts as a taking up of the analytic of finitide at the heart of his philosophical anthropology, in such a way as to assume in all lucidity the problems of the unthought and that of the doublets?" (Knee, 1990: 120).

15. In this light, it is possible to read Foucault's last works, in which his frame of historical reference changes from the well-trodden ground of the birth of modernity to early Christian, and then Greek and Roman, ethics, as an enactment of the inevitable retreat of the origin. As he studied modes of subjectivation, Foucault realized that, no matter how important a place the Enlightenment occupies in our history, "we have to refer to much more remote processes if we want to understand how we have been trapped in our own history" (1983a: 210). The origin inevitable retreats, and it is possible to follow it so long as its traces can be deciphered, whether in the form of documents or pottery fragments. Just as inevitably, however, the traces become rarer and rarer, eventually disappearing, without us ever having glimpsed the original moment. In his essay on "Foucault and psychoanalysis", J.-A. Miller traces exactly this retreat in Foucault's work, though without reference to the retreat and return of the origin double. Miller is wrong, however, in

believing to detect in this retreat "a kind of slide (...) which upsets the archaeological process and also the processes of epistemic scansion" (Miller, 1992: 61). Such a critique would hold only for the archaeological Foucault, in that he upholds a notion of the closed episteme, and only then on condition that this retreat occurred in his works. By the time he came to write those works which are marked by the continual retreat of the origin, Foucault had given up all attempt at defining a closed episteme, was no longer an archaeologist in the sense he had given that word.

16. As Harvey notes, modernity is "characterized by a never-ending process of internal ruptures" (Harvey, 1989: 12). Lyotard recognizes the aptness of this characterization for both modernity *and* postmodernity: "What, then, is the postmodern (...) It is undoubtedly part of the modern. Everything that is received must be suspected, even if it is only a day old" (Lyotard, 1992b: 21). If this is so, then a lucid postmodernity might attempt to break with everything *except* the modern— which, paradoxically (but we are used to these paradoxes by now), would constitute a decisive break with modernity. The paradoxes multiply: for example when Racevski notes that Foucault's "desire to 'se déprendre de soi-même' is an imperative that has its roots in (...) a growing feeling of alienation toward some intellectual currents whose stifling domination Foucault experienced in his youth": Marxism, phenomenology, existentialism (Racevskis, 1988: 28). Not only is the need to break with his past felt only through the very tools provided by it (alienation, domination, experience) the very act of breaking with oneself is paradigmatic of the thought of that one figure who combined all these currents: Jean-Paul Sartre, who, as he tells us in his autobiography, was always concerned to think against himself (Sartre, 1964: 158).

17. For Hoy, "both the modern and the postmodern ways of thinking can be described as thinking the unthought. The difference between them is *how* to think it" (Hoy, 1988: 21). The first such difference lies in the "willingness of postmoderns to accept rather than to lament the inevitable inability to think the 'great unthought'" (22).

18. Moreover, the 'after now' is a structure of the empirico-transcendental doublet. Whereas, as Foucault has shown in *The Order of Things*, in the Classical Age the foundation of being was anterior to that which it founded, in modernity the foundation is simultaneously grounding and grounded— an empirico-transcendetal double. Thus, the foundation occupies the paradoxical position of preceding its own possibility, or the subject is able (partially) to elucidate its hermeneutic horizons only after now; after that 'now' in which it acts.

Chapter Six

1. For a first-hand account of Foucault's political activism, see Mauriac, 1976; 1977; 1981.

2. The definition of consciousness as presence to itself (or for-itself) appears to lie at the root of the misconception that the Sartrean subject as *simply* present to itself. Such a misconception arises from a hasty reading of *Being and Nothingness*, where Sartre, in an attempt to forestall such a misunderstanding, writes: "presence to itself has often been taken for a plenitude of existence", but *"presence to* always implies duality". Thus "[p]resence to self (...) supposes that an impalpable fissure has slipped into being" (BN:

124). As Howells notes, Sartre, as much as Derrida, is concerned "with questioning the identification of Being and presence" (Howells, 1988: 195).

3. On the ways in which Sartre's for-itself anticipates many of themes of post-structuralist thought, see Howell, 1992: 332-3.

4. For an example of such a summation of Sartre's social thought see Aronson, 1980: 128.

5. These similarities have been one of the few points upon which attention has been paid to the affinities between Foucault's work and Sartre's. See, for example, Flynn, T.R., 1993: 285; Spanos, 1993: 294n37; Macey, 1993: 132; Jay, 1986: 179-81 (interestingly, Jay, in the chapter on Foucault in his recent book on antiocularcentricism in French thought, which is fundamentally based upon his 1986 article on the same topic, has minimized the extent to which Foucault owes his analysis of the gaze to Sartre. All mention of a "subterrenean affinity" (1986: 181) has been removed from the later text, and Jay has modified his initial contention that Foucault was implicitly in Sartre's "debt" (1986: 193) to one more in keeping with the usual narrative of rupture between the two: now Foucault simply and implicitly "complemented" Sartre's analysis (1993: 412).

6. Pucciani criticizes Sartre for depicting homosexuality in terms of a "sinister dialectic [...]] of subject-consciousnesses and object-consciousnesses, of the active and the passive [...] where all possibility of *Mitsein* is abolished" (Pucciani 1990: 650). Although it is true that, in his descriptions of homosexuality, Sartre implies that it is particularly non-reciprocal, his actual description of heterosexual relationships, at least in *Being and Nothingness*, finds no more evidence of reciprocity. As we have seen, for Sartre the relation between "subject-consciousnesses and object-consciousnesses, of the active and the passive", is the foundation of all concrete relations between two subjects.

7. As Halperin puts it, Foucault's "gay science" is "based (...) on a notion of gay existence without a gay essence" (Halperin, 1994: 23). Of course, Sartre gives two necessary and sufficient conditions for being an existentialist, which he equates: that which all existentialists have in common, "is simply the fact that they believe that existence comes before essence— or, if you will, that we must begin from subjectivity" (EH: 348, translation modified). It goes without saying that Foucault would not adhere to the second part of the definition, any more than would Heidegger, whom Sartre blithely classes among "the existential atheists" (348).

8. Nevertheless, Deleuze overstates the importance of this element in Foucault's thought in his book-length study of Foucault. In that work, Foucault's entire project is seen as culminating in "a certain idea of Life" as "the force that comes from outside" (Deleuze, 1988: 92-3). Far from culminating in such an idea, it represents the temptation of romanticism from which Foucault never ceased to retreat— without, however, ever entirely expunging its traces. From the notion of a wholly positive power in *Mental Illness and Psychology*, to his 1977 statement that there is no outside to power, to his last works in which a wholly acculturated subject is seen as the only possible agent for change, Foucault's work represents a long and largely successful struggle to free himself from vitalism, and it is in this struggle that his greatest contribution to political philosophy lies.

9. In the period between *The Birth of the Clinic* and *Discipline and Punish*, Foucault had, in *The Archaeology of Knowledge*, denounced his use in the earlier book of the term "*regard médical*", to the extent that it suggested "*the* synthesis or *the* unifying function of *a*

subject" (AK: 54 and n.). Thus, in *Discipline and Punish* he will depersonalize the gaze: it will become more an effect of architecture than of individual persons. In this too, however, Foucault follows the same trajectory as had Sartre before him: as Theunissen has noted, the distance between *Being and Nothingness* and the *Critique* is summed up in the fact that in the latter "it is matter that alienates me. It takes over the task that transcendent social ontology entrusted to the Other" (Theunissen, 1984: 254). It goes without saying, of course, that for both writers matter is a bearer of alienation only insofar as it is the bearer of meaning, which meaning has its source in the activities of acting subjects. That is, matter can alienate only insofar as it is what Sartre has termed the practico-inert.

10. By the time he wrote *Notebooks for an Ethics*, Sartre had already purged his perspective in this regard of much of the abstractness of *Being and Nothingness*. Here, it is no longer the simple, infinitely reversible gaze which is at the basis of oppression, but the gaze upon the foundation of a non-reversible power relation. These must be distinguished, for example, from "cases of reciprocal ignorance":

> I do not know medicine, but the medical doctor does not know philosophy. Each one holds the secret to the other's incompleteness. The one to whom I am an object is an object for me and in this way I deliver myself from my alienation. (NE: 299)

In Foucault's terms, a power relation exists here, but not a state of domination. And it is precisely such a state that Sartre proceeds to sketch:

> It is a quite different case when my ignorance is experienced as definitive and as not being reciprocal, as happens in an oppressive society. (NE: 299)

"An oppressed person reduced to servile labor or a wage earner who cannot get further education" is definitively objectified, definitively constituted "as incomplete and inefficacious" (299). It is not power that is evil in Sartre's work; it is non-reversible power relations, states of domination where the margin of liberty is extremely limited. Ironically, Foucault has himself been widely misinterpreted on this point: commentator after commentator has pointed to what Rorty calls "a crippling ambiguity between 'power' as a pejorative term and as a neutral, descriptive term" (Rorty, 1991: 195; see also Taylor, C., 1986: 90-2).

11. Sartre makes a similar accusation against psychoanalysis in his introduction to a supposed "Psychoanalytic Dialogue", published in *Les Temps Modernes* in 1969. "[T]he psychoanalytical relationship is, *by its very nature*, a violent one", for "[b]y his presence alone, the invisible and silent witness of the discourse of the patient (...) transforms his speech, even as it is uttered, into an object. Why?. For the simple reason that there could never be any reciprocity between these two figures, the one lying on the couch, his back to another sitting down, invisible and intangible". The text of the dialogue, then, represents "the overthrow of the univocal relationship linking the subject to the object" (Sartre, 1974d: 200-202). Sartre's text represents a considerable advance on *Saint Genet* in that here the asymmetry of the power relation is founded upon the materiality of a form of knowledge and the concrete setting in which it develops. It should be compared to Foucault's assertion in *Madness and Civilisation* that "Freud (...) exploited the structure that enveloped the medical personage (...) He focused upon this single

presence (...) all the powers that had been distributed in the collective existence of the asylum; he transformed this into an absolute Observation, a pure and circumspect Silence, a Judge who punishes and rewards in a judgement that does not even condescend to language; he made it the Mirror in which madness, in an almost motionless movement, clings to and casts off itself" (MC: 277-8).

12. For Jay, "the Panopticon (...) was an architectural embodiment of the most paranoid Sartean fantasies about the 'absolute look'" (1993: 410).

13. From this perspective, the following passage from Freud's second volume of *Introductory Lectures* emerges as a profoundly revealing:

    If now we consider the difficult problems that confront the educator— how he has to recognize the child's constitutional individuality, to infer from small indications what is going on in his immature mind, to give him the right amount of love and yet maintain an effective degree of authority we shall tell ourselves that the only appropriate preparation for the profession of educator is a thorough psychoanalytic training. (1988: 184-5)

14. Freud himself provides some warrant for the assimilation of the unconscious to being-for-others: "we have the same relation to our unconscious as we have to the psychical processes of another person" (1988: 102).

Chapter Seven

1. Thus, for Merleau-Ponty, there must be an "interworld" before there is the possibility of choice (1973: 200). In Sartre's world, in which there is only consciousness and things, we cannot speak of "decision (...) that is to say, of the deliberation between possibilities and of the motives which prefigure it (...) the revolutionary will of the militant (...) does not come out of what he was but out of the future, out of nonbeing" (106).

2. In *Notebooks for an Ethics*, Sartre explicitly embraces this consequence, in stating that the original choice of every for-itself is always the same: that of inauthenticity: "His project is inauthentic when man's project is to rejoin an In-itself-for-itself and to identify it with himself; in short, to be God and his own foundation, and when at the same time he posits the Good as preestablished" (NE: 559). Now, since the choice must be made on "the unreflective plane"— the reflective plane implies the unreflective, and thus must be anterior to it— "this freedom does not posit itself as freedom". Thus,

    in freely making itself, it does so unreflectively, and as it is a nihilating escape from being toward the In-itself-for-itself and a perpetual nihilation, it cannot do anything unless it posits the In-itself-for-itself as the Good existing as *selbständig*. (NE: 559)

   It is a matter here, Sartre writes, neither of determinism, nor of obligation. Simply, the ontological structure of the for-itself is such that the initial choice is always the choice of inauthenticity. Freedom, that is choice in the face of genuine alternatives, if it is indeed exists, can only arise subsequently.

3. Stone makes a parallel criticism, in terms of the for-itself's inability to become authentic: "My 'original project' of escaping anguish into bad faith itself confers significance on

worldly events, which merely occasion the realization of my project. But this entails the unwelcome consequence that my anguished flight in the face of interpersonal repression is an endless journey. For if this repression merely occasions a priori undertaking, how can we envision a 'recovery of being which was previously corrupted'? Once enmired in bad faith from inward motivations, I cannot break out, since my anguish endures and my 'corrupted' consciousness remains the only possible source of conversion" (Stone, 1981: 252-3).

4.   Bell recognizes the problem which I have outlined, and concludes, with remarkable understatement, that "it will not be easy to disengage oneself from that fundamental choice, for after all, it delimits all those things that can count as good reasons for an alternative choice" (Bell, 1989: 118). Nevertheless, she holds out the possibility of such a change, so long as "impure or accessory reflection" is abandoned in favour of "pure reflection". It should be clear by now that, were it possible for the for-itself to relinquish its meanings, it would have no basis for adopting new ones. "Pure reflection", strictly speaking, is meaningless. And it should therefore come as no surprise to find Sartre himself abandoning it:

> You know that I never described this kind of reflection; I said it could exist, but I only showed examples of accessory reflection. And later I discovered that nonaccessory reflection was not different from the accessory and immediate way of looking at things, but was the critical work one can do on oneself during one's entire life, through *praxis*. (Sartre, 1977d: 122)

5.   In this regard at least, *The Archaeology of Knowledge* is no improvement on *The Order of Things*. In the former work, the episteme is indeed the "regional" system Foucault describes, but its earlier, all-encompassing, role as a closed and total system reappears under the names "historical a priori" or "archive". On this point, see O'Farrell, 1989: 60.

6.   For Derrida, the ambiguous place Freud and psychoanalysis, especially the complex discourse developed in *Beyond the Pleasure Principle*, occupy in Foucault's work throws into doubt the feasibility of the entire notion of episteme. Derrida asks whether Foucault would "have inscribed this problematic matrix *within* the whole whose history he describes? Or would he have put it on the other side, on the side of what allows one, on the contrary, to delimit the whole, indeed to problematize it? And thus on a side that no longer belongs to the whole, nor, I would be tempted to think, to any whole, such that the very idea of a gathering of problematization or deployment [*dispositif*], to say nothing more of age, *episteme*, paradigm, or epoch would make for so many problematic names, just as problematic as the very idea of problematization?" (Derrida, 1998: 117; translation modified). In essence, Derrida accuses Foucault of being under the spell of the metaphysics of presence; Freudian psychoanalysis appears in Foucault's work simultaneously as that which opens the space for Foucault's critique, and as the object of that critique, "without the consequences being drawn with regard to the identity of all the concepts at work in this history" (102). The point is well made—except that it does not apply to any of Foucault's works after the archaeological period. Ever since Foucault began to advocate minor knowledges, his notion of the episteme has become more and more open, divided and, precisely, problematic. Foucault describes himself as an historian of the present exactly to disturb too great a confidence in "the opposition between

absence and presence, outside and inside" (Derrida, 1998: 89). Derrida persists in reading the later Foucault in the light of the former; that is, he *totalizes* him.

Chapter Eight

1.   John Rajchman sees this passage as being aimed specifically at Sartre (Rajchman, 1985: 44).

2.   Prior to his analysis of the gift, Sartre sketches another possible means for two subjects to enter into a relation of positive reciprocity: the appeal. And this comportment takes as its point of departure the being *in situation* of the Other: "What I recognize is not an unconditioned freedom set above any and all situations (...) In reality, to recognize the other's freedom concretely is to recognize it in terms of its own ends, along with the difficulties it experiences and its finitude" (NE: 283). Unfortunately, the appeal too is founded upon a perspective in which the world is stripped of its significations. In the appeal, "I take it that what is wanted by one freedom must be accepted as such by other freedoms, simply because it is a freedom that wants it (...) Therefore I posit in principle that every end *has* a value and that every human activity is haunted by value. I also thereby posit in principle that it is always better that a value, whatever it may be, should be realized in the world" (274-5). But if I can suspend my values in favor of other values, regardless of what these other values might be, it can only be because I am capable of suspending the meanings inherent in the world. That this is so becomes even clearer when Sartre considers a situation in which the appeal is refused: "One no longer considers my ends with a confidence based on principle and because they are wanted by a freedom, one considers them in themselves and in the *Umwelt* of the person asked to do so, and as internal to his system of values. This would still be admissible if this comparison and this examination were to lead to the bursting of this system of values of the other, but, quite to the contrary, the end is rejected" (292). This criticism of the for-itself for having values in the name of which it evaluates those of the Other can only be predicated on a belief in its ability to step outside of all values (except for the value that values should be realized). But outside of values, of *meaning*, there is nothing: not freedom, and certainly not reciprocity.

3.   In the *Critique of Dialectical Reason*, Sartre adds one more criticism of an ethics which will take the liberty of the for-itself as unconditional end: the for-itself always has the project of changing the world, and therefore of changing itself. "His constant search is for a different *arrangement* of the universe, and a different statute for man; and in terms of this new order he is able to define himself as *the Other whom he will become*". It is thus "impossible for him to treat his own present as an end" (112); his present is project towards...not static being.

4.   It must be recalled, of course, that the *Notebooks* were, as the name suggests, working notes of Sartre's. I will make no attempt to connect the various strands of thought apparent in them to each other, for they are not commensurable with each other. As Kruks points out, the *Notebooks* "point, Janus-like, in two directions" (Kruks, 1990: 186); some point back to the dualist ontology of *Being and Nothingness*, others to the social and historical ontology of the *Critique*.

5.   One of the most influential critiques of Sartre, that developed by Merleau-Ponty in *The Adventures of the Dialectic*, is centrally concerned with this issue of the constitution of meaning. Merleau-Ponty asserts, and many commentators have agreed, that for Sartre

"meaning is wholly spiritual" (Merleau-Ponty, 1973: 124); that between consciousness and meaningless being, and between the for-itself and the Other, there is "no hinge, no joint or mediation" (142, 154), no "interworld" (200). Merleau-Ponty's criticisms are justified with regard to *Being and Nothingness*, but not with regard to the *Critique*, in which, as I have shown, meaning is simply encountered by the individual for-itself in the world, not somehow created new and *ex nihilo* by each one of us. Unfortunately, the debate between Sartre and Merleau-Ponty was cut short by the latter's death, before he had time to reply to the *Critique*.

6. For Hartmann, if Sartre was to overcome the "subjective formalism" of *Being and Nothingness*, it would be necessary for him to provide a theory in which "the world would (...) 'supply' possibilities and constitute a dialectical 'mean' for myself, so that I could make known to myself, in terms of the world, what I want to be" (Hartmann, 1966: 84-5). With the *Critique*, Sartre provides just such a theory.

7. In fact, change is not just possible, it is inevitable, for the project of conserving a given state of affairs in a world in continual motion due to the effects of a countless number of other projects requires constant effort on the part of the for-itself. The bourgeoisie, according to Sartre, in order to conserve its hegemonic position, conceived the project of deflecting the proletariat's energies away from concrete action and toward an imaginary world. Thus it was

    > that the proletariat had to be changed by the priests *so as to avoid* changing the bourgeoisie, and that the bourgeoisie could not avoid change unless it changed itself and grounded the new authority of the priest on the dissolution in it of the (serial) movement of de-Christianization. (CDR: 779)

    Or, as Sartre writes of violence, inasmuch as it defines a state of domination, it must "*create itself* in order to maintain itself, and change in order to remain the same" (CDR: 719). Sartre had, then, already pre-empted Foucault's implied criticism in *The Archaeology of Knowledge* (a text in which the references to Sartre, and especially to a brief interview entitled "Sartre Aujourd'hui" (Sartre, 1971), are transparent):

    > Archaeology (...) considers that the same, the repetitive, and the uninterrupted are no less problematic than the ruptures (...) they too are governed by the rules of formation of positivities; far from manifesting that fundamental, reassuring inertia which we like to use as a criterion of change, they are themselves actively, regularly formed. (174)

    It is not only archaeology which problematizes continuity; Sartre too shows that it is "actively, regularly formed" and, moreover, that it is never more than *local* continuity in discontinuity.

8. Réplique: I (1) "Action de répondre; réponse à ce qui a été dit ou écrit"; (2) "Réponse vive, faite avec humeur et marquant une opposition".

    II(1) "Chose qui en répète une autre (...)" *La Grand Robert de la langue française*, Tome VIII, p.266.

9. Baudrillard, in his critique of Foucault, claims that, for the latter liberation is a mere ruse of repression: "Any form of liberation is fomented by repression: the liberation of productive forces is like that of desire; the liberation of bodies is like that of women's liberation, etc."

(1987: 26). Thus Baudrillard misses the central importance of strategy to Foucault: strategic resistance, resistance to domination in the form of a *réplique* to the dominating power in that power's own discourse, is real, effective resistance. On the specific subject of feminism, Foucault saw resistance as having progressed beyond the stage of such a strategic return of discourse. The move beyond the discourse of domination was, however, prepared for by a necessary stage of *réplique*:

> The real strength of the women's liberation movements is not that of having laid claim to the specificity of their sexuality and the rights pertaining to it, but that they have actually departed from the discourse conducted within the apparatuses of sexuality. The movements do indeed emerge in the nineteenth century as demands for sexual specificity. What has their outcome been? Ultimately, a veritable movement of de-sexualization, a displacement effected in relation to the sexual centering of the problem, formulating the demand for forms of culture, discourse, language, and so on, which are no longer part of that rigid assignation and pinning-down to their sex *which they had initially in some sense been politically obliged to accept in order to make themselves heard.* (Foucault, 1980g: 219-20; italics mine)

"Homosexual liberation movements", in contrast, remain "caught at the level of demands for the right to their sexuality" (220). Nevertheless, such strategic resistance is real and effective; it is not, as Baudrillard would have it, "*the same thing*" as that which it resists (Baudrillard, 1987: 26).

10. Thus strategies do not represent "forces which have come from outside" as Deleuze claims (1988: 87). They are more accurately seen (to use Deleuzian terminology) as a folding of power against itself, and thus necessarily do not result in a passage outside power. The fact that there is no outside to power is precisely the reason why Foucault believes that strategy represents the most effective form of resistance. Strategy confronts power in power's own domain, in its terms, and therefore always faces the danger of being colonized by the power which it seeks to resist. But it has the advantage of representing genuine and potentially effective resistance, rather than an imaginary passage to a fictive 'outside'.

11. The apparent ambivalence in Foucault's assessment of the Enlightenment has escaped many of his commentators, who see in him only "a fierce foe of the Enlightenment" (Merquior, 1985: 101). In discussing Foucault's late essays on Kant, Merquior argues that in Foucault's advice that we keep alive the "historical meaning" of the Enlightenment, rather than preserve its "remains" represents merely another way "to snipe at its intellectual heritage" (149-50). Merquior appears to have forgotten Kant's definition of Enlightenment as a "negative principle in the use of one's cognitive powers", rather than consisting in any determinate knowledge. "[T]hose who are exceedingly rich in knowledge are often least in their use of it", Kant adds (Kant, 1991b: 249).

12. To appreciate Foucault's understanding of the Enlightenment fully, it is necessary to recognize the presence in his work of yet another Sartrean thematic: that of counter-finality. The notion of counter-finality, developed in the *Critique*, explains how our actions are stolen from us, as it were, by their inscription into the practico-inert field. That is, actions become embodied in matter, which matter enters into situation with the field of human actions, forming a complex network with results almost impossible to predict. To put it simply, actions, especially where there is no attempt at coordination among actors,

often have results that the actors neither foresee nor want. It is just such a reversal of the intended consequences of action that Foucault sees in the Enlightenment. Thus, those commentators who see in Foucault's reading of the Enlightenment merely a conspiracy theory, in which "a brutal change in the practices of power" was concealed beneath "the rhetorical umbrella" provided by "concepts of law and morality" (Habermas, 1987: 288) have missed an important dimension of his thought. Counter-finality is, as it were, the negative side of strategy; it represents the réplique made by worked matter to our actions, which réplique is open to being taken up again in a new counter-strategy: thus the strategic use of the failure of the prisons, outlined in *Discipline and Punish*. Most importantly, the inscription of action into the practico-inert field and the subsequent functioning of that field in such a way as to cause systematic, seemingly designed, effects, explains that element in Foucault's thought which has been so puzzling to many of his commentators (for example, Taylor, C., 1986: 86-8) how it is that power relations can be "both intentional and nonsubjective" (HSI: 94). They can be so because they are always exercized with "a series of aims and objectives" (95) by conscious agents, at the local level (what Foucault calls "the local cynicism of power"), but these tactics enter into relations with each other which are not willed by the actors, and which, "finding their base of support and their condition elsewhere, end by forming comprehensive systems" (95). On all these points, see Hendley, 1991: 65-6; Knee, 1990: 121-2.

13. Just as Foucault has often been read as an anti-Enlightenment thinker, so has he been interpreted as seeing in law only a limit to our freedom (eg, Rochlitz, 1992: 254; Deleuze 1988: 136-7, n10; Walzer, 1986: 62-3). In fact, his statements on law can more plausibly be read as advocating a system of justice whish is more, not less, law and rule based, rather than one which judges in terms of norms. Laws, at least insofar as they prohibit rather than prescribe, are compatible with a freedom to invent creative responses to ever-changing situations. Thus Deyfus and Rabinow are correct in pointing out that Foucault suggests that the "ideals of law are in permanent tension with the social order established by political technologies" (Dreyfus and Rabinow, 1983: 131).

14. As Dosse notes, "the fight in which Foucault engages at the end of the 1970s and the start of the 1980s is that for the rights of man" (Dosse, 1992: 424). In the light of these texts, it is clear that many of Foucault's commentators have overestimated the place in his work of the notion of the specific intellectual, or the consistency with which he upheld it.

15. Sawicki suggests such a distinction between the perception of an injustice and the appeal to norms to justify such a perception, when she allows that in "our political struggles against injustice and oppression, feminists may continue to appeal to the standards of rationality and justice that are available in the contexts in which we find ourselves" Sawicki, 1994: 309). In fact, when we decide whether or not to appeal to such standards it is always already too late: we are committed to these standards even in our acts of rejecting them. The perception of injustice itself is made in relation precisely to such standards.

16. Todd May advances a similarly 'pragmatic' interpretation of Foucault's method. For him, "[g]enealogy subverts the attachment to certain claims or sets of claims that have important inferential roles in a variety of discourses. It does so on the grounds of other claims or sets of claims that it holds constant" (May, 1993: 100). Where I disagree with May is in his assertion that Foucault remains a transcendental thinker to the extent that his notion of a power that is not resisted "is a transcendental one. It cannot be had without

conceiving a substance beneath or beyond discourses and practices (...) which is the subject of refusal and the locus of revolt" (115). This is so, May argues, because in fact many practices do go unresisted, or even "prevent (...) the consideration of resistance" (115). Thus, if one persists in speaking of resistance in all cases, one must have a notion of an essential resistance, which essence in some cases goes unrealized. May is led astray by too grand a conception of resistance. Resistance is everywhere there is power simply because resistance *is* power. Practices like psychology which appear to preclude even the thought of resistance may well be successful in preventing any manifest revolt. But these practices are resisted nevertheless, if only in the efforts individuals make to adapt themselves to them.

17. The name of a series of pamphlets which Foucault helped to produce as part of his work with the GIP. On the intolerable as the basis of Foucault's ethics, see Glücksmann, 1992: 336-7.

18. Cited as a "personal communication", Dreyfus and Rabinow, 1983: 187. Of these words Hendley writes: "What Foucault says here could also be applied, without qualification, to Sartre's concept of counter-finality" (Hendley, 1991: 211n10).

19. And it is for this reason that, although Norris is right to suggest that in certain respects there is no great distance between Foucault and Rorty (Norris, 1994: 181), his work, unlike Rorty's, does not consist in "an apologia for existing values and beliefs that would place them beyond reach of counter-arguements or effective oppositional critique" (189). Foucault is a pragmatist to the extent that he recognizes that such a critique must depart from existing values and beliefs, and appeal to them as its ultimate horizon. This does not "place them beyond the reach of counter-arguments"; arguments, by definition, appeal to standards of truth or morality which precede them.

20. From the 'bad', French, side, Auzias is equally wrong in drawing the conclusion that the consequence of Foucault's work is a reformism "within a system which he neither denounces nor demolishes in its essence" (Auzias, 1986: 55). This is to swing Foucault too far back in the other direction: he accepts our values but not our "system", for he believes that as it stands, it gives rise to consequences and practices which are found to be intolerable by the very values which also inform it.

21. At least one commentator on Foucault has read his work as denying the possibility that there can exist a truth about the subject which is not, inevitably, subjugating. According to this reading, "Self-representation means subjectivation and inevitable denial of liberty". Thus Foucault's solution lies in "a training that eliminates the ethical subject" (Scott, 1990: 90). As we shall see, this reading of Foucault ignores the difference between a knowledge of the subject that would reveal the truth of its being, and the practical knowledge, which is directed as much toward the world as the subject who knows it.

22. "The conversion: recognition of myself as ec-static For-itself entails the recognition of spirit as detotalized totality" (NE: 10; translation modified).

23. Both Coles (1991: 109) and, following him, Owen (1994: 105) stress the extent to which Foucault's work on the self, too, is a *social*, not individual, undertaking.

24. Before we make the notion of authenticity central to Sartre's thought, however, it is necessssary to note that the word almost never appears in *Being and Nothingness* itself.

25. Foucault himself believed that the passage through the subject was necessary to critique: "On the critical side— I mean critical in a very broad sense— philosophy is precisely the challenging of phenomena of domination (...) This critical function of philosophy, up to a certain point, emerges right from the Socratic imperative: 'Be concerned with yourself, i.e., ground yourself in liberty, through the mastery of self'" (ECS: 20).

26. In advocating a return to Greek notions of self-formation, Foucault was, in a sense, returning to his own starting-point, in his translation of Kant's *Anthroplogy*. For that work, as much as the Greek texts Foucault analyzes, finds the principle of liberty in the maintenance of "self-control" (Kant, 1978: 174; "maîtrise de soi-même" in Foucault's own translation [Kant, 1991a: 120]). Thus Kant's advice:

    > Young man! Deny yourself satisfaction (of amusement, of debauchery, of love, etc.), not with the Stoical intention of complete abstinence, but with the refined Epicurean intention of having in view an ever-growing pleasure. (Kant, 1978: 54)

    It is also possible to link this theme of "maîtrise de soi-même" to Kant's texts on Enlightenment and the French revolution, to which Foucault would often return in the last years of his life. Establishing such mastery over oneself amounts to a "revolution coming from inside of man", characterized, Kant says, quoting his own earlier "Was ist Aufklärung?", by "'his departure from his self-incurred tutelage'" whereby we begin to think for ourselves (Kant, 1978: 129).

27. One might speculate that Foucault's awareness of the dangers of taking one's being as a theme for reflection is a distant echo in Kant. In the *Anthropology*, translated by Foucault for his *thèse complémentaire*, Kant warns of the risks associated with such a reflection. "observation' of oneself" (in his translation Foucault uses the term "surveiller" [Kant, 1991a: 21]) "is the most direct path to illuminism and terrorism", and leads "ultimately to the madhouse" (Kant, 1978: 16-7).

28. As Flynn notes, Foucault's "claim that every exercise of power is accompanied by or gives rise to resistances opens a space for possibility and freedom in any context. This stance leaves him remarkably close to Jean-Paul Sartre, whose maxim was that we can always make something out of what we have been made into" (Flynn, T., 1994: 35).

29. As Sartre points out (à propos of the group), the relation which one founds with regard to oneself *subsequent* to one's constitution as a subject is itself conditioned by the range of culturally structured possibilities available to one; it is dependent, in other words, on the "system of real possibilities of distance from oneself, of withdrawal, etc." (CDR: 704).

Chapter Nine

1. For Flynn, the "visibility-domination dyad" in Foucault's work "looks suspiciously like the Sartrean looking/looked-at relationship, in that neither allows for positive reciprocity and mutuality (...) Foucault never escapes the stage of reciprocal endangerment in his account of social interaction. For him, too, it appears that 'hell is other people'" (Flynn, T. R., 1993: 285).

2. Barry Smart notes that for Foucault power relations "are conceptualized as existing at the most elemental level of the social domain and might be said to constitute it"; indeed, at the limit, Foucault's conception might be "the equivalence of power relations with sociality itself" (Smart, 1983: 87).

3. Aronson argues that "(s)ociety— and particularly the alienated and contradictory social life of class societies— is the missing term of Sartre's social thought" (Aronson, 1980: 263). For him, Sartre's "description of the hell of the practico-inert" reproduces the capitalist ideology in which there are only separate individuals. In fact, Aronson is confusing the practico-inert with counter-finality. The practico-inert is the domain of worked upon matter; it is that which secures the socialization of the child. It is thus precisely the "'internal' route to sociality" which Aronson demands (265). Counter-finality, on the other hand, is that dimension which is, if not specific to capitalist society, at least much more prevalent in a society in which sheer numbers and complexity combine with a deliberate policy of limited economic intervention to increase exponentially the likelihood of actions having an unforeseen, negative, result. Aronson's contention that Sartre ignores the necessity of cooperation in any society is also based on a misunderstanding of the practico-inert: for Aronson, Sartre's depiction of human relations in the context of scarcity is "simply wrong: wrong because the *Critique* shows no sense that humans are also deeply connected for *positive* reasons" (254). If we replace Aronson's emphasis on cooperation with a concept of interpolation, we see that the only positivity required by Sartre is the notion of a productive power.

4. Nor is it sufficient to adopt a Jungian vocabulary and assert that the body, "is not a ground but an archetype, an exemplar" (Cohen, 1984: 331). The metaphorics of the archetype, like that of the origin and of the ground, is designed to perform an effacement of history. No more than the in-itself does such a stable form exist.

5. This might be an appropriate point to address another persistent misunderstanding of Foucault, namely that his appeal to "bodies and pleasures" in *The History of Sexuality, Volume 1* represents a "recourse to an uncapturable prediscursive spontaneity" (Dews, 1989: 12) or a vague gesture towards a different normative system (Fraser, 1989: 63). The rallying point represented by "bodies and pleasures" is necessarily left undetermined by Foucault: his point is not that there is a prediscursive body which should be expressed, but that those elements of our behaviour which are currently subsumed under the notion of sexuality can and have been articulated differently. If and when such a reconfiguration of subjectivity takes place, the space marked by Foucault's "bodies and pleasures" will be given content. As to the contention that this represents one of the rare occasions upon which Foucault allowed his readers to glimpse the alternative normative system which underlies his work, this is simply based on a misreading: Foucault did not oppose "bodies and pleasures" to current notions of right, but simply to the "deployment of sexuality" (HS: 157). He does not, as Fraser claims, seek to replace "the vocabulary of humanism" with such notions, but simply to help us reconceptualize sexuality.

6. To speak of comprehension as occurring *first*, to be followed later by *evaluation* is to introduce a temporal distinction where none exists, and harks back to Sartre's earlier idealism, in which things and acts could be perceived independently of the values later to be attributed to them. No matter, the idealism is residual in the *Critique*, and without

important consequences: Sartre himself would probably have accepted that the distinction is illegitimate.

7. For Theunissen, the aspect of the *Critique* "that shakes the foundations of Sartre's [earlier] social ontology" is "the concession of the reciprocity of the subject-object relationship" Theunissen, 1984: 247). For him, however, this insight should lead in the direction of a recognition of the other more akin to Merleau-Ponty's chiasm that the conflictual reciprocity with which the *Critique* culminates.

8. Ironically, Foucault may intend his comment here as an implicit critique of Sartre: the full sentence runs: "The coherence of such a history does not derive from the revelation of a project but from a logic of opposing strategies". The project is, of course, a key term in Sartre's vocabulary. This criticism, like many others made by Foucault and his contemporaries, indicates that their in-depth familiarity with Sartre's work stops with "Existentialism is a Humanism".

9. For Ingram, "if it can be said that Foucault interprets communicative action strategically, as a game of power, it can also be said that he interprets strategic action communicatively, as a game of dialogue" (Ingram, 1994: 243).

Chapter Ten

1. I owe this bibliographical information to Cumming, 1991: 115 and 218n21.

2. Quoted by his interviewer in Sartre, 1977b: 22.

3. If we take the events of May 1968 as marking the break between modernity and postmodernity, as many commentators have done, then it is possible to find support for Foucault's contention that Sartre helped to participate in the supersession of modernity. For more than one critic has concluded that the May events, as Jameson put it, "fully bear out" the conclusions of the *Critique* and "testify to its significance as an expression of some of the deepest tendencies of its historical period" (Jameson, 1971: 209). Writing more than a decade later, Martin Jay adds that "what was 'corroborated' was as much the darker elements of that theory as the more hopeful" (Jay, 1984: 359).

4. Macey claims that Foucault's reading at this time was explicitly "'against' Sartre and Hegel".

5. In a much later interview, Foucault treated Sartre's comment with the seriousness it deserved: "Poor bourgeoisie: if it had needed *me* as 'bulwark,' it would have lost power long ago" (Foucault, 1991: 85)

6. To be fair to Foucault, the interview in which he apparently calls "La légende de la vérité" "The History of Truth" is available to me only in an English translation from the original German publication— itself presumably a translation from the French. So the deformation of the title of Sartre's essay may be due as much to repeated translations as to any error of Foucault's.

7. As Derrida notes, Sartre did not have to wait for an epochal shift in order to become untimely. He was out-of-step with his time from the start, for he "rejected or misrecognized so many theoretical or literary events of his time— to be brief, let's say

psychoanalysis, marxism, structuralism, Joyce, Artaud, Bataille, Blanchot" (Derrida, 1984: 371). For Hollier too our age, which "will no doubt have defined itself as an epoch (...) by evolving under the sign of the sign" is nevertheless "dominated by that immense exercise in untimeliness, the work of Jean-Paul Sartre, whose will to modernity (...) issues on this specific point in an unprecedented anachronism" (Hollier, 1986: 59). Now that Sartre has been "essentially relegated to the past", Hollier adds, he is doubly untimely, and with him all who still write about him (92).

8. Deleuze notes that "[i]f Foucault is a great philosopher, this is because he used history for the sake of something beyond it: as Nietzsche said, acting against time, and thus on time, for the sake of a time one hopes will come" (Deleuze, 1992: 164-5). But it should be added, as Mahon points out, that whereas Nietzsche emphasizes "active forgetting" in the *Untimely Meditations*, Foucault placed on the accent more on memory than forgetting (Mahon, 1992: 180)

9. Sawicki has noted the extent to which the adoption of Foucault's discourse by feminists may be "risky": "Risky practices are those about which there is conflicting evidence concerning their practical and political implications" (Sawicki: 1991: 102-3). In particular, she identifies Foucault's "practices of self-erasure and self-refusal" (104) as questionable for a movement which seeks to give a voice and a political identity to women, and instead argues for "the strategic value for feminism of building identities" (106). It is worth pointing out, however, the extent to which this critique of Foucault is compatible with—perhaps even reliant upon—Foucault's work. In the first place, Foucault himself endorsed the strategic value of the affirmation of identity—with regard to homosexuals, for example. In the second, the identification of the 'risky' elements in all discourses is precisely the kind of analysis that Foucault is calling for by his "hyperactive pessimism". As an enlightenment thinker, of a sort, the only element of Foucault's work which he would be happy for us to retain uncritically is the negative principle of permanent critique.

10. Though Foucault regarded the *work* as out-of-date, the man himself was another matter entirely. Sartre joined the generation whose philosophical project was the dissolution of subjectivity of the Sartrean kind, in the political mobilization of the 1960s. Thus, Foucault says, "Sartre died contemporary with those who were educated in the image of a thought formed in rupture with him" (1994b: 263).

11. Since we have been taking Derrida as one of our fixed reference points to which we can refer any thought in order to measure the extent of its postmodernity, it is worth noting here his appeal to the untimely in order to justify his recent re-examination of Marx. In returning to a certain "spirit" of Marx, Derrida says:

> I would be today, here, now, less insensitive than ever to the appeal of the contretemps or of being-out-of-step, as well as to the style of an untimeliness that is more manifest and more urgent than ever. Already I hear people saying: "You picked a good time to salute Marx!" Or else: "It's about time!" Why so late? I believe in the political virtue of the contretemps. (Derrida, 1994: 88)

Chapter Eleven

1. Bell notes that "the prevailing opinion seems to be (...) that Sartre's published work renders ethics impossible, not just problematic" (Bell, 1989: 9).

2. For Megill, Foucault, who is "implicitly committed to the notion that the reigning order, whatever its nature, is degraded", is "much more conscious than Sartre ever was of the oppressive potential that rests in every state, in every mass movement" (Megill, 1985: 239, 246).

3. On the Rome and Cornell lectures, see Stone and Bowman (1991a and b).

4. Richard McCleary translates *futur antérieur* as "prior future" (246, 248), and as "previous future" (243). Though *futur antérieur* is the normal French expression for the grammatical tense we call the future perfect, McCleary's translation is appropriate given the context. I shall follow this translation, giving the French in brackets.

5. This distinction between prior future and future perfect provides an outline of a response to the inevitable objection that Sartre, far from writing in the future perfect, always and explicitly "put the accent on the present ekstasis and not on the future", as he advises in *Being and Nothingness* (202). Such an objection, moreover, could point to Sartre's explicit rejection of a future perfect attitude to our own time, in his "Présentation des *Temps Modernes*": "We write for our contemporaries; we do not want to look at our world with future eyes" (Sartre, 1948: 14). What Sartre here rejects, however, is not the notion of the future perfect as I have defined it, but only the elevation of the future over a present considered as *already* having been, a dead present. For those who regard our time from the vantage point of such a future, "we are already dead" (14). They see our present without its living future, for they regard the future as already existing, a prior future. But that means they do not see our present at all, for "an epoch, like a person, is first of all a future" (14). As Hollier notes, "if the future perfect must be condemned, it is not so much because it kills the present by making of it a past future, but more fundamentally because it authorizes the belief that the future is a present future". It is in this sense, and this sense alone, that "the Sartrean definition of the future excludes precisely the case that it might ever be transformed into a future perfect" (Hollier, 1986: 200). Bennington too, in his argument that the future perfect, as opposed to "the future proper", is antithetical to postmodernism, takes the future perfect as a future anterior: a "future perfect [that] has always already been contained in the past (...) future perfect because *perfectum*, complete already, and therefore not future at all" (Bennington, 1990: 20). The future perfect is thus an ambivalent tense: it points both towards the future which cannot be expected, and the future which, like Heidegger's *a priori* perfect, is a repetition of the lost origin.

6. Deleuze's denial of agency in Foucault is also a denial of such intelligibility. For Deleuze, "forces are in a perpetual state of evolution (...) Suddenly, things are no longer perceived or propositions articulated in the same way" (Deleuze, 1988: 85). But while change, in Foucault's and Sartre's later work, is complex and often unpredictable, this does not imply, however, that it is random: "History has no 'meaning', though this is not to say that it is absurd or incoherent. On the contrary, it is intelligible (...) in accordance with the intelligibility of struggles" (Foucault, 1980d: 114). Once again, Deleuze's account of Foucault ignores the dimension of strategy and therefore conscious agency. As we have

seen, in the cases of both Sartre and Foucault, the denial of the possibility of agency is connected to the postulation of a closed system for the interpretation of meaning: an episteme. We should not be surprised, therefore, to find implicit in Deleuze's Foucault just such a closed system. And, as in the cases of the early Foucault and Sartre, the assumption of such a system necessitates the postulation of an 'outside', a source for the disruption of the episteme. Thus, for Deleuze, change occurs when "something breaks the series and fractures the continuums" (127). The epistemic is the region of *Gelassenheit*, of waiting for the unknown. It is apolitical or conservative, for change cannot be directed, only expected. And when it arises, it can only be different, neither better nor worse (though Deleuze— judging, of course, from within the episteme— ventures to hope that "the new form that is neither God nor man (...) will not prove worse than its two previous forms" (132)).

7. We need go no further to see the potential for an initial misunderstanding arise. With the notion of an aesthetics of existence, Foucault indeed wishes to place the emphasis on the second aspect of morality, at the expense of the first. But that is not to say that he wishes to oppose an ethic of subjectivation to our current ethic of codes. As Foucault had shown in *The History of Sexuality, Volume I*, our current ethic, as much as the Greek, emphasizes subjectivation. The "attempt to transform oneself into the ethical subject of one's behavior" can be achieved, not only through a stylization of one's existence, but also through

> a decipherment as painstaking, continuous, and detailed as possible, of the movements of desire in all its hidden forms, including the most obscure. (UP: 27)

That is, Freudianism is not, in and of itself, incompatible with an aesthetics of existence. But the difference between the hermeneutics of desire and the kind of stylization which Foucault is advocating lies in the form of subjectivation. For the modern subject, *subjectivation* takes the form of *subjection*: the individual is tied to their identity, conceived of as an essence. Foucault, as is clear from a reading of the second two volumes of the *History of Sexuality* in conjunction with the first, does not seek to free us from codes, but to free us from a relationship to self which is felt to be overly restrictive.

8. As Morris puts it, "in his later work Foucault not only shares with the early Sartre the view that there is no fixed original essence of an individual, but also shares the view that instead of seeking to discover a nonexistent, original, true self, one might engage in actively forming the self as a work of art" (Morris, 1996: 544). Of course, the aesthetic activity Sartre and Foucault (and for that matter Lyotard) take as their model is distinctly modern in its insistence on novelty.

9. Thus Manfred Frank is wrong to see in Foucault a thinker trapped in a mode of understanding which is too exclusively concentrated upon codes and rules. Foucault, as much as Derrida, recognizes that "(d)iscursive orders (...) are unstable and uncontrollable (...) for internal reasons" (Frank, 1989: 187), because the rules governing their uses are always open to interpretation.

10. This is also an untimely ethics, as should already be apparent, for the future perfect is the site of the untimely *par excellence*. If confirmation of its untimely character is needed, however, it is to be found in the *Untimely Meditations*. The ethics of the future perfect mirrors Nietzsche's notion of virtue as that which swims "against the tide of history", that is, "against the blind power of the actual" (1983: 106).

11. In his recent exploration of the *The Moral Theory of Poststructuralism*, Todd May argues that these late texts of Foucault's ought not to be seen as concerned with ethics at all—with questions of right and wrong—but instead as focusing on matters of what is beautiful and ugly in individual lives. Such a thesis is necessary for May to rescue his thesis that Foucault's ethical thought is informed by what he calls the "principle of antirepresentationalism" (48), for these works do seem to be informed by a notion of certain lives as exemplary, and thus to violate May's principle. But while I agree with May that the "principle of antirepresentationalism" is an important force within Foucault's thought, it neither exhausts the latter's ethical thought, not can the consequentialism which flows from it occupy the entire field of morality. Just as analytic philosophers have seen the need to supplement consequentialist (and deontic) theories with a theory of the virtues, so Foucault saw the need to include the notion of examplary lives within the purview of ethics. It was not representations *per se* to which Foucault objected, but the notion that any (set of) representations were obligatory, that the subject essentially *is* in some way or other. That cultures should make available a range of representations is inevitable, and in no way undesirable, so long as they do not essentialize the subject in so doing. We are not, therefore, simply to reject representations, but to assess them; assess them in the same way we assess the other element of moralities, their codes:

> the important question (...) is not whether a culture without restraints is possible or even desirable but whether the system of constraints in which a society functions leaves individuals the liberty to transform the system. (Foucault, 1988a: 294)

12. Whether, in adopting the term 'game', Foucault wishes to indicate the similarity of his approach to rule-following to Wittgenstein's, I do not know. But the similarities are striking. It is true that Wittgenstein's examples of rule-following are drawn from situations in which "everything is a matter of course" (Wittgenstein, 1958: § 240), whereas ethics is concerned primarily with "hard cases" (Blackburn, 1981: 170). But far from invalidating the applicability of Wittgenstein's analysis to ethical rule-following, the relative lack of determinacy in such cases makes the analysis even more convincing. For Foucault, as for Wittgenstein, ethical decisions, like all examples of rule-following, are ultimately founded on "*forms of life*" (Wittgenstein, 1958, II: 226). When a hard case arises and the way in which the rules are to be followed is unclear, therefore, a situation has arisen which, in its ethically relevant aspects, is unlike those previously and routinely encountered. It is at this point that the need for creativity, for invention, arises most clearly: this is the case in which "we play—and make up the rules as we go along", or "we alter them—as we go along" (§ 83). But the element of invention is never completely absent, not even from the most routine applications of rules. Despite the fact that, in the routine case, I "obey the rule *blindly*" (§ 219), I have still "to apply the rule in the particular case without guidance" (§ 292). None of our games is completely "bounded by rules"—in fact, we cannot even imagine what such a game would look like, since we would need to have rules determining the applications of our rules, and further rules governing our meta-rules, and so on (§ 39). In the absence of such meta-rules, however, "every course of action can be made to accord with the rule" (§ 201). Rule-following, whether in ethics, aesthetics, or daily life, is *never* simply the mechanical application of determining regulations, or the following of "a visible section of rails invisibly laid to infinity" (§ 218) but is the creative employment of the precepts implicit

in our forms of life in order to achieve a result which is in no way given beforehand. Thus, as Wittgenstein says, to make an aesthetic judgment, we need not only to know the rules, but to "develop a feeling for the rules", to "interpret the rules" (Wittgenstein, 1967: 5). On the compatibility of Sartre's analysis of rule-following with Wittgenstein's, see Dwyer (1989).

13. As Sawicki notes, Foucault writes "from the perspective of a future historian in order to defamiliarize present practices and categories" (Sawicki, 1991: 101).

14. Baudrillard's critique of Foucault appreciates neither the future perfect stance of the historian of the present, nor the necessary tension between the empirical and the transcendental poles of enquiry. For Baudrillard, the fact that Foucault can reach a "definitive understanding about power" implies that his object, power, is in the past: "*all this is now over with* (...) Foucault can only draw such an admirable picture since he works at the confines of an area (...) now in the process of collapsing entirely" (Baudrillard, 1987: 11). Thus Baudrillard believes that Foucault must be assuming a transcendental (present) position in relation to some empirical (past) reality. Similarly, for Baudrillard, Foucault's (and, *a fortiori*, Sartre's) "theory of controls by means of a gaze that objectifies (...) is passé" (16). In these passages, it is Baudrillard who appears as "the last great dinosaur" of an earlier, more simplistic, understanding of postmodernism, an understanding which fails to appreciate— in all senses of that word— the necessarily untimely nature of its thought.

15. The 'anachronistic' element in Foucault's history of the present has, unfortunately, been lost in translation. Why, Foucault asks in *Discipline and Punish*, is he interested in writing the history of the prison:

> Simply because I am interested in the past [*Par un pur anachronisme*]? No, if one means by that writing a history of the past in terms of the present. Yes, if one means writing the history of the present. (DP: 31)

16. By this definition, and as he himself acknowledges, Derrida, too, might be called an Enlightenment thinker. For him, too, Enlightenment thoughts are those "that, while attempting to think reason and the history of reason, necessarily exceed its order, without becoming, simply because of this, irrational, and much less irrationalist. For these thoughts may in fact also try to remain faithful to the idea of the Enlightenment (...) while yet acknowledging its limits, in order to work on the Enlightenment of this time, this time that is ours— *today*" (Derrida, 1992b: 79).

Chapter Twelve

1. Claude Mauriac reports that just such a humanism was imputed to Foucault by his friend, Maurice Clavel, who once asked Foucault why, if he rejected humanism, "do you do what you do? In the name of what?" Foucault responded: "In the name of what? In the name of the excluded and of the confined— of those confined and excluded *by humanism*". "Therefore in the name of a wider humanism?", Clavel asked, but Foucault's only response was a smile (Mauriac, 1977: 519).

2. The interview from which this quotation is drawn is included as an afterword to Dreyfus and Rabinow's *Michel Foucault: Beyond Structuralism and Hermeneutics*. Oddly, the French

translation of Dreyfus and Rabinow's book contains a markedly different response of Foucault's to precisely the same question:

> There is a tension in Sartre between a certain conception of the subject and a morality of authenticity. And I always ask myself if this morality of authenticity does not in fact dispute what is said in *The Transcendence of the Ego*. The theme of authenticity refers, explicitly or not, to a mode of being of the subject defined by its adequation to itself. Now it seems to me that the relation to self is structured as a practice which can have its models, its conformities, its variants, but also its *creations*. The practice of the self is a complex and multiple domain. (quoted in Colombel, 1994: 270)

The recording held by the Bibliothèque de Saulchoir which contains the interview (conducted in English) with Dreyfus and Rabinow transcribed and edited to form their "Afterword" contains nothing like the above passage. Despite the fact that here too Foucault fails fully to appreciate the extent to which Sartre's notion of authenticity (at least in its more careful formulations) supports precisely the 'creative' interpretation of the relation to self which Foucault developed, this formulation, more than the one quoted in the original edition of Dreyfus and Rabinow's book, appears to open the way for the interpretation that I have here attempted to offer of the relation between Foucault and Sartre. That is, it suggests that Foucault developed certain possibilities opened up by Sartre's work, possibilities which Sartre himself did not fully develop.

3. Mark Poster has noted, in regard to this interview, that Foucault "ignores aspects of Sartre's writing that go in the other direction, toward undoing the universal subject" (Poster, 1993: 66). Jeanette Colombel, too, with explicit reference to the interview quoted above, finds in both men "the care of constructing a morality after the death of God which appeals to the *internal movement of creation*" (Colombel, 1994: 271). In Foucault's defence Colombel asserts that he could not have been aware of the importance of creation to Sartre, for the *Notebooks for an Ethics* had not yet been published at the time of the interview. In fact, even in *Being and Nothingness* the notion of authenticity as being truly oneself is explicitly rejected. Jana Sawicki, on the other hand, has retreated from a position in which she recognized the affinities between Foucault and Sartre ("The subject presupposed in Foucault's later discourses resembles the creative, nihilating subject found in the writings of French existentialist, Jean-Paul Sartre" Sawicki, 1991, 125n18) to one in which she endorses Foucault's own assessment ("I now think that Foucault's subject is more Nietzschean than Sartrian" Sawicki, 1994: 313n31). Unfortunately, both Sawicki's comments, offered as asides in footnotes, are undeveloped, so the reasons for her change of mind are not made explicit.

4. For the contention that Foucault advocates a humanism in the future perfect, I find unexpected support from Deleuze:

> It's difficult, all the same, to say that Foucault's philosophy is a philosophy of the subject. At most, it 'will have been' [«aura été»] one, when Foucault discovers subjectivity as a third dimension. (Deleuze, 1995: 126; translation modified)

BIBLIOGRAPHY

Arac, Jonathan (ed.) (1988) *After Foucault: Humanistic Knowledge, Postmodern Challenges*. New Brunswick: Rutgers University Press.

Armstrong, Timothy J. (trans. and ed.) (1992), *Michel Foucault Philosopher*. New York: Routledge.

Aronson, Ronald (1980) *Sartre - Philosophy in the World*. London: Verso.

Auzias, Jean-Marie (1986) *Michel Foucault*. Paris: La Manufacture.

Balan, B., et. al. (1968) "Entretiens sur Foucault" *La Pensée* 137.

Barrett, Michele (1991) *The Politics of Truth: From Marx to Foucault*. Cambridge: Polity Press.

Baudrillard, Jean (1987), *Forget Foucault*. trans. N. Dufresne, New York: Semiotext(e) [1977].

Bell, Linda A. (1989) *Sartre's Ethics of Authenticity*. Tuscaloosa: The University Of Alabama Press.

Bennington, Geoffrey (1990) "Towards a Criticism of the Future" in Wood, D. (1990).

Bernauer, James (1990) *Michel Foucault's Force of Flight: Toward an Ethics for Thought*. New Jersey: Humanities Press.

Bernauer, James and Rasmussen, David (1987) *The Final Foucault*. Cambridge: The MIT Press.

Blackburn, Simon (1981) "Reply: Rule-Following and Moral Realism" in Holtzman, Steven H., and Leich, Chistopher M. (eds.) *Wittgenstein: To Follow a Rule*. London: Routledge & Kegan Paul.

Bourdieu, Pierre (1984a) *Distinction: A Social Critique of the Judgement of Taste*. Trans. Richard Nice, London: Routledge & Kegan Paul.

———(1984b) "Le plaisir de savoir" *Le Monde* 27 June.

———(1985) "Les intellectuels et les plaisirs" in Ewald, et.al. (1985).

———(1991) *The Political Ontology of Martin Heidegger*. Trans. Peter Collier, Cambridge: Polity Press.

Bradbury, Malcolm, and McFarlane, James (1983) "The Name and Nature of Modernism" in Bradbury and McFarlane (eds.), *Modernism*. Penguin Books.

Caputo, John and Yount, Mark (eds) (1993) *Foucault and the Critique of Institutions*. The Pennsylvania State University Press.

Caws, Peter (1984), *Sartre*. London: Routledge & Kegan Paul.

Clark, Timothy (1986) "Being in Mime: Heidegger and Derrida on the Ontology of Literary Language" in *MLN*, Vol 101, No.5.

Clifford, Michael (1990) "Dasein and the Analytic of Finitude" in Dallery, Arleen B., and Scott, Charles E., *Crises in Continental Philosophy*. Albany: State University of New York Press.

Cohen, R.A. (1984) "Merleau-Ponty, the Flesh and Foucault" *Philosophy Today*, Winter.

Coles, R. (1991) "Foucault's Dialogical Artistic Ethos" *Theory, Culture & Society*, Vol. 8.

Colombel, Jeannette (1994) *Michel Foucault: La clarté de la mort*. Paris: Éditions Odile Jacob.

Cumming, Robert Denoon (1991) *Phenomenology and Deconstruction I: The Dream is Over*. The University of Chicago Press.

Defert, Daniel (1990) "Lettre à Claude Lanzmann" in *Les temps modernes*, Oct-Dec.

Deleuze, Gilles (1988) *Foucault*. Trans. Sean Hand, University of Minnessota Press.

———(1992) "What is a *dispositif*?" in Armstrong (1992).

———(1995) *Negotiations: 1972-1990*. Trans. Martin Joughin, New York: Columbia University Press.

Derrida, Jacques (1978a) "Cogito and the History of Madness" in *Writing and Difference*, trans. Alan Bass, London: Routledge & Kegan Paul [1967].

———(1978b) "From Restricted to General Economy: A Hegelianism without Reserve", in *Writing and Difference*.

———(1978c) "Structure, Sign and Play in the Discourse of the Human Sciences", in *Writing and Difference*.

———(1981) *Positions*, University of Chicago Press [1972].

———(1982a) "Différance", in *Margins of Philosophy*. Trans. Alan Bass, University of Chicago Press [1972].

———(1982b) "The Ends of Man", in *Margins of Philosophy*.

———(1984) "Derrida l'insoumis", in Muchnik, Nicole (ed.), *De Sartre à Foucault: Vingt ans de grands entretiens dans Le Nouvel Observateur*. Paris: Hachette.

———(1985) *The Ear of the Other: Otobiography, Transference, Translation*, Christie V. McDonald (ed), trans. Peggy Kamuf and Avital Ronnel, New York: Schocken Books.

———(1989a) *Of Spirit: Heidegger and the Question*, trans. Geoffrey Bennington and Rachel Bowlby, University of Chicago Press.

———(1989b) "Desistance" trans. Christopher Fynsk, in Lacoue-Labarthe, Philippe, *Typography: Mimesis, Philosophy, Politics*, Cambridge: Harvard University Press.

———(1990) "Heidegger's Silence" in Neske, Gunther, and Kettering, Emil (eds), *Martin Heidegger and National Socialism* Lisa Harries and Joachim Neugroschel (trans), New York: Paragon House.

————(1992) *The Other Heading: Reflections on Today's Europe.* trans. Pascale-Anne Brault and Michael B. Naas, Bloomington: Indiana University Press.

————(1993) *Aporias.* Trans. Thomas Dutoit, Stanford University Press.

————(1994) *Specters of Marx.* Trans. Peggy Kamuf, New York: Routledge.

————(1998) "'To Do Justice to Freud": The History of Madness in the Age of Psychoanalysis', in *Resistances of Psychoanalysis.* Trans. Peggy Kamuf, Pascale-Anne Brault and Michael Naas, Stanford University Press.

Dews, Peter (1987), *Logics of Disintegration: Post-Structuralist Thought and the Claims of Critical Theory.* London: Verso.

————(1989) 'Adorno, Poststructuralism and the Critique of Identity', in Andrew Benjamin (ed.) *The Problems of Modernity: Adorno and Benjamin.* London: Routledge.

Docherty, Thomas (1992) "Criticism, History, Foucault". *History of European Ideas*, vol. 14, no. 3.

Le Doeuff, Michele (1991) *Hipparchia's Choice: An Essay Concerning Women, Philosophy, etc.* Trans. Trista Selous, Oxford: Basil Blackwell.

Dosse, François (1992) *Histoire du structuralisme, tome 2: le chant du cygne, 1967 à nos jours.* Paris: Éditions la Découverte.

Dreyfus, Hubert L. (1984) "Beyond Hermeneutics: Interpretation in Late Heidegger and Recent Foucault", in Shapiro, Gary and Sica, Alan (1984) *Hermeneutics: Questions and Prospects.* Amherst: The University of Massachussets Press.

————(1987) "Intoduction" to Foucault *Mental Illness and Psychology.* Alan Sheridan (trans), Berkeley: University of California Press.

————(1992) "On the Ordering of Things: Being and Power in Heidegger and Foucault" in Armstrong (1992).

Dreyfus, Hubert L. and Rabinow, Paul (1983) *Michel Foucault: Beyond Structuralism and Hermeneutics.* Chicago: The University of Chicago Press.

During, Simon (1992) *Foucault and Literature: Towards a Genealogy of Writing.* London: Routledge.

Dwyer, Philip (1989) "Freedom and Rule-Following in Wittgenstein and Sartre", *Philosophy and Phenomenological Research*, Vol. 50, No. 1.

Eribon, Didier (1991) *Michel Foucault.* Trans Betsy Wing, Harvard University Press.

————(1994) *Michel Foucault et ses contemporains.* Paris: Fayard.

Ewald, François, et. al. (1985) *Michel Foucault: Une histoire de la vérité.* Paris: Syros.

Fell, Joseph P. (1979) *Heidegger and Sartre: An Essay on Being and Place.* New York: Columbia University Press.

Ferry, Luc, and Renaut, Alain (1990) *French Philosophy of the Sixties: An Essay on Antihumanism.* Trans. Mary H.S. Cattani, Amherst: The University of Massachussets Press.

Flynn, Bernard C. (1978) "Michel Foucault and the Husserlian Problematic of a Transcendental Philosophy of History", *Philosophy Today*, Fall.

Flynn, Thomas R. (1993) "Foucault and the Eclipse of Vision" in Levin, David Michael (ed) *Modernity and the Hegemony of Vision*. Berkeley: University of California Press.

———(1994) 'Foucault's mapping of history' in Gutting (1994).

———(1997) *Sartre, Foucault and Historical Reason, Volume One: Towards an Existentialist Theory of History*. The University of Chicago Press.

Foucault, Michel (1963a) 'Guetter le jour qui vient' *La Nouvelle Revue Française* (October)..

———(1963b) 'Distance, aspect, origine' *Critique* 198 (November).

———(1966a) 'Entretien' *La Quinzaine Littéraire* 5, May 16.

———(1966b) 'Une histoire restés muette' *La Quinzaine Littéraire* 8 (July 1).

———(1968a) 'Une mise au point de Michel Foucault' *La Quinzaine Littéraire*, March 15-31.

———(1968b) 'Réponse au Cercle d'épistemologie' *Cahiers pour l'analyse* 9, Summer.

———(1971) *Madness and Civilization: A History of Insanity in the Age of Reason*. Trans. Richard Howard, London: Tavistock.

———(1972a) *Histoire de la folie à l'âge classique*. Paris: Gallimard. [1961]

———(1972b) *The Archaeology of Knowledge*. Trans A. M. Sheridan Smith. London: Routledge, 1972.

———(1972c) 'The Discourse on Language', trans. Rupert Swyer. Published as an appendix to the American edition of AK (New York: Harper and Row).

———(1973) *The Birth of the Clinic: An Archaeology of Medical Perception*. Trans. A.M. Sheridan Smith, New York: Vintage Books.

———(1974) (with Noam Chomsky) 'Human Nature: Justice versus Power', in Fons Elders (ed). *Reflexive Water: The Basic Concerns of Mankind*. London: Souvenir Press [originally televised in November, 1971]

———(1975a) *Surveiller et punir: Naissance de la prison*. Paris: Gallimard.

———(1977a) 'The Father's "No"', in *Language, Counter-Memory, Practice: Selected Essays and Interviews*. Trans. Donald Bouchard and Sherry Simon. Ithaca: Cornell University Press [1962].

———(1977b) 'A Preface to Transgression', in *Language, Counter-Memory, Practice*. [1963].

———(1977c) 'Language to Infinity', in *Language, Counter-Memory, Practice*. [1963].

———(1977d) 'Theatrum Philosophicum', in *Language, Counter-Memory, Practice* [1970].

———(1977e) 'La grande colère des faits', *Le Nouvel Observateur* 652.

———(1979a) 'Lettre ouverte à Mehdi Bazargan', *Le Nouvel Observateur* 753.

————(1980a) `On Popular Justice: A Discussion with Maoists', in *Power/Knowledge: Selected Interviews and Other Writings 1972-1977*. Colin Gordon (ed). New York: Pantheon Books [1972]

————(1980b) `Body/Power' in *Power/Knowledge*. [1975]

————(1980c) `Two Lectures', in *Power/Knowledge*. [1976]

————(1980d) `Truth and Power', in *Power/Knowledge* [1976]

————(1980e) `The Eye of Power', in *Power/Knowledge* [1977]

————(1980f) `Power and Strategies', in *Power/Knowledge*, [1977]

————(1980g) `The Confession of the Flesh' in *Power/Knowledge*.[1977]

————(1981) `Is it useless to revolt?', trans. James Bernauer, *Philosophy and Social Criticism*, Vol. 8, No. 1.

————(1982) `Pierre Boulez ou l'écran traversé', *Le Nouvel Observateur*, October.

————(1983a) `The Subject and Power', in Dreyfus and Rabinow (1983).

————(1983b) `On the Genealogy of Ethics: An Overview of Work in Progress", in Dreyfus and Rabinow (1983)

————(1984) `What is Enlightenment?', in *The Foucault Reader*. ed. Paul Rabinow, New Yo————(rk: Pantheon Books.

————(1986a) `Dream, Imagination and Existence'. Trans. Forrest Williams, in Ludwig Binswanger and Michel Foucault, *Dream and Existence*. Seattle: Review of Existential Psychology and Psychiatry [1954]

————(1986b) *Discipline and Punish: The Birth of the Prison*. Trans. Alan Sheridan. London: Penguin Books [1975]

————(1986c) *The Use of Pleasure*. Trans. Robert Hurley, New York: Vintage Books [1984]

————(1986d) *The Care of the Self*. Trans. Robert Hurley, London: Penguin Books [1984]

————(1987a) *Mental Illness and Psychology*. Trans. Alan Sheridan. Berkeley: University of California Press [1962]

————(1987b) `Maurice Blanchot: The Thought from Outside'. Trans. Brian Massumi, in *Foucault/Blanchot*. New York: Zone Books. [1966].

————(1987c) `The ethic of care for the self as a practice of freedom', trans. J.D. Gauthier, in Bernauer and Rasmussen (1987) [1984]

————(1988a) `Sexual Choice, Sexual Act: Foucault and Homosexuality' in *Politics, Philosophy, Culture: Interviews and Other Writings, 1977-1984*. Ed. Lawrence D. Kritzman, trans. Alan Sheridan a.o., Routledge. [1982]

————(1988b) `Truth, Power, Self: An Interview with Michel Foucault", in Martin, Luther H., Gutman, Huck, and Hutton, Patrick H. (eds), *Technologies of the self: A Seminar with Michel Foucault*. London: Tavistock Publications. [1982]

———(1988c) `Critical Theory/Intellectual History', in *Politics, Philosophy, Culture* [1983]

———(1988d) `The Art of Telling the Truth", in *Politics, Philosophy, Culture* [1984]

———(1988e) `Return of Morality', in *Politics, Philosophy, Culture* [1984]

———(1989a) *The Order of Things: An Archaeology of the Human Sciences*. Tavistock/Routledge. [1966]

———(1989g) `Introduction', to Georges Canguilhem, *The Normal and the Pathological*. Trans. Carolyn R. Fawcett, New York: Zone Books. [1978]

———(1989h) *Résumé des cours: 1970-1982*. Paris: Julliard. [1989]

———(1990) *The History of Sexuality, Vol. I: An Introduction*. Trans. Robert Hurley, Penguin Books. [1976]

———(1991) *Remarks on Marx: Conversations with Duccio Trombadori*. Trans. R. James Goldstein and James Cascaito. New York: Semiotext(e). [1978]

———(1993) `About the Beginning of the Hermeneutics of the Self: Two Lectures at Dartmouth', in *Political Theory*, Vol. 21, No. 2. [1980]

———(1994a) `Foucault, Michel, 1926-'. Trans. Catherine Porter, in Gary Gutting (ed.), *The Cambridge Companion to Foucault*. Cambridge University Press. [1984]

———(1994b) `Appendice' in Didier Eribon, *Michel Foucault et ses contemporains*. Paris: Fayard.

———(1995) `Madness, the Absence of Work', trans. Peter Stastny and Deniz Şengel, *Critical Inquiry* 2 (Winter 1995). [1964].

———(1996a) `Madness Only Exists in Society', trans. Lysa Hochroth, in *Foucault Live*, Sylvère Lotringer (ed), New York: Semiotext(e). [1961]

———(1996b) `The Order of Things', trans. John Johnston, in *Foucault Live*. [1966]

———(1996c) `The Discourse of History', trans. John Johnston, in *Foucault Live*. [1967]

———(1996d) `Foucault Responds to Sartre', trans. John Johnston, in *Foucault Live*. [1968]

———(1996e) `The Archaeology of Knowledge', trans. John Johnston, in *Foucault Live*. [1969]

———(1996f) `An Historian of Culture', trans. Jared Becker and James Cascaito, in *Foucault Live*. [1972]

———(1997) `For an Ethics of Discomfort', in Foucault, *The Politics of Truth*. Sylvère Lotringer and Lysa Hochroth (eds), New York: Semiotext(e). [1979]

Frank, M. (1989) *What is Neostructuralism?* Trans, Sabine Wilke and Richard Gray, Minneapolis: University of Minnesota Press.

Fraser, Nancy (1989) *Unruly Practices: Power, Discourse and Gender in Contemporary Social Theory*. Cambridge: Polity Press,

Freud, Sigmund (1988) *New Introductory Lectures on Psychoanalysis*, trans J. Strachey, Penguin Books [1933].

Glücksmann, André (1992) "Michel Foucault's nihilism" in Armstrong (1992).

Gutting, Gary (1989) *Michel Foucault's Archaeology of Scientific Reason*, Cambridge: Cambridge University Press.

———(ed.) (1994) *The Cambridge Companion to Foucault*, Cambridge University Press.

Haar, M. (1980) "Sartre and Heidegger", in Silverman, H.J., and Eliston, F.A., (eds), *Jean-Paul Sartre: Contemporary Approaches to His Philosophy*, Pittsburgh: Duquesne University Press.

Habermas, Jürgen (1983), "Modernity–An Incomplete Project", in Foster, H. (ed), *The Anti-Aesthetic: Essays on Postmodern Culture*, Seattle: Bay Press.

———(1987) *The Philosophical Discourse of Modernity*, trans F. Lawrence, Cambridge, MIT Press (German orignal: 1985).

Halperin, D. M. (1994) "Historicizing the Subject of Desire: Sexual Preferences and Erotic Identities in the Pseudo-Lucianic *Erôtes*", in Goldstein, J. (ed.), *Foucault and the Writing of History*, Cambridge: Basil Blackwell.

Hartmann, Klaus (1966) *Sartre's Ontology: A Study of Being and Nothingness in the light of Hegel's Logic*, Evanston: Northwestern University Press.

Harvey, David (1989) *The Condition of Postmodernity: An Enquiry into the Origins of Cultural Change*, Basil Blackwell.

Martin Heidegger (1962) *Being and Time*, John Macquarrie and Edward Robinson (trans), Oxford: Basil Blackwell [1927].

———(1971a) "The Origin of the Work of Art", in *Poetry, Language, Thought*, Albert Hofstadter (trans), New York: Harper and Row [1950]

———(1971b) "What are Poets For", in *Poetry, Language, Thought* [1950].

———(1971c) "The Thing", in *Poetry, Language, Thought* [1951].

———(1971d) "Building, Dwelling, Thinkimg", in *Poetry, Language, Thought* [1952].

———(1971e) "Language", in *Poetry, Language, Thought* [1959].

———(1975a) "What is Metaphysics", in Kaufmann, W., *Existentialism from Dostoeusky to Sartre*, New York: New American Library [1949].

———(1975b) "The Way Back into the Ground of Metaphysics", in *Existentialism from Dostoeusky to Sartre* [1949].

———(1977a) "Letter on Humanism", in *Basic Writings*, David F. Krell (ed.), Frank A. Cappuzi with J. Glenn Gray (trans), HarperSan Francisco [1947].

———(1977b) "The Age of the World Picture", in *The Question Concerning Technology and Other Essays*, William Lovitt (trans), New York: Harper and Row [1950].

———(1977c) "The Word of Nietzsche: 'God is dead'", in *The Question Concerning Technology* [1950].

———(1977d) "The Question Concerning Technology", in *The Question Concerning Technology* [1954].

———(1977e) "Science and Reflection", in *The Question Concerning Technology* [1954].

———(1977f) "What Calls for Thinking?", in *Basic Writings* [1954].

———(1977g) "Modern Science, Metaphysics, and Mathematics", in *Basic Writings* 1962].

———(1977h) "The Turning", in *The Question Concerning Technology* [1962].

———(1977i) "The End of Philosophy and the Task of Thinking", in *Basic Writings* [1966].

———(1982a) "Language in the Poem: A Discussion on Georg Trakl's Poetic Work", in *On the Way to Language*, Peter D. Hertz (trans), San Francisco: Harper and Row [1959].

———(1982b) "A Dialogue on Language" in *On the Way to Language* [1959].

———(1982c) "The Nature of Language", in *On the Way to Language* [1959].

———(1985) "Who is Nietzsche's Zarathustra?", trans. Bernd Magnus, in Allison, D.B., *The New Nietzsche: Contemporary Styles of Interpretation*, MIT Press [1954].

———(1990) *"Der Spiegel* Interview", in Neske and Kettering, (eds), *Martin Heidegger and National Socialism*, Lisa Harries and Joachim Neugroschel (trans), New York: Paragon House [1977].

Hendley, Steven (1991) *Reason and Relativism: A Sartrean Investigation*, State University of New York Press.

Hill, R.K. (1989) "Foucault's Critique of Heidegger", in *Philosophy Today*, Winter.

Hollier, Denis (1986), *The Politics of Prose: Essay on Sartre*, trans. J. Mehlman, Minneapolis: University of Minnesota Press.

———(1992) "The Word of God: 'I am dead'", in Armstrong (1992).

Howells, C. (1988), *Sartre: The Necessity of Freedom*, Cambridge: Cambridge University Press.

———(1992) "Conclusion: Sartre and the deconstruction of the subject", in Howells, C. (ed), *The Cambridge Companion to Sartre*, Cambridge University Press.

Hoy, David Couzens (1986) *Foucault: A Critical Reader*, Oxford: Basil Blackwell.

———(1988) "Foucault: Modern or Postmodern?", in Arac (1988).

Hutcheon, L. (1988) *A Poetics of Postmodernism: History, Theory, Fiction, Routledge*.

Ijsseling, S. (1986) "Foucault with Heidegger", in *Man and World* 19.

Ingram, D. (1994) "Foucault and Habermas on the subject of reason", in Gutting (1994).

Jameson, F. (1971) *Marxism and Form: Twentieth-Century Dialectical Theories of Literature*, New Jersy: Princeton University Press.

———(1984) "Foreword" to Lyotard (1984).

———(1991) *Postmodernism, or The Cultural Logic of Late Capitalism*, Verso.

Jay, Martin (1984) *Marxism and Totality: The Adventures of a Concept From Lukács to Habermas*, University of California Press.

————(1986) `In the Empire of the Gaze: Foucault and the Denigration of Vision in Twentieth Century French Thought' in Hoy (1986).

————(1993) *Downcast Eyes: The Denigration of Vision in Twentieth-Century French Thought*, Berkeley: University Of California Press.

Kant, Immanuel (1978) *Anthropology from a Pragmatic Point of View* Trans. Victor Lyle Dowdell. Carbondale: Southern Illinois University Press. [1798]

————(1991a) *Anthropologie du point de vue pragmatique*, trans. M. Foucault, Paris: Vrin [1798]

————(1991b), *Political Writings*, trans. H.B. Nisbet, Cambridge University Press.

Kemp, P. (1984) "Review Essay", *History and Theory*, Vol. 23.

Knee, P. (1990) "Le cercle et le doublet: Note sur Sartre et Foucault", in *Philosophiques*, Vol. xvii, no. 1.

Kofman, S. (1984), "Sartre: Fort! Ou Da?", *Diacritics*, Winter 1984.

Krell, D.F. (1987) "The Perfect Future: A Note on Heidegger and Derrida", in Sallis, J. (ed) (1987) *Deconstruction and Philosophy: The Texts of Jacques Derrida*, The University of Chicago Press.

Kremer-Marietti, A. (1974) *Michel Foucault*. Paris: Seghers.

Kruks, Sonia (1990) "Sartre's 'First Ethics' and the Future of Ethics" in Wood, D. (1990).

LaCapra, D. (1978) *A Preface to Sartre*, Ithaca: Cornell University Press.

Lacoue-Labarthe, P. (1989) "On the Sublime", trans. G. Bennington, in Appignanesi, L. (ed) *Postmodernism*, London: Free Association Press.

Lebrun, Gerard (1992) "Notes on phenomenology in *Les Mots et les Choses*" in Armstrong (1992).

Lyotard, Jean-François (1984) *The Postmodern Condition: A Report on Human Knowledge*, trans. Geoff Bennington and Brian Massumi, Minneapolis: University of Minnesota Press.

————(1990) *Heidegger and 'the jews'*, Andreas Michel and Mark S. Roberts (trans.). Minneaopolis: University of Minnesota Press.

————(1992a) "Note on the meaning of 'post-'", in *The Postmodern Explained to Children: Correspondence 1982-1985*, trans J. Pefanis and M. Thomas, Sydney: Power Publications.

————(1992b) "Answer to the question: what is the postmodern?" in *The Postmodern Explained to Children.*

————(1993a) "Intellectual Fashions", in *Political Writings*, trans. B. Reading and K. Paul, Minneapolis: University of Minnesota Press.

————(1993b) *"Heidegger and 'the jews'*: A Conference in Vienna and Freiburg", in *Political Writings*.

Macey, David (1993) *The Lives of Michel Foucault*, London: Vintage.

McGowan, J. (1991) *Postmodernism and Its Critics*, Cornell University Press.

McKenna, A.J. (1988) "Postmodernism: It's Future Perfect", in Silverman, H.J., and Welton, D., *Postmodernism and Continental Philosophy*, State University of New York Press.

McNay, L. (1992) *Foucault and Feminism: Power, Gender and the Self*, Cambridge: Polity Press.

Mahon, Michael (1992) *Foucault's Nietzschean Genealogy: Truth, Power, and the Subject*, Albany: State University of New York Press.

Mauriac, Claude, *Le Temps immobile*, Paris: Bernard Grasset.

———(1976) Tome 3: *Et comme l'espérance est violente*.

———(1977) Tome 4: *La terrasse de Malagar*.

———(1981) Tome 6: *Le rire des pères dans les yeux des enfants*.

May, Todd (1993) *Between Genealogy and Epistemology: Psychology, Politics, and Knowledge in the Thought of Michel Foucault*, The Pennsylvania Sate University Press.

———(1995) *The Moral Theory of Poststructuralism* The Pennsylvania State University Press.

Megill, A. (1985) *Prophets of Extremity: Nietzsche, Heidegger, Foucault, Derrida*, Berkley: University of California Press, 1985.

Melville, S.W. (1986) *Philosophy Beside Itself: On Deconstruction and Modernism*, University of Minnesota Press.

Merleau-Ponty, Maurice (1968) *The Visible and the Invisible*, trans. A. Lingis, Evanston: Northwestern University Press.

———(1973), *Adventures of the Dialectic*, trans, J, Bien, Evanston: Northwestern University Press [1955].

Merquior, J.G. (1985) *Foucault*, London: Fontana.

Miller, J. (1993) *The Passion of Michel Foucault*, New York: Simon and Schuster.

Miller, J.-A. (1992) "Foucault and psychoanalysis" in Armstrong (1992).

Morris, Phyllis Sutton (1996) 'Self-Creating Selves: Sartre and Foucault' *American Catholic Philosophical Quarterly*, Vol. LXX, No. 4 (Autumn).

Muchnik, N. (1984) (ed.), *De Sartre à Foucault: Vingt ans de grands entretiens dans Le Nouvel Observateur*, Paris: Hachette

Nietzsche, F. (1983) "The Uses and Disadvantages of History for Life" in *Untimely Meditations*, trans. R. Hollingdale, Cambridge University Press [1874].

Norris, C. (1994) "'What is enlightenment?' Kant according to Foucault" in Gutting (1994).

O'Farrel, Clare (1989), *Foucault: Historian or Philosopher?*, Macmillan.

Owen, D. (1994) *Maturity and Modernity: Nietzsche, Weber, Foucault and the ambivulence of reason*, London: Routledge.

Owens, T.J. (1970) *Phenomenology and Intersubjectivity: Contemporary Interpretations of the Interpersonal Situation*, The Hague: Martinus Nijhoff.

Ozouf, M. (1984), 'Préface', to Muchnik, N. (ed.), *De Sartre à Foucault: Vingt ans de grands entretiens dans Le Nouvel Observateur*, Paris: Hachette.

Palmer, R. E. (1984) "On the Transcendability of Hermeneutics (A Response to Dreyfus)", in Shapiro and Sica (1984).

Palmier, J.-M. (1969) "La mort du roi", *Le Monde*, 3 May, p.viii.

Palonen, K., and Subra, L. (1990) *Jean-Paul Sartre - un philosophe du politique*, University of Jyväskylä.

Poster, Mark (1979) *Sartre's Marxism*, London: Pluto Press.

———(1984a) *Foucault, Marxism and History: Mode of Production Versus Mode of Information*, Cambridge: Polity Press.

———(1984b) "Sartre's Concept of the Intellectual: A Foucauldian Critique", *Notebooks in Cultural Analysis: An Annual Review*, Durham: Duke University Press.

———(1993) "Foucault and the Problem of Self-Constitution", in Caputo and Yount (1993).

Pucciani, O.F. (1990) "Saint Sartre et l'homosexualité", *Les Temps Modernes*, Oct-Dec.

Rabinow, Paul (1994) "Modern and countermodern: Ethos and epoch in Heidegger and Foucault" in Gutting (1994).

Racevskis, K. (1988) "Michel Foucault, Rameau's Nephew, and the Question of Identity" in Bernauer and Rasmussen (1987).

Rajchman, J. (1985) *Michel Foucault: The Freedom of Philosophy*, New York: Columbia University Press.

———(1991) *Truth and Eros: Foucault, Lacan, and the Question of Ethics*, New York: Routledge.

Rorty, Richard (1986) 'Foucault and Epistemology', in Hoy (1986).

———(1991) *Essays on Heidegger and others: Philosophical Papers Vol. 2*, Cambridge University Press.

———(1993) 'Paroxysms and Politics', *Salmagundi* 97.

Roudinesco, E., et. al. (1992) *Penser la folie: Essais sur Michel Foucault*, Paris: Galilée.

Said, E. W. (1988) "Michel Foucault, 1926-1984", in Arac (1988).

Sartre, Jean-Paul (1948) 'Présentation des *Temps Modernes*', in *Situations* II. Paris: Gallimard.

———(1955) *No Exit and Three Other Plays*, trans. S. Gilbert and L. Abel, New York: Vintage Books.

———(1956) *Being and Nothingness: A Phenomenological Essay on Ontology*, trans. Hazel E. Barnes, Washington Square Press [1943]

———(1961) *The Condemned of Altona*, trans. S. and G. Leeson, New York: Alfred A. Knopf.

———(1964) *The Words*, trans. B. Frechtman, Greenwich: Fawcett Premier.

————(1968) *Search for a Method*, trans. H.E. Barnes, New York: Vintage Books [1960]

————(1969) *The Communists and Peace*, trans. I. Clephane, London: Hamish Hamilton [1954]

————(1970) "Intentionality: A Fundamental Idea of Husserl's Phenomenology", trans. Joseph P. Fell, *Journal of the British Society for Phenomenology*, Vol I, No. 2 (May).

————(1971) "Replies to Structuralism: An Interview", trans. R. D'Amico, *Telos*, Fall [1966].

————(1974a) "We Write for Our Own Time" in *Selected Prose*, trans, R. McCleary, Evanston: Northwestern University Press [1946].

————(1974b) "Determinism and Freedom", in *Selected Prose* [1964].

————(1974c) "A Plea for Intellectuals", in *Between Existentialism and Marxism: Sartre on Philosophy, Politics, Psychoanalysis and the Arts*, New York: Pantheon Books [1965].

————(1974d) "The Man with the Tape-Recorder", in *Between Existentialism and Marxism* [1969].

————(1974e) "The Itinerary of a Thought", in *Between Existentialism and Marxism* [1969].

————(1974f) (With Gavi, P. and Victor, P.) *On a raison de se revolter*, Paris: Gallimard.

————(1975) "Existentialism is a Humanism" trans. P. Mairet, in Kaufmann, W. (ed), *Existentialism from Dostoeusky to Sartre*, New York: New American Library [1946].

————(1976) *Critique of Dialectical Reason: Volume One*, trans. A.S. Smith, London: Verso [1960].

————(1977a) "Justice and the State", in *Life/Situations*, trans. P. Auster and L. Davis, New York: Pantheon Books [1972].

————(1977b) "Self-Portrait at Seventy", in *Life/Situations*.

————(1977c) "Simone de Beauvoir Interview Sartre", in *Life/Situations*.

————(1977d) "On *The Idiot of the Family*", in *Life/Situations* [1971].

————(1984) "Conversations with Jean-Paul Sartre", in de Beauvoir, S. *Adieux: A Farewell to Sartre*, London: Penguin.

————(1985) *War Diaries: Notebooks from a Phoney War, November 1939-March 1940*, Quintin Hoare (trans), Verso [1983].

————(1988) *Saint Genet: Actor and Martyr*, trans. B. Fretchman, London: Heinemann [1952].

————(1992) *Notebooks for an Ethics*, trans D. Pellauer, Chicago: University of Chicago Press [1983]

Sawicki, Jana (1987) "Heidegger and Foucault: Escaping Technological Nihilism", *Philosophy and Social Criticism*, Vol 13, No.2.

————(1991) *Disciplining Foucault: Feminism, Power and The Body*, New York: Routledge.

————(1994) "Foucault, feminism and questions of identity" in Gutting (1994).

Scott, C.E. (1990) *The Question of Ethics: Nietzsche, Foucault, Heidegger*, Bloomington: Indiana University Press.

Shapiro, G., and Sica. A. (1984) *Hermeneutics: Questions and Prospects*, Amherst: The University of Massachussets Press.

Silverman, H.J. (1987) *Inscriptions: Between Phenomenology and Structuralism*, New York: Routledge & Kegan Paul.

——(1991) (ed) *Writing the Politics of Difference*, State University of New York Press.

Smart, B. (1983) *Foucault, Marxism and Critique*, London: Routledge & Kegan Paul.

Spanos, W.V. (1993) *Heidegger and Criticism: Retrieving the Cultural Politics of Destruction*, Minneapolis: University of Minnesota Press.

Stone, R.V. (1981) "Sartre on Bad Faith and Authenticity" in Schilpp, P.A. (ed) *The Philosophy of Jean-Paul Sartre*, La Salle: Open Court.

Stone, R.V. and Bowman, E.A. (1991a) "Sartre's *Morality and History*: A First Look at the Notes for the Unpublished 1965 Cornell Lectures", in Aronson, R. and van de Hoven, A., *Sartre Alive*, Detroit: Wayne State University Press.

——(1991b) "'Making the Human' in Sartre's Unpublished Dialectical Ethics", in Silverman (1991).

Taylor, Charles (1986) 'Foucault on Freedom and Truth' in Hoy (1986).

Taylor, Mark C. (1987) *Altarity*, The University of Chicago Press.

Theunissen, M. (1984) *The Other: Studies in the Social Ontology of Husserl, Heidegger, Sartre, and Buber*, C. Macann (trans), Cambridge: MIT Press (German orignal: 1977).

Wittgenstein, Ludwig (1958) *Philosophical Investigations*, trans. G.E.M. Anscombe, Oxford: Basil Blackwell [1953].

——(1967) *Lectures and Conversations on Aesthetics, Psychology and Religious Belief*, Berkeley: University of California Press.

Wolin, R. (1992) The Terms of Cultural Criticism: The Frankfurt School, Existentialism, Poststructuralism, New York: Columbia University Press.

Wolin, S.S. (1988) "On the Theory and Practice of Power" in Arac (1988).

Wood, D. (1990) (ed) *Writing the Future*, London: Routledge.

Wood, D. (1991) "Translating the Differences: The Futures of Continental Philosophy" in Silverman (1991).

Wood, P.R. (1989) "Derrida Engagé and Poststructuralist Sartre: A Redefinition of Shifts In Recent French Philosophy", *MLN*, Vol. 104, No. 4.

STUDIES
IN
EUROPEAN
THOUGHT

This series of monographs, translations, and critical editions covers comparative and interdisciplinary topics of significance from the early eighteenth century to the present. Volumes, both published and projected, include a collection of essays on German drama, a study of the Künstlerroman, and a study on the aesthetics of the double talent of Kubin and Herzmanovsky-Orlando.

For additional information about this series or for the submission of manuscripts, please contact:

Peter Lang Publishing
Acquisitions Dept.
516 N. Charles St., 2nd Floor
Baltimore, MD 21201

To order other books in this series, please contact our Customer Service Department at:

800-770-LANG (within the U.S.)
(212) 647-7706 (outside the U.S.)
(212) 647-7707 FAX

or browse online by series at:

www.peterlang.com

Learning Resources
Centre